The Third Step East
Zen Masters of America

by

Richard Bryan McDaniel

Portraits by Molly Macnaughton
Foreword by James Ishmael Ford

For Joan,

who has been my partner in life

for nearly 45 years

THE THIRD STEP EAST
Zen Masters of America
Richard Bryan McDaniel

Text © Richard Bryan McDaniel, 2015
Portraits © Molly Macnaughton, 2015
All rights reserved

Designed by Karma Yönten Gyatso

Published by
The Sumeru Press Inc.
PO Box 2089, Richmond Hill, ON
Canada L4E 1A3

LIBRARY AND ARCHIVES CANADA CATALOGUING IN PUBLICATION

McDaniel, Richard Bryan, author
    The third step East : Zen masters of America / by Richard Bryan McDaniel;
    portraits by Molly Macnaughton ; foreword by James Ishmael Ford.

Includes bibliographical references and index.
Issued in print and electronic formats.
ISBN 978-1-896559-22-3 (pbk.).--ISBN 978-1-896559-23-0 (epub)

    1. Zen Buddhists--United States--Biography. 2. Buddhist monks--United States--Biography. 3. Zen Buddhism--United States--History. I. Title.

BQ9298.M34 2015   294.3'927092273   C2015-900189-7
                                                          C2015-900190-0

 For more information about The Sumeru Press
visit us at *www.sumeru-books.com*

Contents

7   Foreword
9   Preface
17 Prologue in Japan
23 D. T. Suzuki
41 Nyogen Senzaki
57 Sokei-an and Ruth Fuller Sasaki
75 "Beat" Zen
93 Alan Watts
109 Robert Aitken
125 Shunryu Suzuki
145 Soen Nakagawa and Eido Tai Shimano
165 Taizan Maezumi
183 Walter Nowick
199 Philip Kapleau
215 Dainin Katagiri
233 Epilogue in Clatskanie
239 Acknowledgements
241 Endnotes
251 Bibliography
255 Index of Names
263 About the Author
265 About Sumeru

Foreword

WHAT WE HAVE HERE ARE STORIES, specifically Rick McDaniel's delightful telling of the stories of the beginnings of a convert community of Zen Buddhist practice in North America.

Of course it isn't a complete story. The fact that one of the principal Rinzai teachers is omitted due to the unsettled nature of current revelations of his misbehaviors, some of the allegations quite serious, points directly to how this is still a story in the making.

At the same time I find my heart beating faster as I read these stories, brought together with attention and care. And how they tell us of something quite real, a human enterprise, with heroes and villains, sometimes the same person. And something more. This book sings to us of something coming to form, a living and dynamic spiritual tradition taking shape today, sinking roots into new soil.

And, out of this, I find myself invited into the stories. My own, of course. And, in some ways more important, into the big story, the story of Zen and its way of healing broken hearts, and giving people new life, of a dynamic discipline, an ethical code that makes sense, and a living community.

I hope as you read this volume, you will be entertained, and informed. But, most of all, I hope you, too, feel invited into this continuing, rich, story.

It is something important.

James Myoun Ford
Benevolent Street Zendo
Providence, Rhode Island

Preface

ONE HUNDRED YEARS AGO, in 1914, there were no Zen teachers in North America. There were, however, two practitioners. But Nyogen Senzaki, in California, had been told by his teacher—Soyen Shaku—not to utter even the "B" of Buddhism for 17 years after their parting in 1905. Senzaki would not give his first public talk about Zen until 1922. Sokei-an Sasaki and his wife, Tomeko, had been members of an abortive attempt to establish a Zen farming community in California. In 1914, she left him to return to Japan. Sasaki then set out to work his way across North America, ending up in New York City, where he would not begin teaching until 1928.

The year before, 1927, D. T. Suzuki's *Essays in Zen Buddhism* was published in Britain, and Europeans and Americans slowly became aware of a tradition unlike anything they had previously encountered. Something of a publishing boom followed which inspired a small group of individuals—such as the beat poet, Gary Snyder—to seek formal Zen training, but they had to go to Japan in order to do so.

Fifty years ago, in 1964, Snyder returned to the United States from Japan and was surprised to discover that a Zen priest, Shunryu Suzuki, was teaching in San Francisco. Other Zen centers were soon operating in Los Angeles, Rochester, New York City, and even Minneapolis.

A mere twenty years later, by 1984, the nascent Zen movement appeared to be foundering. Shunryu Suzuki's heir in San Francisco, Richard Baker, had been forced to resign his position in disgrace. The Zen teacher in Los Angeles, Taizan Maezumi, admitted to being an alcoholic and had entered the Betty Ford Clinic. Possibly the most renowned Zen Center in the country, Philip Kapleau's in Rochester, had been decimated when one of his former students led away half the membership. And in Surry, Maine, the first American to be authorized to teach Zen, Walter Nowick, gave up teaching in order to focus on music.

The past thirty years have been a time of regrouping, redefining, and revisioning exactly what Zen is and should be in America. Like the Chinese and Japanese before them, North Americans have taken an Indian tradition which pre-dates Christianity and reformed it into something uniquely their own. However, it has not been a birth without complications.

This is the first of two books in which I profile the men and women who have established Zen on this continent. The focus of this volume is deliberately narrow, limited to the pioneers who brought Japanese Zen to America and to those whose stories are, in a sense, complete. With two exceptions, none of the people I profile were living at the time of writing. The most notable omission from this book is Joshu Sasaki, who died in July 2014 at the age of 107. The controversies surrounding him, however, made it difficult to include him in the present work, and I will discuss him in the sequel to this book—*Cypress Trees in the Garden*.

The story of Zen in America naturally becomes more complex with the passage of time, and therefore that second book will have a broader perspective, including chapters on Korean and Vietnamese Zen teachers in the United States. It will also examine the way in which contemporary Zen practitioners have dealt with the challenges left in the wakes of the pioneers described in this book.

The present volume is probably better thought of as a collection of stories than a history. My approach, as in my earlier books on the Zen Masters of China and Japan, is not that of a historian or even a biographer but essentially that of a story-teller.

As with my earlier work, I depend largely on existing sources for the material I recount in *The Third Step East*. These are the stories of American Zen as they have begun to be told and retold; they are part of the public record. There is some new material, gleaned from conversations I have had with Zen teachers in the United States and Canada; my goal, however, is not so much to cast new light on the individuals as to gather together the stories already in circulation.

Story-tellers are not necessarily historically accurate sources of information, even when telling stories about themselves. It is, after all, inevitable that stories reflect a point of view. Mihoko Okamura's recollection and description of the evening Jack Kerouac and Allen Ginsberg dropped in on D. T. Suzuki differs from their versions. Even a single narrator may give alternate renditions of particular events. Sokei-an Sasaki provided his students in New York two different accounts of the story in which his teacher instructed him to "carve a Buddha." In one, it was Soyen Shaku who gave the order; in another, it was Sokei-an's personal teacher, Sokatsu Shaku. The specifics of the stories also vary, although the point of both remains the same.

A historian or a biographer might try to determine which version was closer to the actual events. A story-teller, on the other hand, simply opts for the version which—in his or her opinion—seems to best reflect the subject's personality, understanding, and method of presenting Zen.

And, of course, story-tellers have been known to dramatize details for effect.

Perhaps the best analogy for the profiles in this volume might be popular films based on the lives of actual persons. The scripts for such movies are not written to provide a strict historical account of the subject's life—that is precisely how they differ from documentaries—but to convey a feeling or impression about the subject.

Documentaries will, of course, be made; histories and biographies have been and will continue to be written. But—as has been the case with the Zen tradition from its beginning—stories will be told, and, in the telling, embellishments and alterations will occur. That is because what is important about a good story is not so much its accuracy as its effectiveness. In Zen, that effectiveness has always been measured by the degree to which the story helps others with their practice and with the attainment of awakening. When Sokei-an told the "Carve a Buddha" story, he was not imparting personal information; he was instructing his students.

Richard Bryan McDaniel
Fredericton, New Brunswick, Canada
November 2014

The Third Step East
Zen Masters of America

"Why did the First Patriarch come east?"

Prologue in Japan

*Z*EN IS THE JAPANESE PRONUNCIATION of the character that the Chinese pronounce *chan*, which, in turn, is a rendering of the Sanskrit word *dhyana*, usually translated into English as "meditation." The etymology of the word reflects the steadily eastward movement of the meditation school of Buddhism from India to China, thence to Japan (as well as to Vietnam and Korea), and eventually beyond Asia to North America and the rest of the globe.

Although Buddhism is generally considered a religion, it differs from the theistic traditions more familiar in the West in that it lacks a deity—a Supreme Being external to creation. Writing specifically of the Zen tradition, Alan Watts described Buddhism as

> —a way and a view of life which does not belong to any of the formal categories of modern Western thought. It is not religion or philosophy; it is not a psychology or a type of science. It is an example of what is known in India and China as a "way of liberation."[1]

The Buddha was not a supernatural being but rather an "enlightened" teacher. In fact, the word "Buddha" is a title rather than a name. It means the "Enlightened" or the "Awakened One," and it usually—but not always—refers to Siddhartha Gautama, also known as Shakyamuni (the sage of the Shakya clan), who flourished five hundred years before the birth of Christ. Buddhism, as a doctrine, is the body of teachings attributed to him—generally referred to as the Dharma. The teachings were originally received orally and passed on in the same manner. Eventually they were written down in the Pali language in documents known as *Suttas* (the Pali term) or *Sutras* (the Sanskrit term). Over time, as the followers of the Buddha reflected on his teachings, new interpretations evolved. Sometimes these interpretations were composed as Sutras which were also attributed to the Buddha, even centuries after his death. Competing theories and interpretations of these teachings led to a proliferation of schools, including the establishment of two broad traditions:

the conservative Theravada (the Teaching of the Elders) which spread to Sri Lanka, Burma and Thailand, and the more liberal but also at times more fanciful Mahayana which spread north to Tibet as well as into China, Vietnam, and Korea. It was out of the Mahayana tradition, and partially in reaction to it, that Zen evolved.

Mahayana Buddhism was practiced in China for 400 years before the development of the Chan School. Tradition has it that the school was brought to China from India in the 6th Century by a legendary missionary named Bodhidharma; more probably, Chan evolved from the encounter between Indian Buddhism and Chinese culture, in particular Daoism with its emphasis on the rhythms of nature—the natural flow, or "way" (Dao), of things.

Chan Buddhism came into full flower during the late Tang Dynasty. By the end of the 9th Century, there were Five Houses of Chan, each of which traced its lineage back to a particular group of teachers. The two most prominent of these schools were known, in Japanese, as the Rinzai and the Soto.

Japanese political leadership at that time had a great admiration for all things Chinese, and, throughout much of the Tang Dynasty, courtiers, scholars, craftsmen, and monks traveled to the Asian mainland, returning with ideas which the Japanese assimilated and modified in their unique fashion. Governance, the legal system, the calendar, and other branches of learning were all modeled after Chinese examples. The Chinese mode of writing was adopted, with the result that while a particular character would have the same meaning in both languages, the word it represented, the sound, could be entirely different—thus 禅 is pronounced *chan* in China and and *zen* in Japan.

Religious ideas were also borrowed from China, although the earliest forms of Buddhism to be brought back to Japan were those popular in the port cities of the Chinese coast; it would take another three centuries before Japanese visitors made contact with the remote Chan communities sequestered in the mountains. The Tendai, Shingon, and Pure Land forms of Buddhism were all established in Japan well before Zen.

The first Rinzai temple in Japan was established by Myoan Eisai in 1191. Dogen Kigen[2] brought the Soto School of Zen back to his homeland from China thirty-five years later.

The Zen School differs from other forms of Buddhism in the emphasis it puts on the practice of seated meditation (*zazen*) and the achievement of "awakening" (*kensho* or *satori* in Japanese). With "awakening," the Zen practitioner attains the same insight and perception that Siddhartha Gautama had when he achieved enlightenment and became the Buddha. A poem attributed to Bodhidharma sums up the Zen tradition in four lines:

A special transmission outside the scriptures;
Not dependent on words or letters;
By direct pointing to the mind of man,
Seeing into one's true nature and attaining Buddhahood.

Both the Rinzai and Soto schools view awakening as the goal, although not necessarily the culmination, of Zen practice. The traditional methods by which they seek to guide the practitioner to this end, however, differ.

In China, the Rinzai developed the use of *koans* as an *upaya* or "skillful means" by which the student could be led to awakening and later to the deepening and integration of that awakening into all aspects of his or her life. The term koan[3] refers to a "public record," or "case," in the sense of records kept by a court of law in order to establish precedent in jurisprudence. Koans were largely based on stories about the Zen Masters of the Tang Dynasty. In many instances the koan consists of a question posed by a student and the master's reply, which may appear to be a wholly illogical *non sequitur*. For example, on one occasion when the Zen Master Joshu Jushin[4] was asked the significance of Zen, he replied, "The cypress tree in the garden." When Ummon Bun'en[5] was asked who the Buddha was, he said, "A dried shit-stick."[6] The Rinzai student who is assigned such a koan meditates on it to discover why the teacher's answer is appropriate.

The koan most students begin with is called "Joshu's Dog" or *Mu!* A monk asked the 9th century master, "Does a dog have Buddha-nature?" Joshu replied, "*Mu!*" Mu literally means "no" or "nothing," and Joshu appears to be contradicting the generally accepted Buddhist belief that all things—not only dogs but even insects and trees—have "Buddha-nature." The meditator, however, is warned not to think of the literal meaning of Mu, but to absorb himself in the koan until he achieves the insight (*kensho*) which will allow him to answer correctly when asked, "What is Mu?"

In contrast, the Soto student is usually taught a subjectless meditation known in Japanese as *shikan taza* or "just sitting." The meditator sits alert without focusing attention on anything in particular.

The Rinzai tradition had the reputation of being more demanding than the Soto and put a greater emphasis on attaining awakening. Soto practice, especially in Japan, was considered gentler and stressed the practice of sitting meditation (*zazen*) over attainment. In his writings, Dogen maintained that practice and enlightenment were one. The Buddha had taught that all beings, just as they are, are whole and perfect, that all beings had "Buddha-nature" even though they were not aware of it. From this, Dogen concluded that when the practitioner was properly seated in meditation, enlightenment was present even if the individual was unaware of it. The man who brought the Soto style of meditation to North America, Shunryu Suzuki, made the same point.

The teaching techniques were not exclusive. The Soto School made occasional use of koans, and Rinzai students could be advised to practice *shikan taza*. What they shared was the belief that Buddhahood—awakening—is achieved not through study, acquiring knowledge of the teachings, but through direct spiritual experience.

Meditation and the quest for awakening were primarily the concern of monks attached to Zen temples and not always all of them. Zen temples were also centers for devotional activities carried out by a professional clergy on behalf of lay people who spent little or no time in regular meditation practice. Rites were conducted in the temples for the welfare of the nation or personal prosperity; funeral and memorial services were conducted for the benefit of families.

The Rinzai School was prominent in the major urban centers of Japan and was popular with both government and military leaders; the much larger Soto School was prominent in rural areas. Rinzai Temples received government support and became the basis of an education structure for the upper classes known as the Gozan System. The temples in this network not only provided religious training, they also came to be centers of academic and artistic instruction. As a result, a Zen sensibility came to infuse many aspects of Japanese culture including the visual, literary, and even military arts.

In the last years of the 19th century, the abbot and primary teacher at the prestigious Rinzai temple, Enkaguji[7] was Soyen Shaku. Shaku had trained under Imakita Kosen, one of the most influential Zen masters of the Meiji Era. This was a time of significant change in Japan. In a matter of a few years, the country was transformed from a feudal society into an industrially developed nation. Kosen was a staunch nationalist and supported the government's efforts to modernize Japan by adopting those western institutions, such as universities, which could best assist its advancement. So when his most promising disciple, Shaku, completed his Zen training, rather than sending him on the traditional pilgrimage to other Zen temples in the country, Kosen encouraged him to enroll in the newly established Keio University.

Shaku stayed there three years, after which he traveled to Ceylon (now Sri Lanka), where he familiarized himself with the Theravada tradition. After three years in Ceylon, Shaku returned to Japan. A year later, Kosen died, and his young disciple succeeded him as abbot of Engakuji.

Like his teacher, Shaku was a political conservative who generally accepted the social and economic policies of the Meiji government. He was a product of his era and environment and, as such, took for granted the belief that the Japanese people were the unique descendants of a sacred royal household. He supported Japan's expansionist policies in Asia and took time from his duties at Engakuji to serve as a chaplain in the army during the Russo-Japanese War (1904-05). Later he would argue that the Japanese victory in that combat was due, in part, to the strength the nation drew from Buddhist culture and specifically from Zen training which helped instill a "Samurai spirit" in the population.

In 1893, when Shaku had been abbot of Engakuji for a year, he was invited to take part in the World Parliament of Religions being held in conjunction with the Chicago World's Fair. Some of his colleagues advised him to refuse the invitation on the grounds that the barbarians of the United States could not possibly understand or appreciate Buddhism; after careful consideration, however, Shaku decided to take part. He composed two papers to be presented at the Parliament and, because he had only a rudimentary knowledge of English, asked one of his students, Teitaro Suzuki, to translate them for him.

During the late 19th Century, a number of western academics had become familiar with Buddhism. Some even felt it was a faith more in accord with the post-Darwinian scientific perspective than was Christianity; however, following the lead of the founder of the Pali Text Society, Professor Thomas William Rhys-Davids of the University of London, there was a consensus that the Theravada School was a purer expression of the Buddha's teaching than the later and, so it was believed, corrupted Mahayana. The Japanese delegation which took part in the Parliament—including, besides Shaku, representatives of the Nichiren and Tendai Schools—provided the attendees with an alternative vision of the Mahayana as a progressive and evolving system of thought.

Shaku's principle paper dealt with Buddhist teachings regarding "cause and effect." It was read to the participants by the Parliament's chairman, John Henry Barrows, and was received politely but without that enthusiasm which the audience demonstrated for some of the more charismatic Asian presenters, such as the Ceylonese Buddhist and Theosophist, Anagarika Dharmapala, and the Hindu, Swami Vivekananda. One attendee who was impressed by Shaku's paper, however, was Paul Carus, a prolific writer, publisher, and editor interested in the relationship between religion and science. He was one of those who believed Buddhism might be better able to overcome the rift between the two than could Christianity. Shaku's paper was in accord with his own thought, so Carus invited the Zen master to his home in LaSalle, Illinois, about seventy miles west of Chicago. While Shaku was his guest, Carus asked him to consider collaborating on a project to prepare translations of Buddhist—in particular, Mahayana—texts for publication in English. Shaku demurred, stating that he was not qualified to do so and that his duties at Engakuji prevented him from taking on other responsibilities; he noted, however, that he had a student whom he thought would be suitable for the task.

Chapter One
D. T. Suzuki

TEITARO SUZUKI WAS BORN in 1870 in Kanazawa, the capital of Kaga (later Ishikawa) Prefecture. The city, on the coast of the Sea of Japan, is a damp place, noted for its high humidity and rainfall (averaging nearly 200 days a year). It was a gloomy but moderately important center, and Suzuki's family was of the Samurai class, which—prior to the Meiji Era—had held a privileged position in feudal Japan. After the Meiji reforms, however, those privileges were lost.

Suzuki's father, grandfather, and great-grandfather had all been physicians, and it had been expected that young Teitaro, who showed some aptitude in the field, would also train in medicine. His father died, however, when the boy was only six years old, leaving the family in poverty. Suzuki's mother received a small widow's pension which she supplemented by taking in boarders, but even with this extra income the family could not afford for Teitaro to pursue a medical degree.

The dominant forms of Buddhism in the region were Soto Zen and Pure Land. Mahayana Buddhism recognizes that in addition to Shakyamuni Buddha there are many other Buddhas both in the past and yet to be born. It maintains that one of these, Amida Buddha—who reigns in the "Western Paradise" (the Pure Land)—once vowed that anyone who called upon him with faith would be reborn in that Paradise. Devotees are taught to repeat the *nembutsu*—"*Namu amida butsu*"—a short prayer meaning, "I take refuge in Amida Buddha." Like many Samurai, however, the Suzuki family was affiliated with neither of these but with a Rinzai Temple, although they were not active members. Suzuki's father had been a Confucianist, and his mother, while not particularly devout, was a Pure Land adherent.

A year after their father died, Teitaro's older brother also passed away. Their mother was shaken by these two losses, and, when her eyesight began to fail as well, she went on a pilgrimage to visit the shrine of Fudo-myoo, a popular devotional figure. She took her young son with her, and Suzuki later said that the grimacing image of Fudo, holding a sword and a rope, aroused his earliest interest in religion. When he was eight years old, his mother arranged for him to be formally received into the Hijibomon sect of the Pure Land School.

While still very young, Teitaro came to wonder why he had had to face so many difficulties and challenges in his life—the loss of family status, the deaths of his father and brother, the family's straitened financial circumstances. In a biographical essay written years later for the journal of the British Buddhist Society, he reflected that in those days the loss of a father was even more devastating than it would be in later times

—for so much depended on him as head of the family—all the important steps in life such as education and finding a position in life afterwards. All this I lost, and by the time I was about seventeen or eighteen these misfortunes made me start thinking about my karma. Why should I have these disadvantages at the very start of life?[8]

He brought his questions to the priest at the Rinzai temple where the family was registered; the man, however, was an appointee with little actual experience of Zen practice, and nothing came of the meeting. Suzuki also spoke with a couple of Christian missionaries, one of whom gave him a Japanese translation of the Book of Genesis. But the concept of a God external to, and responsible for, creation was a foreign one, and Suzuki could make little sense of it.

At school, he was considered a good pupil. In addition to his regular studies, he taught himself an idiosyncratic form of English from old textbooks. It was in Upper Middle School that he was first introduced to Zen. His mathematics teacher, a man named Jikei Hojo, was a disciple of Imakita Kosen. Suzuki joined the discussion group about Zen which Hojo hosted at the school. To further the young student's interest, Hojo gave him a copy of the *Orategama,* a collection of letters written by Zen master Hakuin Ekaku.[9] The book caught Teitaro's interest, although he found it difficult to understand. It was enough, however, to goad him into visiting an authorized Zen teacher.

The nearest was Michizu Setsumon at Kokutaiji in the adjacent prefecture of Etchu. Suzuki made the journey through the mountains over the Kurikara Pass in a small horse drawn bus. When he arrived, the teacher was absent, but the monks provided him a room and told him he could practice zazen there. They left him, however, with no instruction about how to do so, and there he waited until the teacher—addressed as Roshi[10]—returned.

During his first formal interview (*sanzen*) with Setsumon, Suzuki was unfamiliar with the appropriate protocol for such meetings. He brought his copy of the *Orategama* and asked the Roshi to explain some of the more obscure terms Hakuin had employed in it.

"What a stupid question!" Setsumon barked, dismissing him.

He returned to the room he had been assigned, but still no instruction was provided. No one spoke to him, not even the monks who brought his meals. After a few days, frustrated and homesick, he left to return home.

Fiscal constraint prevented him from completing secondary school, but he was able to find work teaching English at a primary school in a nearby fishing village. Doing so, he was able to contribute to the family's finances. After a year, he returned to Ishikawa to teach at Mikawa Primary School.

The family recognized Teitaro's academic talents, and, after their mother died in 1890, his older brother provided him funds to attend classes at Waseda University in Tokyo. There, for the first time, he encountered spoken English and discovered that what he had been teaching bore little resemblance to the actual language.

Residing in Tokyo, he was relatively close to Kamakura where Engakuji was located. The concerns which had preoccupied him remained unresolved, and one day he determined to visit Engakuji. It was thirty miles away, and he walked the whole distance. Imakita Kosen accepted him as a lay student, and Suzuki began his formal Zen training.

Kosen assigned him Hakuin's koan, "What is the sound of one hand clapping?" Suzuki focused on the koan during zazen but found it entirely opaque. When he went to sanzen with Kosen, the teacher would put his left hand forward without saying anything; Suzuki had no idea how to respond. Whenever he attempted to express his thoughts about the koan, Kosen dismissed these as nothing more than ideas.

Within a year, Kosen died. His heir, Soyen Shaku, changed Suzuki's koan to Mu. Suzuki applied himself to the new koan with all his energy, feeling as if his life would be meaningless if he were unable to resolve it.

When Shaku learned that his student was able to read and write English, he assigned him a number of translation tasks, including his correspondence with the organizing committee of the World Parliament of Religions. He also had Suzuki translate Paul Carus' *The Gospel of Buddhism*, for which Shaku had provided an introduction. Throughout all of this work, Mu remained at the back of Suzuki's mind, but he came no closer to understanding it. Because he had nothing to say, he stopped attending sanzen with Shaku, except those mandated during the formal retreats known as *sesshin*, and, on those occasions, Shaku often dismissed him with a blow.

This continued for four years. Suzuki wondered if his difficulty was due to a lack of familiarity with Zen literature; perhaps, he thought, he could find the answer to Mu in one of the books in the Temple library. He immersed himself in these, which would be a great help to him when later he began writing, but nothing he read helped him understand Mu any better.

When, after the Parliament, Paul Carus asked Soyen Shaku to consider remaining in the United States in order to assist him in preparing translations of Eastern texts, Shaku suggested that Teitaro Suzuki would be better suited for the position. In a letter to Carus, Shaku described the future scholar as an "honest and diligent Buddhist" but also noted that he was "not thoroughly versed with Buddhist literature." [11]

It was a great opportunity, but Suzuki was aware that going to the United States also meant that he might not be able to partake in sesshin for many years. If he did not resolve the koan during the upcoming sesshin, he would not have another opportunity until he returned to Japan, and he had no idea when that would be.

The next sesshin was the December Rohatsu Sesshin which marks the anniversary of the Buddha's awakening. Traditionally, it is the most demanding retreat of the year; the periods of zazen are extended, and the participants are spurred on by frequent blows from the *kyosaku*—or "encouragement" stick.

Suzuki concentrated on Mu with all his might, synchronizing it with his breath. By the final days of the seven day retreat, the koan was no longer something separate from him. There was not the koan on the one hand, and the person repeating it on the other; there was only Mu. This deep state of concentration is known as *samadhi*.

> Up till then I had always been conscious that *Mu* was in my mind. But so long as *I* was conscious of *Mu* it meant that I was somehow separate from *Mu*, and that is not a true *samadhi*. But towards the end of that *sesshin*, about the fifth day, I ceased to be conscious of *Mu*. I was one with *Mu*, identified with *Mu*, so that there was no longer the separateness implied by being conscious of *Mu*. This is the real state of *samadhi*.[12]

Then, after a round of meditation, he was roused from this samadhi by the sound of a bell being rung, and Mu was resolved. This was the "satori"—or awakening to one's true nature— the *raison d'être* of Zen about which Suzuki would write so tantalizingly in the future.

> Without the attainment of satori no one can enter into the mystery of Zen. It is the sudden flashing of a new truth hitherto altogether undreamed of. It is a sort of mental catastrophe taking place all at once after so much piling of matters intellectual and demonstrative.[13]

Suzuki rushed to *sanzen* and was able to answer all but one of the testing questions Shaku put to him; the next morning, he was able to answer that question as well. Shaku acknowledged the validity of his awakening and gave him the Buddhist name "Daisetz" which means "Great Simplicity." Suzuki retained the name for the rest of his life, joking that it actually meant "Great Stupidity."

Suzuki arrived in San Francisco in 1897 and was welcomed to the United States by being placed in quarantine on the suspicion that he had tuberculosis. After a period of observation, as well as interventions on his behalf by Carus and Dharmapala, who had made such an impression at the Parliament of Religions, he was allowed to proceed to Illinois.

In La Salle, Suzuki stayed in the expansive residence which Carus had inherited from his father-in-law, Edward Hegeler. The house had been designed by William Boyington, who also designed the Chicago Water Tower, one of that city's most distinctive architectural features. From this house, Carus operated the Open Court Publishing Company.

Carus was one of a number of thinkers at the turn of the 19th and 20th centuries who were trying to reconcile the growing conflict between religion and science. He sought to identify what he called a "Religion of Science"—a religious perspective shorn of mythology and superstition, in harmony with current scientific understanding, which could be globally accepted. He believed that Buddhism had the potential to fill this role. To that end, Open Court Publishing made Eastern texts available to the West. Suzuki would work with Carus on this project for eleven years.

In addition to his translation, proof-reading and editing duties, Suzuki also functioned as a kind of houseboy. He was responsible for hauling water from the well and fetching firewood. He did not resent having to carry out these tasks, which were considered honorable in the Zen tradition, lauded in the famous verse of Pangyun[14] who, like Suzuki, was a layman:

> How miraculous! How wondrous!
> Hauling water and carrying wood!

Suzuki's first assignment was to assist Carus with a translation of the *Tao Te Ching*.[15] Suzuki was not happy with the rendition, believing that Carus distorted the work by his use of abstract Western terminology which did not adequately reflect the intention of the text. Suzuki took it upon himself to translate Ashvaghosha's *Awakening of Faith in the Mahayana*, which would be the first of many books in English that he would release under his own name. This was published in 1900, after which Suzuki began work on *Outlines of Mahayana Buddhism*, in which he sought to counter the perception of western scholars who viewed the Mahayana, with its esoteric teachings and plethora of Bodhisattvas (roughly equivalent to Christian Saints), as a degenerate form of Buddhism compared with the older Theravada School.

There was growing academic and popular interest in Buddhism after the World Parliament of Religions, although the number of Westerners who gave serious thought to adopting the Buddhist faith was miniscule. There were a few, however, some of whom even found their way to Engakuji and undertook Zen training under Shaku's tutelage. In 1905, one of these, a San Francisco resident named Ida Russell, invited Shaku to make a second visit to the United States as the guest of her and her husband.

Shaku accepted the invitation and arranged for Suzuki to meet him in San Francisco. On the passage over the Pacific, Shaku composed a poem in which he reflected that he was carrying on the tradition of Bodhidharma by travelling eastward in order to bring Zen to new lands.

Shaku remained with the Russells long enough to introduce Ida to koan study, and she became the first person in North America known to work on koans with an authorized teacher. Arrangements were made for Shaku to give a number of talks to the Japanese immigrant communities in San Francisco, Los Angeles, Sacramento and Oakland. Then in 1906, attended by Suzuki, he proceeded across the country by train. They stopped in Illinois so Shaku could visit Carus before continuing to the East Coast.

During his tour, Shaku met a range of political and academic figures, including President Theodore Roosevelt, and he gave public lectures on Zen. Like Suzuki in his *Outline of Mahayana Buddhism*, Shaku sought to correct popular misconceptions. Christian critics had been vociferous in condemning Buddhism as a negative and life-denying doctrine whose goal was the total extinction of the person in Nirvana. Shaku argued instead that Buddhism was life-affirming, and that through meditation practice the individual came into direct contact with

> —the most concrete and withal the most universal fact of life.... It is the philosopher's business to deal with dry, lifeless, uninteresting generalizations. Buddhists are not concerned with things like that. They want to see the fact directly and not through the medium of philosophical abstractions. There may be a god who created heaven and earth, or there may not; we could be saved simply by believing in his goodness, or we could not.... True Buddhists do not concern

themselves with propositions such as these.... Buddhists through [meditation] endeavor to reach the bottom of things and there to grasp with their own hands the very life of the universe, which makes the sun rise in the morning, makes the bird cheerfully sing in the balmy spring breeze, and also makes the biped called man hunger for love, righteousness, liberty, truth, and goodness.[16]

Shaku's tour lasted nine months, and, while they were in New York, Suzuki met Beatrice Erskine, whom he would later marry. When Soyen Shaku returned to Japan, Suzuki resumed his work in LaSalle and continued there for another two years.

In 1908, he left Open House Publishing, went to New York, and renewed his acquaintance with Beatrice. Then he did a tour of Europe before returning to Japan, where Beatrice would eventually follow him.

Beatrice's family were practicing Bahá'ís, a faith which teaches the concept of continuing revelation. There is not a single prophet or messenger in the Bahá'í tradition, but rather a succession of "Manifestations of God," each of whom provides humankind with a new "dispensation" in which a broader understanding of the Divine Will is presented suitable to the current stage of human knowledge and understanding. The Manifestation for the current era is Bahá'u'lláh, who lived in Persia (now Iran) from 1817-92. Previous Manifestations included the Buddha and Jesus, as well as Krishna and Muhammad.

Beatrice, who was an alumnus of Radcliffe and did graduate work at Columbia, was also interested in the Theosophical Society established in 1875 and headquartered in Madras, India. Theosophists also believed in continuing revelation and were particularly interested in Eastern philosophy. Their stated objectives were:

1) To establish a universal brotherhood of all humankind without distinction of race, gender, or creed;
2) To promote the study of comparative religion, philosophy, and science; and
3) To investigate "unexplained laws of nature and the powers latent in" human beings.

Such were some of the issues thoughtful persons were considering at the time.

Beatrice and Suzuki were married in Yokohama in 1911. They adopted a son, Paul, who was of mixed European and Japanese descent. Both their marriage and the adoption flouted the ethnocentric attitudes common throughout Japan. The family lived in a small cottage in the Engakuji compound until 1919, when they moved to

Kyoto, where Suzuki taught at Otani University. At one point, the couple operated an animal shelter, much to the annoyance of their neighbors.

They founded the Eastern Buddhist Society and published an English language journal, *The Eastern Buddhist*, to which they both frequently contributed articles. A number of D. T. Suzuki's pieces were collected and published by the British company, Rider, in 1927 under the title, *Essays in Zen Buddhism*. The book related Tang dynasty koans and tales never before heard in the west and was surprisingly successful. More than any other work to that date, it would be responsible for promoting a popular interest in Zen both in North America and Europe.

Suzuki was 57 when *Essays in Zen Buddhism* was released; his output after its publication was prodigious. A second and third volume of Essays were brought out by Rider. He released a translation of the *Lankavatara Sutra* in 1932; *The Training of the Zen Buddhist Monk* was published in 1934; and *Zen Buddhism and Its Influence on Japanese Culture* came out in 1938, the same year that Beatrice published *Mahayana Buddhism*.

The appeal of Suzuki's books was the portrait he gave of a religion which stood in stark contrast to the Judaeo-Christian heritage of the West—a religion without a deity, a religion which held that the practitioner could attain the same insight and awareness its founder had had. In response to those critics who viewed the Mahayana as a distortion of the Buddha's original teaching, Suzuki insisted that a vital religion must not be limited to its earliest expression but must demonstrate the ability to evolve. Zen, he argued, was Buddhism "shorn of its Indian garb," the cultural and historical trappings of the original teaching. What was central to Zen, after all, was not a "dependence on words and letters" but the transmission of the original awakening experience by which Siddhartha Gautama became the Buddha and which he passed onto his disciple, Mahakasyapa.[17]

Later scholars would accuse Suzuki of providing a distorted description of Zen. He largely ignored the Soto school and even his presentation of Rinzai teaching and practice was very personal. Regardless of whether it was objective or not, it was a presentation which would resonate with a much larger audience than he—or anyone else—could have foreseen. A talk he gave at Oxford in 1953 provides a summary of some of the main themes to which he returned time and again in his writing.[18]

He posited that Zen was "a combination of Chinese psychology and Indian philosophy" which provided a practical demonstration of "the highly abstract teachings" of Indian Buddhism. The goal of Zen Buddhism is not to understand the Buddha's teaching but to share his experience of awakening or satori. The Buddha was not—as was Jesus in Christianity—a being of a different order; he was an ordinary man. So what he attained, others could attain as well.

The Buddha's understanding came from his quest to answer the great questions of life and death and all other forms of duality

> —or, as we might say nowadays…the bifurcation of subject and object. When we are faced with this bifurcation, when subject and object oppose one another, the result is the anxiety and fear which troubles us all.

The Buddha first sought to resolve this issue through philosophical analysis, and, when that proved inadequate, "he turned to moral discipline and ascetic practice" as undertaken by the yogic tradition of the time. This, too, proved futile. "Thus neither intellectual discipline nor moral discipline availed to solve this problem."

> Now the religious or spiritual life is something which transcends an intellectual attempt to reach reality. Other religions emphasize moral discipline, but moral endeavour can never reach the realm of spirituality. When we have attained the spiritual plane, moral life emanates naturally, but moral discipline and intellection will never bring us to this spiritual life. We must transcend the subject-object aspect of existence.
>
> How are we to reach this transcendental realm? It is reached when the personality and the teaching, or the questioner and the question, are identified. So long as Buddha had his question before him; so long as he had it outside and separate from himself, as if it could be solved by external means, it could never be solved. The question comes out of the questioner. But when it is out, the questioner mistakenly thinks it is something outside himself. The question is answered only when it is identified with the questioner.

To analyze a problem philosophically is to separate oneself from the problem. "When the question goes out from the questioner and becomes separated from him, he cannot solve it." It is precisely the "bifurcation" of subject/object which is the root of the problem of life and death. Humankind, according to Suzuki, has

> —a persistent desire to return to the state of innocence prior, epistemologically speaking, to creation, to the state where there is no

division, no knowledge—prior to the subject-object division, to the time when there was only God as He was before He created the world. The separation of God from the world is the source of all our troubles. We have an innate desire to be united with God.

After failing to do so through intellectual or moral effort, the Buddha sought to address the matter of duality by turning inward through meditation. He took his place beneath what would come to be called the Bodhi Tree and sat. At first his mind remained in "great turmoil," but eventually consciousness sank

—back into itself. This is what is called *samadhi*, being absorbed in meditation, and when we come to this everything is lost. There is psychologically a complete state of unconsciousness. But when this state is reached, even this is not final. There must be awakening, and this awakening usually takes place through sense-stimulation.

In Suzuki's case it had been the sound of the bell. For the Buddha, it was the sight of the morning star. When he saw the star on the horizon, he saw into his own true nature and was awakened to that unity which precedes and underlies dualism. The full significance of this awareness can only be appreciated when one comes to awakening oneself. Buddhism, therefore, is the

—religion of enlightenment. To understand it, we have to become enlightened ourselves. By being enlightened we attain *bodhi*[19] and become Buddha; it is by experiencing *bodhi* that we become real Buddhist followers.

Although Suzuki made it clear that one came to awakening through the practice of zazen, he did not provide instruction on how to do zazen. Still, readers sought a way to practice. A group of such readers in England, known as the Buddhist Lodge, had been established by a London barrister named Christmas Humphreys. Humphreys had come to Buddhism via Theosophy and was an enthusiastic reader of Suzuki's books and the *Eastern Buddhist*. The books and articles were the subject of many of the lodge discussions. In 1936, they were delighted to learn that Suzuki was coming to London to participate in the World Congress of Faith. When they met him, the lodge members were all entranced by Suzuki, but none more so than a young man, just turned 21, named Alan Watts.

The topic of the symposium in which Suzuki participated was "The Supreme Spiritual Ideal." A number of papers were presented before his, in which the subject was addressed in a suitably serious and generally humorless fashion. When it was Suzuki's turn at the podium, he began his address by telling the audience that he did not know what was meant by the terms "Spiritual" or "Ideal" and so had no idea what the "Supreme Spiritual Ideal" was. After that, he used the remainder of the time allotted to him to describe his small cottage and its garden in Kyoto. The audience, Christmas Humphreys later reported, responded enthusiastically.

Beatrice died in 1939, just as most of the northern hemisphere became involved in the Second World War. The Second Sino-Japanese War had already begun two years earlier. Suzuki, as a much younger man, had been on record as supporting Japanese territorial ambitions following the first Sino-Japanese War (1894-95).[20] It would have been difficult for a young man in his twenties to resist the tide of public opinion and nationalism of the day.

He was a more mature man by 1939 and had had an American wife to whom he had been happily married for twenty-eight years. A number of articles he had written on *bushido* (the Japanese "art of war") and Zen have since been referenced to suggest that he supported Japanese actions during the Second World War, but the evidence is weak. In his personal correspondence during the Russo-Japanese and the Second Sino-Japanese wars, Suzuki decried the conflicts and Japanese military policies, and what he wrote about bushido in general cannot easily be interpreted as supporting the government policies of the day. In fact, during the war he remained in seclusion at his old cottage in the Engakuji compound, suspected by Japanese authorities of holding anti-militaristic and leftist views. When military officials came to the University where Suzuki had been teaching and told the young men that it was their duty to die for their country, Suzuki risked arrest and imprisonment by arguing, on the contrary, that it was their duty to come back to their country alive because without its youth, a country has no future. Later Suzuki would state that the "Pacific War was a ridiculous war for the Japanese to have initiated; it was probably completely without justification."[21]

After the war, Christmas Humphreys was appointed an assistant prosecutor in the War Crimes trials held in Japan. Although fraternization with the occupied population was prohibited, Humphreys made his way to Engakuji to visit Suzuki. Humphreys wrote that when they first met, Suzuki raised his arm so the sleeve of his kimono hid the emotion on his face.

In spite of the natural ill-will engendered by the war, several other members of the occupying forces had sufficient interest in Zen to seek out Suzuki. Among them was Richard DeMartino, an American who spoke Japanese fluently and had been seconded to assist the team acting as defense counsel for those Japanese military officers accused of war crimes. He brought a friend, Philip Kapleau, to visit Suzuki. Kapleau had been a court reporter during the Nuremburg Trials in Germany and was now in Japan to cover the Tokyo trials. It was during his visits to Suzuki with DeMartino that Kapleau was first introduced to the importance of satori in the Zen tradition.

Suzuki was a prolific writer. Over his career, he composed more than a hundred books in Japanese and another thirty in English. His sales increased after the war. A*n Introduction to Zen Buddhism*, originally published in Japan in 1934, was reissued by Rider and Company in 1948 with a Foreword by Carl Jung; then came *The Zen Doctrine of No-Mind* and *Manual of Zen Buddhism* in 1949 and 1950.

In 1949, he was invited to Honolulu to give a series of lectures at the University of Hawaii. From there, he proceeded onto California and eventually made his way to Columbia University in New York. Philip Kapleau was one of those who attended the talks at Columbia. Suzuki was also a visiting lecturer at several other universities.

The people who attended the lectures were drawn in many cases by a naïve interest in Zen. For most westerners, Zen had an aura of the *outré* about it, and it drew the attention of individuals who, earlier, would have been drawn to spiritualism or the Theosophical Movement. During the discussion period following one of Suzuki's lectures, an attendee tried to bring the topic around to the psychic abilities popularly believed to be attained through meditation, in particular the ability to read the thoughts of others. Finally, the usually mild-mannered Suzuki put an end to the questioning by asking, "What is the use of knowing someone else's mind? What is important is to know your own."

There were occasionally individuals who still harbored hostile feelings about the war. At Yale University, a faculty member questioned Buddhism's claim to be the religion of compassion. "It's well known that war criminals like General Tojo practiced Zen meditation," he pointed out. "How 'compassionate' can Zen Buddhism be if it has people like that in its temples?"

Suzuki considered the question for a long while in a silence which grew increasingly uncomfortable for those in attendance. Finally he said, "Doesn't a soldier, who must confront death every day in his activities, need as much compassion as a civilian?"

The critics in his audiences, however, were a minority, and by the late mid-1950s Suzuki had achieved celebrity status. Supporters in New York established the Zen Studies Society in order to promote his work. Photos were published in popular magazines showing a small, Japanese man, with an engaging smile, sometimes dressed in cardigans and bowties, sometimes in kimonos, with enormous eyebrows sprouting like spiky vegetation above the lenses of his rimless glasses. In Japan, he was awarded the Medal of Culture by the Emperor. In North America and Britain, his books continued to sell well.

Through it all he continued to remain accessible to almost anyone who called upon him, as in the case of the evening when Jack Kerouac and Allen Ginsberg, both inebriated after attending a party to celebrate the publication of Kerouac's *Dharma Bums*, phoned to say they wanted to come over to see him. The person who took that call before passing it onto Suzuki—who later admitted she eavesdropped, with some apprehension, on the conversation going on in the other room—was the young woman in whose parents' apartment Suzuki had his rooms at the time. Her name was Mihoko Okamura.

When Mihoko had been a freshman in high school, she skipped classes one day in order to attend one of Suzuki's lectures at Columbia. She was struggling with depression at the time. She had grown up in California where her sense of personal security had been destroyed when her family was exiled to an internment camp during the war years. After the war, her father found work as a gardener at the Brooklyn Botanic Gardens, and the family left behind everything with which they had been familiar in order to move to New York.

She had the usual questions about the purpose of life to which reflective young people are subject, but these were exacerbated by her experiences during the war. After listening to Suzuki speak, she visited him in his rooms at Butler Hall and told him of her feelings. He let her talk at length without interrupting her or making light of anything she said. When she fell quiet, he sat a moment in silence, then said, "Well!"

He told her that her feelings were examples of the "Great Doubt" which often provides the energy behind Zen practice. Traditionally it is held that three elements are necessary for the practice of Zen: Great Faith, Great Perseverance, and Great Doubt. Great Doubt is the driving concern which compels one's practice.

Mihoko became Suzuki's personal assistant and remained with him for the last fifteen years of his life. When Suzuki retired from Columbia in 1957, Mihoko accompanied him to Cuernavaca where he attended a conference on Zen and Psychology organized by the Mexican Psychoanalytic Society and held at the home of the German psychoanalyst, Erich Fromm, then living in Mexico. Fifty people attended the conference, many coming specifically in order to meet Suzuki.

An often repeated story about Suzuki, originally told by Fromm, took place during this conference. Suzuki was late for one of the sessions, so Mihoko and Fromm's wife, Annis Freeman, went to look for him. They searched the conference grounds without success, and were becoming concerned when they found him seated by a tree meditating. As Fromm put it, Suzuki had become so "at one" with the tree that it was difficult to see him.

In 1959, Suzuki was awarded an honorary doctorate of law degree from the University of Hawaii. While in Honolulu to accept it, he attended a reception hosted by the Young Buddhist Association. Anne Aitken, wife of the pioneer American Zen master, Robert Aitken, related that after the meal was served, she chanced to see Suzuki "browsing among the tables, and picking off parsley from the plates, and eating it. Catching her eye, he grinned like a little boy and said, 'People don't eat their parsley, and it is so good for them.'"[22]

Alan Watts told of an incident at one of Suzuki's presentations when

> —a member of the audience asked him, "Dr. Suzuki, when you use the word 'reality,' are you referring to the relative reality of the physical world, or to the absolute reality of the transcendental world?" He closed his eyes and went into that characteristic attitude which some of his students call "doing a Suzuki," for no one could tell whether he was in deep meditation or fast asleep. After a minutes' silence, though it seemed longer, he opened his eyes and said, "Yes."[23]

For much of the 1950s and 1960s, Suzuki's name was synonymous with Zen. He was the recognized authority on the subject. Western understanding of Zen was almost wholly based on his writings or those of Alan Watts, whose early books on Zen were largely a reworking of Suzuki. But as more Westerners went to Japan and studied with masters there, that authority began to be questioned. A frequent criticism was that he "wrote about" Zen rather than "taught" Zen. Western practitioners, like Philip Kapleau, decried how little attention he paid to the mechanics of meditation practice.

Other critics argued that his presentation of Zen was too narrow, focusing almost exclusively on Rinzai Zen. Although in later life he would write about the Pure Land School and about Western mystics such as Meister Eckhart, he wrote very little about the largest Zen school in Japan—the Soto—and what he did write was often dismissive. It was also suggested that his portrayal of the Rinzai School overlooked the devotional and ritual practices common in Rinzai temples. Other critics chastised him for separating Zen from its foundations in traditional Buddhism and presenting it as something fundamental to all spiritual traditions—as he put it, "the ultimate fact of all philosophy and religion."[24]

In many cases, these criticisms amounted to little more than complaints that Suzuki did not present Zen the way the critic would have. Suzuki was not an authorized Zen teacher, nor did he claim to be. What he did do was inspire people like Kapleau to undertake Zen training. It was through Suzuki's writing that the concept of satori—no matter how misunderstood—was first presented to the west, raising the possibility of a way of perceiving reality in a manner outside the common dualistic framework of Western thought. His belief in the universality of Zen insight allowed Western readers, still attached to their own religious heritages, to investigate how those traditions could be enhanced or deepened through Zen.

There have been more profound writers on Zen since Suzuki, and there have, no doubt, been many whose Zen insight was deeper than his. But no matter how flawed his presentation may have been, it was his exposition of Zen that introduced it to the West and inspired the first Western practitioners to seek out teachers.

Daisetz Teitaro Suzuki died on July 12, 1966, at the age of 96. Mihoko reported that his final words were: "Don't worry. Thank you. Thank you."

Chapter Two
Nyogen Senzaki

As a young man at Engakuji, Suzuki briefly shared accommodations with another of Soyen Shaku's students, a monk named Nyogen Senzaki. At Shaku's behest, Senzaki would also come to the United State where his work complemented and fulfilled Suzuki's. Suzuki introduced the West to the theory of Zen; Senzaki introduced North Americans to the practice of Zen.

The story is told that in 1876, a Japanese fisherman—or possibly an itinerant Kegon monk—named Senzaki came upon the body of a recently deceased woman on the Russian Kamchatka peninsula which extends southward towards the archipelago of Japan. At the woman's breast, there was a newborn child which the fisherman rescued and brought back to his homeland. The dead woman had clearly been Japanese, but the baby grew up with Chinese features as a result of which Nyogen Senzaki assumed his natural father was either from Siberia or China.

The child was officially adopted by the fisherman and registered as the first-born son of the Senzaki family. His given name was Aizo. His adoptive mother died when he was five after which he was sent to the house of his grandfather, who was the abbot of Sokoji, a Buddhist temple in the Pure Land Tradition. There, under his grandfather's supervision, the boy was educated in classical Chinese and Buddhist literature.

The grandfather was a devout man who instilled a strong moral sense in his grandson, but he was also a man who lamented the degraded condition to which Buddhism and, in particular, the clergy had fallen. When he sensed that his grandson was drawn to religious life, he encouraged the boy to live by the Buddhist precepts but discouraged him from becoming ordained. When Aizo was sixteen, the grandfather became ill and his last words to the boy were: "Corruption among Buddhist priests keeps getting worse. Although you have always wished to leave secular life and seek the great Dharma, entering monkhood may, ironically, hinder your goal. Beware of joining that pack of tigers and wolves called monks."[25]

Aizo returned to his adoptive father's house, where he began a course of study intended to prepare him for a medical degree. He remained drawn to Buddhist studies, however, and, by the age of eighteen, had read the entire Tripitaka—the three collections of Buddhist scriptures.[26] Around this time, he also read the autobiography of Benjamin Franklin and took up Franklin's habit of maintaining a journal in which he daily recorded his deeds, both good and bad, marking the bad deeds with a black dot. The young Aizo was saddened by the frequency of black dots in his diary. Attracted to the highly disciplined lifestyle of foreign missionaries then proselytizing in Japan, he briefly considered becoming a Christian.

He felt a strong sense of obligation to the members of his grandfather's temple; their donations had provided the old man with an income and, thus, helped pay for Senzaki's education. He wondered how he could repay the debt he owed them and, despite his grandfather's warning, kept coming back to the idea that he might best do so by entering religious life.

He first learned of Zen through a friend who composed haiku and introduced him to the poetry of Matsuo Basho.[27] This led him to investigate others works on Zen. In his reading, he happened upon the story of Tokusan,[28] who had been a student of the *Diamond Sutra*. Tokusan came to realize that his academic study was not furthering his spiritual development so one day burned all the notes he had gathered on the *Diamond Sutra* and began his formation anew under the direction of Zen Master Ryutan.[29] Inspired by this example, Senzaki gave up his medical studies and sought ordination as a monk. His head was shaved, and he was given the Buddhist name Nyo Gen, "Like a Phantasm." Appropriately, the name came from a passage in the *Diamond Sutra* which states that all "composite things" are like phantasms, like figures in a dream.

Although he had been ordained in a Soto Temple (there was no Rinzai Temple in the area), he began a correspondence with Soyen Shaku who had recently been elevated to the post of abbot at Engakuji. In 1896, Senzaki left his home and traveled to Kamakura in order to work with Shaku.

At their first meeting, Shaku was concerned by the physical appearance of the young man who presented himself at the temple. A physician was consulted, and it was discovered that Senzaki had tuberculosis and needed to be kept in isolation. His first year at Engakuji was spent quarantined in a small hut on the temple grounds. From time to time, Shaku would visit Senzaki, whose condition continued to worsen. On one occasion, he asked Shaku, "What will happen if I die?"

"If you die, just die," Shaku told him.

Eventually Senzaki's health improved, and Shaku accepted him as a student. Senzaki did koan study with Shaku for five years but at some point became disturbed by the disparity he saw between the Buddhist vow to "liberate" all creatures and the secluded and comfortable life monks led far from the daily cares of lay life. He was also disillusioned with many of the Buddhist priests he met who, in contrast to the austere lives exhibited by Christian missionaries, paid slack attention to the precepts. He never questioned Shaku's commitment to the Dharma nor the sincerity of his teacher's vows, but Senzaki saw little of that same zeal among the majority of priests in the Zen establishment. He recalled his grandfather's last words and found himself in sympathy with the criticisms common during the Meiji Restoration about the Buddhist clergy. In a commentary on a koan he wrote many years later, Senzaki derided those who proclaimed themselves

> —Zen masters, just because they passed several hundred koans in the secret rooms of their teachers. They teach their students in their own secret rooms and produce similar Zen teachers. It is a sort of school for magic and tricks. It has nothing to do with the understanding of Buddha Shakyamuni and Bodhidharma. The whole matter is nothing but a joke. No wonder most Zen teachers in Japan now have wives and children. They drink and smoke, and accumulate money for the comfort of themselves and their families.[30]

Senzaki aspired to live the life not of a married priest but of a celibate monk in the manner of the earliest followers of the Buddha. But even as a monk, he did not feel it was his calling to remain sequestered from the world at large. In a letter to Shaku, Senzaki explained his reasons for wishing to leave Engakuji: "Though it was my original vow to attain Buddha's Dharma for the benefit of all beings, the present flood of corruption does not permit me to focus on the eternal. I believe I must sacrifice my own practice to work in the here and now."

He goes on to describe the conditions he found during a visit to his home village of Fukaura:

> The rich were arrogant and had no sympathy for the poor. Ethics were secondary to profits. The clash of greed was seen even between parents and children. Being a small coastal village, there were many prostitution houses (in earlier times, it is said that prostitutes numbered in the three hundreds). Moral decay defied description; the only youths not corrupted were the blind and the mute. Inferior education, pathetic religious life, and loss of chastity were all regarded as routine; rape, theft, and gambling had spread to ordinary homes as if the police did not exist. Bribery of officials was taken for granted....
>
> Although the village had four temples, funerals and religious events were the monks' only activities. Even at Buddhist rituals, monks merely joined in drinking alcohol and singing. With the village as it was, few educators were willing to respond to a request to come

to Fukaura. Even those who came lost their integrity to the decadence, and left the village in debt and shame.³¹

Soyen Shaku supported his disciple's decision to interrupt his training at Engakuji and return to his village in order to set up a primary school, which he termed a "Mentorgarten." His intention was to create an environment in which both students and teachers were mentors to one another. Although he remained a monk, he did not operate the Mentorgarten as a religious institution but rather as a secular school where he hoped students would have an opportunity to develop both their intellectual and spiritual capacities.

It was a struggle to find the funds necessary to operate the school, and Senzaki was disappointed by the lack of support he received from the community he sought to serve. The Buddhist establishment, in spite of interventions on his behalf by Shaku, was equally unsupportive and considered the school heterodox. Senzaki was also disturbed by the increasingly militaristic atmosphere in Japan which was then engaged in the Russo-Japanese war. Unlike Shaku, Senzaki was openly critical of the Zen establishment's support of the war effort.

Despite their political differences, Shaku invited Senzaki to accompany him as attendant when he accepted an invitation to visit the Russells in San Francisco, and Senzaki gratefully agreed to do so. The Russells, apparently not understanding the relationship between the Zen master and his attendant, took Senzaki on as a houseboy. His duties included doing laundry and general cleaning. The housekeeper, however, decided the new houseboy's English was not adequate for his duties and soon dismissed him.

Senzaki gathered his few possessions into a suitcase and set out on foot to find one of the hotels in San Francisco which catered to Japanese clients. Shaku, who had not intervened on his behalf, accompanied him, carrying the suitcase. When they came to Golden Gate Park, Shaku handed over the suitcase and told Senzaki: "This may be better for you than being hampered by being my attendant. Just face the great city and see what happens—whether it conquers you or you it." He instructed Senzaki to find work in the city which would help him learn as much as he could about the country and its people. "Do not utter even a syllable, don't even pronounce the 'B' of Buddhism for seventeen years. You must come to understand these Americans before you will be able to teach them. Find work, no matter how modest; work in anonymity for at least seventeen years. Then you will be ready." After these final words, the two separated, and, although they maintained a correspondence until Shaku's death in 1919, they never again met in person.

Following his teacher's instruction, Senzaki worked for a while as a household servant. When conditions in San Francisco forced him to leave the city during the 1920 Anti-Japanese Crusade and Congressional Hearings on Immigration, he worked on a farm near Oakland. After the hysteria in the city abated, Senzaki returned and found employment in a hotel. He held a number of positions there: porter, elevator operator, telephone operator, and book-keeper. He eventually became the manager and even, for a while, was a part-owner of a hotel. But he was not a natural businessman, and it did not flourish. When it failed, Senzaki became a cook. He was also a language tutor, teaching English to Japanese students, and Japanese to American students. In his spare time, he meditated in the Japanese Gardens in Golden Gate Park and spent long hours at the public library, reading American and European philosophy and improving his understanding of the written language. He later confided to Robert Aitken, "I enjoyed reading Immanuel Kant. All he really needed, you know, was a good kick in the pants." All the while, he continued to write articles on Zen which he sent back to Japanese periodicals, but he did not make any effort yet to teach Americans.

In 1919—the year Soyen Shaku died—Senzaki found a publisher in Japan for *101 Zen Stories*. He included two stories about his teacher in the collection. *101 Zen Stories* would eventually be translated into English with the help of Paul Reps and then be included in a small volume entitled *Zen Flesh, Zen Bones*, which also contained their translation of the koan collection known as the *Mumonkan* or *Gateless Gate*. *Zen Flesh, Zen Bones* would become one of the most influential books on Zen in America in the 1950s. The stories in it became some of the best known Zen tales in the Western world.

Senzaki had not completed his Zen training in Japan, and he never received *inka*, or formal sanction to teach, but he took Soyen's words to him in Golden Gate Park as authorization to do so after the specified time had passed. So when the seventeen year period of silence came to an end in 1922, Senzaki rented a hall and gave a public lecture on Zen. The subject was meditation although no meditation instruction was provided. He based it upon an earlier talk given by Soyen Shaku on the subject.

From time to time after this initial lecture, Senzaki would present another. He had no permanent temple to work from and called this series of talks a "Floating Zendo."

His first audiences were primarily Japanese, but eventually a number of Occidentals also began to attend. As the number of American participants increased, Senzaki started holding separate sessions for the Americans during which he spoke in highly accented English often having to clarify the word he was trying to say by writing it on a blackboard. His command of the written language would always be better than his spoken English. When he felt some of the members of his audience were ready, he began to instruct them in meditation.

In 1931, he moved to Los Angeles where he continued the practice of holding separate lectures for Japanese and non-Japanese audiences. He called the Los Angeles zendo the Mentorgarten Meditation Hall. By now, periods of zazen were a regular part of the evening's activity.

Senzaki informed his students that the purpose of both Buddhism and zazen was to come to the realization that from "the very beginning we are all buddhas, for our minds as well as our bodies are nothing but Dharmakaya, the Buddha's true body, with infinite light and eternal life. It is our delusion to see ourselves in the small cells of individual egos."[32]

This, however, was something each student had to discover on his own; it was not something one could acquire from another. Echoing Isan Reiyu's words to Kyogen,[33] he told them:

> I am a senior student to you all, but I have nothing to impart to you. Whatever I have is mine, and never will be yours. You may consider me stingy and unkind, but I do not wish you to produce something that will dissolve and perish. I want each of you to discover your own inner treasure.[34]

During meditation, Senzaki's students sat in chairs rather than on cushions. He assigned them koans and held sanzen interviews after the meditation periods. He used the koans of the *Mumonkan* but also at times assigned a passage from Meister Eckhart, as a koan.

> Meister Eckhart, a Christian mystic, said, "The eye with which I see God is the very eye with which God sees me." We use these words as a koan to cut off all attempts at conceptualizing. When you work on this koan, you will see that there is no God, no "me," but just one eye, glaring eternally. You are at the gate of Zen at that moment. Don't be afraid, just keep on meditating, repeating the

koan in silence: "The eye with which I see God is the very eye with which God sees me." There is no reality other than this one eye.[35]

He insisted that their practice needed to continue beyond the periods set aside for formal meditation. One also practiced by being mindful of the everyday tasks with which one was involved:

> —no matter what your everyday task may be, it will turn into Zen if you quit looking at it with a dualistic attitude. Just do one thing at a time, and do it sincerely and faithfully, as if it were your last deed in this world.

There is a pleasing Japanese Zen poem that applies here:

> Buddhism is practiced on the doorknob,
> On the pine tree of yonder hill,
> On the matches and cigarette,
> And in the songs of spring birds.

When you open the door, you hold only the doorknob in your hand. After you open the door and see the pine tree on yonder hill, you think no more of the doorknob. Then you take some matches and a cigarette from your pocket and enjoy a smoke, and you no longer have the pine tree in your mind. Then, when you hear the songs of the spring birds, you forget about smoking, even though the cigarette is still between your lips. This whole process shows you the secret of Buddhist happiness.[36]

Senzaki recognized that Zen did not have a monopoly on spiritual insight. He respected Eckhart and other Christian mystics, and he told the following story about his visit with the Sufi master, Hazrat Inayat Khan. The meeting took place at the home of a western Sufi instructor, a woman identified as Mrs. Martin. A psychologist, Dr. Hayes, was also present. The meeting began with pleasantries, Dr. Hayes asking the visiting Sufi master his opinion about America.

Then the Sufi asked, "Mr. Senzaki, what, please, is the significance of Zen?"

Senzaki smiled at the master; the master smiled back. Their dialogue, as Senzaki expressed it, was over.

Dr. Hayes, however, thought Senzaki was having difficulty finding the appropriate English words to use, and he explained, "*Zen* is the Japanese expression for the Sanskrit term *dhyana*, which means meditation."

The Sufi raised his hand and shook his head, silencing the psychologist. Mrs. Martin got up, saying, "I have a copy of a book written in English which I believe gives a very good introduction to Zen." But the Sufi told her it was not necessary.

Senzaki and Hazrat Inayat Khan smiled at one another once more.

Senzaki's life style was almost ascetic; he tried to live as much like a mendicant monk as was possible in America. But he avoided the outward trappings. He did not shave his head and came to have a distinctive and distinguished head of white hair in later life. He did not wear special garb and was critical of the Japanese Zen priests who came to California and made a show of their purple robes. He viewed with suspicion and kept separate from both the official Zen hierarchy in Japan and the one being established in North America.

He seldom had any money even when he was working, and whenever students tried to give him some he tended to pass it on to others. If students left money in the meditation hall, it was Senzaki's habit to discover who the donor was and invite them to dinner at a café he enjoyed patronizing.

On one occasion, Senzaki took his dirty clothes to a laundry in his neighborhood but did not have the money to reclaim them. Shubin Tanahashi—the woman who operated the laundry with her husband, Shuji—saw him walking by their establishment one day and ran out to ask him why he had not picked up his clothing. When Senzaki explained that he could not afford to do so, she made an arrangement with him. Her son, Jimmy, had Down's Syndrome and was confined to a wheelchair. He was non-verbal and needed extensive personal care. Mrs. Tanahashi offered to do Senzaki's laundry without charge if he would occasionally assist them with the care of their son.

The boy was thought to be incapable of speech but with gentle patience Senzaki taught him to repeat, in Japanese, *"Shujo muhen seigando."* This is the first of the four Bodhisattva vows:

> All beings, without number,
>   I vow to liberate.
> Endless blind passions,
>   I vow to uproot.
> Dharma gates, beyond measure,

> I vow to penetrate.
> The Great Way of Buddha,
> I vow to attain.³⁷

The Tanahashis were so grateful for the care Senzaki provided their son that they offered him accommodations in their home. Mrs. Tanahashi became his first disciple in Los Angeles.

Like many Zen Masters in Asia, Senzaki was a talented poet:

> When I bow before the altar
> Offering Buddha a bunch of daffodils,
> The fragrance of the flowers
> Fills the sleeves of my robe.³⁸

And although he often struggled with the spoken English language, he was a skillful translator. A number of artists, poets, and members of the "bohemian" community were drawn to his Zen meetings. Among these was the poet and artist, Paul Reps, who had spent fourteen years in Japan studying Zen and haiku writing. Reps worked with Senzaki to translate *101 Stories* into English, after which the two collaborated on a translation of the *Mumonkan* and the verses accompanying the series of paintings known as the *Ten Bulls*³⁹ which illustrate the stages of growth in Zen practice.

In 1934, Mrs. Tanahashi showed Senzaki a magazine from Japan with some poems and prose passages written by a young Japanese Zen monk named Soen Nakagawa. The poet was reported to be living as a hermit on Dai Bosatsu Mountain near Mount Fuji. Like Senzaki, Nakagawa was openly critical of the lax moral lives and careerism of Zen clerics as well the vain ritualism that preoccupied temple life. Recognizing a fellow soul, Senzaki and Reps wrote to Nakagawa, sending him a copy of the translation work on which they were engaged. As a result of this initial correspondence, Senzaki and Nakagawa began an enduring long-distance friendship. In 1940, the younger monk made preparations to visit Senzaki in Los Angeles, but the outbreak of war between the United States and Japan prevented those plans from being carried out.

After the 1941 attack on Pearl Harbor, public attitude towards Japanese residents in America, particularly those living on the west coast, was highly charged. Anti-Japanese sentiment had been common in California for many years. There had been legislation segregating schools, banning inter-racial marriages, and preventing people of Asian descent from acquiring US citizenship. Senzaki had been so fearful for his own safety in San Francisco during his first years there that he had carried a pistol.

With the outbreak of war, all persons of Japanese descent were excluded from California as well as parts of other west coast states. Families were relocated to internment camps set up inland. Senzaki was sent to Heart Mountain in the Wyoming desert where he shared quarters with a family. He continued to host a meditation group in the small hut in which they lived, sometimes crowding in as many as twenty attendees. He was free to continue corresponding with his American students in Los Angeles, and he wrote to them once a month, encouraging them to continue their Zen practice.

Several of Senzaki's most moving poems were written during the period of his internment. He composed his poetry in classic Chinese forms then translated them into English. The original kanji, done in ink with a brush, and the typed translation were placed on the same page.

On Christmas day, 1942, he wrote:

> Evacuees make poinsettia,
> With colored papers,
> To celebrate Christmas,
> In this desert of internment
> They think of the scarlet cymes
> In their own gardens in California.[40]

From July 1944:

> This desert on the plateau
> Became a village of evacuees.
> The birds began to visit us from distance,
> To sing their beautiful songs, these summer mornings.[41]

The following poem, not dated, is typed and inked on Heart Mountain stationary:

> The mother was named an enemy-alien
> And forced to stay within the fences.
> Her son answered the call of Uncle Sam,
> And gave his life to the battle field abroad.[42]

And on being allowed to return to California on VJ Day:

> Fellow students:
> Under the Heart Mountain,
> We formed Sangha three years,
> And learned to practice
> The wisdom of Avalokitésvara[43]
> The gate of the barbed wire fence opens
> You are now free,
> To contact with the other students
> Who join you to save all sentient beings
> From ignorance and suffering.[44]

When the displaced Japanese returned to what had been their homes in the "exclusion area," they often found their properties had been confiscated or foreclosed; former neighborhoods where they had dwelt were now occupied by people of other ethnic backgrounds. Many found themselves homeless. In 1945, forty years after he had parted from Soyen Shaku in Golden Gate Park, Senzaki had as little as he had had when he first arrived in North America.

Immediately after release, Senzaki spent two months in Pasadena at the home of one of his disciples, Ruth Strout McCandless, to whom he had given the Buddhist name, Kangetsu. He had entrusted her with his books when he learned he was being sent to Wyoming. Ruth McCandless had taken over from Paul Reps the responsibility of acting as Senzaki's editor, and she and Senzaki would collaborate on two books published after the war, *Buddhism and Zen* in 1953 and *The Iron Flute* in 1961. The first provided basic background information on Zen; the second was a collection of 100 koans and commentaries.

After spending two months with the McCandless family, Senzaki returned to Los Angles. In a poem he wrote on the anniversary of Shaku's death, he described his current situation:

> For forty years I have not seen
> My teacher, So-yen Shaku, in person.
> I have carried his Zen in my empty fist,
> Wandering ever since in this strange land.
> Being a mere returnee from the evacuation
> I could establish no Zendo
> Where his followers should commemorate
> The twenty-sixth anniversary of his death.
> The cold rain purifies everything on the earth
> In the great city of Los Angeles, today.
> I open my fist and spread the fingers
> At the street corner in the evening rush hour.[45]

Senzaki rented a small apartment in Little Tokyo over a hotel which was a popular rendezvous point for prostitutes and their clients. His rooms consisted of a bed-sitting room and a small kitchen. Here he continued meeting with his Japanese and American students seated on wooden folding chairs he had purchased from a funeral home. The formal part of the sessions consisted of an hour's meditation, a short talk, and the recitation of the four vows. Following this, the members of the group shared a cup of tea, then departed. There was little socializing, and, if members tarried too long, Senzaki would gently encourage them to leave.

Senzaki had remained in America in large part because he thought the American psyche was suited to Zen; he considered it "more inclined to practical activity than philosophical speculation."[46]

> Because Buddhism is not a revealed religion, its wisdom is not derived from any Supreme Being, nor from any agents of His. The Buddhist believes that we must attain wisdom through our own striving, just as we obtain scientific and philosophical knowledge only by independent effort. To attain *prajna* [wisdom], we strive in meditation and avoid conceptual speculation.[47]

The American mind, "with its scientific cast," was naturally drawn to Zen. "The alert adaptability of the American mind finds in Zen a quite congenial form of spiritual practice."[48]

Senzaki even enumerated

—eight aspects of American life and character that make America fertile ground for Zen:
1. American philosophy is practical.
2. American life does not cling to formality.
3. The majority of Americans are optimists.
4. Americans love nature.
5. They are capable of simple living, being both practical and efficient.
6. Americans consider true happiness to lie in universal brotherhood.
7. The American conception of ethics is rooted in individual morality.
8. Americans are rational thinkers.[49]

After years of correspondence, Senzaki finally met Soen Nakagawa in 1949 when the younger man visited him in Los Angeles. Nakagawa stayed almost six months. Senzaki had hoped to entice him to remain in America and become his heir, but Nakagawa felt obligated to return to Japan and to Ryutakuji, where the following year he was appointed abbot.

In 1955, accompanied by Ruth McCandless, Senzaki made his only return visit to Japan after fifty years in America. He visited Soyen Shaku's grave and Soen Nakagawa at Ryutakuji.

Because it had been so long since Senzaki had been in Japan, Nakagawa was concerned that he might be uncomfortable with—among other things—the traditional Japanese latrines over which one squatted. So he drew a diagram of a western-style toilet and had the monastery carpenters build one. They were not able to connect the toilet to running water, but it did provide a seat for the visitor.

Nakagawa recognized that his friend was becoming more feeble with the passing years, and he kept apprised of his condition after Senzaki returned to America. In 1958, Nakagawa asked one of his younger monks who spoke English, Tai Shimino, to go to America to act as Senzaki's attendant, but before Shimino was able to leave, they received word that Senzaki had died on May 7.

At his funeral, Japanese priests chanted the traditional funeral rites. Before the ceremony ended, a recording was played. On it a woman, Seiko-an, read a document which Senzaki had entitled his "Last Words." Senzaki himself could also be heard laughing in the background and cheerfully correcting Seiko-an's pronunciation from time to time.

I imagined that I was going away from this world, leaving all you behind and I wrote my last words in English. Friends in the Dharma, be satisfied with your own heads. Do not put on any false heads above your own. Then, minute after minute, watch your step closely. These are my last words to you.... Each head of yours is the noblest thing in the whole universe. No God, no Buddha, no Sage, no Master can reign over it. Rinzai said, "If you master your own situation, wherever you stand is the land of Truth. How many of our fellow beings can prove the truthfulness of these words by actions?"

Keep your head cool but your feet warm. Do not let sentiments sweep your feet. Well trained Zen students should breathe with their feet, not with their lungs. This means that you should forget your lungs and only be conscious with your feet while breathing. The head is the sacred part of your body. Let it do its own work but do not make any "monkey business" with it.

Remember me as a monk, nothing else. I do not belong to any sect or any cathedral. None of them should send me a promoted priest's rank or anything of the sort. I like to be free from such trash and die happily.[50]

Nyogen Senzaki's ashes were divided in two. Half were buried in Los Angeles. The other half was reserved and would eventually be mixed with a portion of Soen Nakagawa's ashes and buried at the Dai Bosatsu Zendo established by Tai Shimino in the Catskill Mountains of New York.

Nyogen Senzaki compared himself to mushroom—without a deep root, no branches, no flowers, and probably no seeds. He underestimated the legacy he was to leave behind. He never acquired the celebrity which D. T. Suzuki attained, but through his students—several of whom went to Japan to study with Soen Nakagawa—the practice of Rinzai Zen obtained a foothold in North America.

CHAPTER THREE
Sokei-an and Ruth Fuller Sasaki

D. T. SUZUKI WAS A SCHOLAR. Nyogen Senzaki was an effective teacher, but he had not been formally authorized as one. The first fully approved, or transmitted, Zen Master to teach in North America was Sokei-an Sasaki.

His birth name had been Yeita, and he was the son of a Shinto Priest, Tsunamichi Sasaki. Tsunamichi's wife, Kitako Kubota, was unable to conceive, so the priest took a young girl, the daughter of a tea-master, as a concubine. She gave birth to Yeita in 1882 and looked after the child for his first two years of life. Afterwards, Tsunamichi provided her a dowry, and she moved to Tokyo where she later married and had a successful career as an entertainer. Kitako, who had withdrawn from the household for this period, returned and raised the boy as her own. Sasaki always referred to her as his mother, and there was a lifelong affection between the two. His earliest memory was of crying because she was in another room rather than beside him in bed as he expected her to be.

As a small child, he wondered, as do many children, where he had come from, how he had come into being. Kitako told him she had picked him up somewhere and brought him home; his father told him he had been found on a tree branch. This childish question, Sasaki later said, was his gateway to Zen.

Yeita's father put his son to bed each evening and taught the boy Chinese by telling him bedtime stories in that language. Tsunamichi was insistent that his son receive a classical education and ensured that he was familiar with the principal Confucian texts.

Yeita was a naturally reflective child. He observed his own mind and marveled at its chaos, at the way his thoughts evaded control. He wondered where dreams came from and kept a journal in which he wrote them down. Later he expanded the journal in an attempt to make a record of all the thoughts that passed through his mind during the course of a day. He was writing ten or more pages a day before he abandoned the effort as futile.

Tsunamichi died in 1897, when Yeita was fifteen years old. After the funeral, Yeita wandered among the trees behind the Shinto shrine where the service had taken place wondering what had become of his father's soul now that the body had been disposed of.

There was some expectation that the boy would follow his father's career as a Shinto priest, but his natural inclination was to art, and his mother's family arranged for him to be apprenticed to a sculptor at the Imperial Academy in Tokyo where he learned traditional Japanese wood work and specialized in carving dragons.

As he matured, he found himself returning to the issues which had troubled him as a child. Years later he described his state of mind to his students in New York:

> At seventeen or eighteen, we open a doubtful eye: Why do we live? Where do we come from? Were we here before? Where do we go? If we have no such period of seeking, I should say that we are sleeping. This questioning comes to every young man's eye.[51]

These concerns remained with him as he pursued his art studies, and those, he realized in retrospect, helped prepare him for Zen practice. He learned samadhi—meditative absorption—not in a monastery but from an art teacher who instructed his students when they sought to paint the sea

> —not to sketch the waves on the seashore or to copy the waves in the ancient masterpieces. "Without brush or palette," he said, "go alone to the seashore and sit down on the sands. Then practice this: forget yourself until even your own existence is forgotten and you are entirely absorbed in the motion of the waves."[52]

There were, he was to discover, many kinds of samadhi, and Zen itself was—as he put it—an art form. "I found this knack of going back to the bosom of nature because I was an artist and worshipped Nature. From this feeling, I entered Zen very quickly."[53]

One day he set up his easel to paint but found himself stymied, unable to draw a line. He understood that it was time to put away his canvas and palette and seek a Zen teacher. The master he approached was one of Soyen Shaku's disciples, Sokatsu Shaku.

Soyen Shaku had assigned Sokatsu responsibility for overseeing Ryomokyokai—the Institute for the Abandonment of Concepts—which Imakita Kosen had established in order to foster the practice of Zen among lay persons. An old farm house outside of Tokyo, surrounded by rice fields, had been converted into a temple. It could only be reached by the narrow paths between the paddies. There were two buildings in the temple enclosure. One was the teacher's residence, the other served as the meditation hall or *zendo*. Here Soyen Shaku and Sokatsu carried on Imakita's hope of revitalizing the Zen tradition which had become corrupted by the careerism common among the members of a professional priesthood; they sought to do so by working with well-educated and culturally talented lay practitioners. Members included university students, a handful of professionals, and even a few members of the nobility.

Sasaki was nineteen years old when he presented himself at the temple and asked to be accepted as a student. Sokatsu asked him, "What career do you follow?"

"I'm a sculptor," Sasaki replied.

"And for how long have you practiced this craft?"

"Six years."

"Very well. Carve me a Buddha."

Sasaki returned to his studio and began work on a carving which, when completed, he brought back to Ryomokyokai and presented to Sokatsu. The Zen master took the statue and demanded, "What is this?" Then he tossed it into a nearby pond.

In that way, Sasaki's Zen training began.

He was given the Buddhist name Shigetsu (Finger Pointing to the Moon) but remained a layman. He was still enrolled in the Imperial Academy of Arts and earned a modest living travelling about Japan repairing old temple carvings. After graduation, he was drafted to serve in the Russo-Japanese War and was sent to Manchuria, where he drove a dynamite wagon. The experience made him all the more aware of the precariousness of human life.

The war ended two months later and, once discharged, Sasaki returned to Tokyo to continue his studies with Sokatsu.

Encouraged by Soyen Shaku, Sokatsu planned to take a small group of disciples to America in order to establish a Zen community there. He invited Sasaki to join them but insisted that he would need to be married if he chose to participate. So a marriage was arranged with another lay student at Ryomokyokai, a woman named Tomeko who was a student at Japan's only college for women.

In September of 1906, Sokatsu and six disciples left for California where they purchased a ten acre farm in Hayward. None of the Japanese had any agricultural experience, and the land was poor and exhausted. The enterprise failed after a single crop of strawberries was harvested. Sasaki and Tomeko left the farm to go to San Francisco where he enrolled at the California Institute of Art. While in San Francisco he met and was befriended by Nyogen Senzaki. The two would remain in contact throughout their lives though they did not always see eye to eye. Sasaki, for example, felt it was inappropriate for Senzaki to introduce his students to koans when he had not finished his own koan training.

Sokatsu and the other disciples, meanwhile, were unable to maintain the farm and eventually also moved to San Francisco where they established an American Branch of Ryomokyokai. At its height, it had about fifty members, most of whom were Japanese. Eventually, Sokatsu returned to Japan, and all of his disciples, save for Sasaki and Tomeko, went with him.

Sasaki then began to explore the United States. For a while, he was able to find work in California repairing statues for an importer of Asian sculpture. Then he hiked north to Oregon where he was able to make use of his wartime experience by dynamiting tree stumps for a farmer. He also worked as a janitor in a bar and for a time as a professional dance partner at a roller rink. In the evenings, he sat in meditation on a rock by the river with a dog to protect him from snakes.

Eventually he and Tomeko came to Seattle, where he worked as a picture framer. He could not afford the studio and tools necessary for carving, so took up writing and began a series of humorous reflections on American life for Japanese periodicals.

One day a policeman stopped Sasaki and a friend on the street in Seattle, demanding to see their identification and asking what work they did. Sasaki replied that he was a mendicant—a professional beggar—and only escaped arrest when the friend hastened to explain that he meant he was a Buddhist monk.

Sasaki and his wife lived in humble circumstances. For a while, they stayed with the Salish people on an island in the Puget Sound. The Japanese couple had faced a great deal of prejudice elsewhere in America, and Tomeko felt more at ease with the Native Americans than she had anywhere else. By this time, they had two young children, and when, in 1914, Tomeko became pregnant a third time, she informed Sasaki that she wanted her children to be raised in Japan. She left him and went to live with her mother-in-law who was aging and had written to ask her daughter-in-law to come care for her.

Unencumbered by family obligations, Sasaki wandered about the United States for the next two years, arriving in New York City in 1916, at the age of 34. Although he continued his Zen practice, he focused on developing his artistic talents during this period and naturally gravitated to Greenwich Village.

Sasaki was fascinated with the wide variety of life-styles he came across during his travels, ranging from the conservative values of small-town America to the sophisticated charlatanism of the Bohemian community he fell in with in the Village. There he encountered people like Aleister Crowley, the British occultist and self-proclaimed mystic. The essays Sasaki sent back to Japan about the people he met and the events he encountered were popular, and he began to acquire a literary reputation. He also wrote in English, making translations of classic Chinese poetry which were published in *The Little Review*, famed for its serialization of James Joyce's *Ulysses*.

He was welcomed into the artistic milieu of the Village and led a comfortable life, but he still had not resolved the issues which had originally drawn him to Buddhism. Then on a hot and humid day in July 1919, he came upon the putrefying carcass of a horse lying in the street. The sight struck him so strongly that he immediately made arrangements to return to Japan.

He resumed his study with Sokatsu and even tried reconciling with Tomeko but remained restless and soon returned to the US. For several years, he travelled back and forth by steamship between Japan and America, studying Zen with Sokatsu at Ryomokyokai and working as an art restorer in New York. Eventually, during one of his return trips to Japan, he realized that if he were serious about his Zen practice, he needed to commit to it until he achieved full awakening.

There are three koans most commonly given to beginning Zen students: Mu, Hakuin's "sound of one hand," and the question posed by the Chinese Sixth Patriarch of Zen, Huineng,[54] who demanded "Show me your original face, your face before your parents were born." Sokatsu assigned Sasaki this last koan. Sasaki had been reading German philosophy and, for a while during his sanzen meetings with Sokatsu, tried to reply to the koan in the light of his understanding of those writers. Often, however, he barely began to speak before Sokatsu rang the bell dismissing him. Finally Sokatsu bellowed at him, "Before father and mother there were no words! Show me your face before their births without words!"

Sasaki struggled for years before resolving the koan. Then, one day

> —I wiped out all the notions from my mind. I gave up all desire. I discarded all the words with which I thought and stayed in quietude. I felt a little queer—as if I were being carried into something, or as if I were touching some power unknown to me. I had been near it before; I had experienced it several times, but each time I had shaken my head and run away from it. This time I decided not to run, and Ztt! I entered. I lost the boundary of my physical body. I had my skin, of course, but I felt I was standing in the center of the cosmos. I spoke, but my words had lost their meaning. I saw people coming towards me, but all were the same man. All were myself! I had never known this world. I had believed that I was created, but now I must change my opinion: I was never created; I was the cosmos; no individual Mr. Sasaki existed.[55]

When Sasaki next met with Sokatsu in sanzen, the teacher immediately recognized that his student had had a break through. "Tell me about this new experience of yours," he demanded.

Sasaki looked at him without speaking. Sokatsu smiled.

Sasaki was 47 years old when he completed his training and received *inka*—the authorization to teach—from Sokatsu. To mark the occasion, Sokatsu also gave him the name Sokei-an, which referred to one of the locations where Huineng had lived. Sasaki would be known by this name for the remainder of his life, although he continued to sign his personal correspondence with his birth name, Yeita.

Sokatsu encouraged him to return to the United States, telling him that interest in Zen was diminishing in Japan; the tradition needed to be carried to North America if it were to survive. He instructed his student to be diligent in familiarizing himself with the people and culture of the United States because it would now be his responsibility to ensure that Buddhism was successfully transplanted there. Because of his reservations about the Zen hierarchies in Japan, Sokatsu wanted Sokei-an to remain a lay teacher. Sokei-an, however, felt that he would have more credibility in America if he were ordained. When Sokatsu refused to carry out the ordination, Sokei-an went to another priest who was willing to perform the ceremony. Sokatsu considered this a betrayal and the two remained estranged for the remainder of their lives.

To raise the funds he needed in order to return to America, Sokei-an worked in a factory for eight months. Then, in 1928, he returned to New York City, determining to be the first Zen Master to "bury his bones in America" and thus "mark this land with the seal of the Buddha's teaching."[56] He avoided his former haunts in Greenwhich Village and, instead, took up a number of apartments elsewhere in the city, including, for a time, in Harlem. He supported himself by doing art restoration while he tried to determine how best to go about promoting the Dharma. He tried, like Christian evangelicals, going door to door offering to tell people about Buddhism; but residents complained, and he was asked to leave the building. He then gave public talks in Central Park and at a bookstore on East Twelfth Street—the Orientalia—which specialized in Asian studies.

His first students were a group of eight Japanese businessmen who, in spite of the rupture between Sokei-an and Sokatsu, were successful in petitioning Ryomokyokai headquarters in Japan to authorize a branch in New York. They were incorporated in 1931 as the Buddhist Society of New York. He tried, for a while, to teach his students to sit in full or half lotus posture (cross-legged with either both feet or one resting on the opposite thigh) and encouraged them to practice sitting in that way at home. Even the students of Asian heritage, however, found the posture challenging so, instead, they used chairs during the meditation sessions.

The focus of his teaching was the one-on-one sanzen interview—he called the sanzen room a "battlefield"—but he also gave powerful talks, *teishos,* which could be witty and sharp. It was his physical presence, however, which most inspired his students.

One of these, Mary Farkas, described the format of the meetings of the Buddhist Society in an article published by the First Zen Institute of America in 1966. The gatherings took place in Sokei-an's apartment where there was a small altar bearing only a stone. Sessions began with a short period of meditation. Farkas suggested it was Sokei-an's silence which drew the participants into the meditation. "It was as if, by creating a vacuum, he drew all into the One after him." Students working on koans were then called into sanzen in an adjacent room. During sanzen there were

> —no psychological or philosophical discussions, no worldly advice or explanations, just the business of Zen. When I was in recent years asked if we were given "instruction" in Zen my considered answer had to be "no." To those of us who received Sokei-an's teaching, the word "instruction" must be a misnomer, for his way of transmitting the Dharma was on a completely different level, to which the word "instruction" could only clarify the state of ignorance of the questioner. If I were to say he "demonstrated" SILENCE, even that would be true but would give no indication of how he "got it across" or awakened it, or transmitted it.[57]

Following sanzen, Sokei-an returned to the main room and took his seat behind a small desk on which he kept notes on the texts he was translating. He would read a passage from one of these then give an extemporaneous talk.

> —the same subject might be given many times. Each time the details would vary, as would the emphasized points....
>
> When Sokei-an would come to a story, his dramatic side would take over. Now all the roles would be played rather than told.... For Sokei-an played not only the human roles, but also the animal, mineral, and vegetable as well. Sometimes he would be a huge golden mountain, sometimes a lonely coyote on the plains. At other times a willowy Chinese princess or Japanese geisha would appear before our eyes. Best of all were the Zen stories in which he would be the arrogant samurai, the uneasy monk, the frightening ghost, and, on the other side, the stern, abrupt, or kindly Master.[58]

Sokei-an believed it was necessary to ensure that there were adequate Buddhist texts available for those who were serious about their pursuit of Zen, so he began an extensive translation project which included rendering the *Platform Sutra of the Sixth Patriarch* into English. He also translated *The Record of Rinzai* and various koan collections.

The group grew slowly but steadily. After seven years, there were thirty members. Sokei-an was not in a hurry. He reminded his students that it had taken hundreds of years for Zen to become established in China and Japan. What was required, he told them, was patience and perseverance. He told them of a monk he had once seen at a temple in Japan preaching to the rocks in the garden because there was no one there to hear him. Years later, when he chanced to pass the temple again, he found the same monk now preaching to a crowd of more than two hundred people.

> I brought Buddhism to America. It has no value here now, but America will slowly realize its value and say that Buddhism gives us something that we can certainly use as a base or a foundation for our mind. This effort is like holding a lotus to a rock and hoping it will take root.[59]

In 1938, the Buddhist Society acquired an unlikely wealthy sponsor, Ruth Fuller Everett. Ruth was the wife of a prominent Chicago attorney, Edward Warren Everett, and their daughter, Eleanor, was married to Alan Watts. Ruth had only been eighteen years old when she married Everett, who was twenty years older than she. The marriage was not a happy one, and, in self-defense, Ruth developed a forceful personality in order to resist her husband's tendencies to bully her. Once she gained the self-confidence to stand up to him, Everett resigned himself to allowing her to pursue her own interests.

In 1923, Ruth took her five-year-old daughter with her to participate in a retreat at a country club outside New York City operated by Pierre Bernard, who called himself "Oom the Magnificent" and purported to be a master of yoga and a spiritual guide. Although Bernard was a fraud and a con-man, the time Ruth spent with him fostered a genuine interest in Eastern Philosophy. When she returned to Chicago, she took up a serious study of Asian philosophy and languages at the University of Chicago.

In the 30s, she and Eleanor traveled to Japan where she introduced herself to D. T. Suzuki. He gave her some preliminary instruction in Zen but advised her that if she were serious she would need to practice with an accredited Zen master. He introduced her to Nanshinken Roshi, who, at first, was reluctant to accept her as a student. He had no other female students, and he doubted that pampered Westerners would even been able to sit properly on cushions. Ruth persisted in seeking admission to the zendo, and finally Nanshinken arranged for a plush arm chair which he installed in his house, telling her she could use it for meditation; however, only cushions were permitted in the zendo itself. Ruth learned to sit cross-legged and in a short time was practicing with the men in the zendo. Nanshinken came to admire Ruth's perseverance and eventually introduced her to koan meditation.

In 1938, Warren Everett was confined to a nursing home with arteriosclerosis, and Ruth moved to New York. She took an apartment in the city and arranged for her recently married daughter and son-in-law to occupy the one next to it. Learning there was an authorized Zen teacher in the city, she sought him out. She was not a passive student.

When Ruth met him, Sokei-an's students were still seated in chairs when meditating. From her own experience in Japan, she knew that westerners were capable of adopting formal meditation postures, and she took on the responsibility of teaching them how to sit on cushions. Soon she was tightening up other aspects of the Buddhist Society program.

Everett died in 1940, leaving Ruth more time to spend with Sokei-an. Part of their time together was work; Ruth remained a committed scholar as well as a dedicated Zen practitioner and, with Sokei-an's help, she had undertaken to do an English translation of the eighth century Chinese *Sutra of Perfect Awakening*. But part of their time together was, to her daughter and son-in-law's surprise, courtship. In his autobiography, Watts described Sokei-an teasing Ruth from her usual reserved composure by telling risqué jokes which, as much as she tried to resist, inevitably caused her to blush and giggle.

In November 1941, just a few weeks before the attack on Pearl Harbor, Ruth arranged for the Buddhist Society to move into more spacious quarters on East 65th Street. With the outbreak of war, the institute drew the suspicion of government officials. Suited FBI agents kept watch over who came and went. That July, Sokei-an—like Nyogen Senzaki—was arrested as an "enemy alien."

He was sent to an internment camp in Maryland. The camp commander turned out to be a decent man who had some sympathy for those in his charge; Sokei-an took up his old calling and carved the commander a staff in the shape of a dragon. Conditions in the camp, however, were harsh, and Sokei-an was not in good health. When he was first interred, he was still recovering from an operation for hemorrhoids, a condition to which monks who spent long times in seated meditation were prone. He lost so much weight in the camp that he was able to tighten his belt four notches.

Ruth used her social connections to intervene on his behalf and was successful in arranging for his release in August 1943. The following year, Ruth and Sokei-an were married, in part to provide him some protection from still suspicious authorities. But his health continued to deteriorate. He had high blood pressure and suffered a number of small strokes.

After his release, Sokei-an told the members of the Buddhist Society that it was probably still too early for Zen to take root in America. The lotus still needed to be held to the rock a while longer:

> I came too soon to this country. These two civilizations [Japan and America] will meet in the future. Now they are fighting, but the fighting is a sign that there will be some contact later. Physical contact is fighting, but mental contact is exchanging minds. Buddhism came into China after the war between China and Central Asia. Buddhism came into Japan after the war between Korea and Japan. War is always introducing Buddhism to the other country....
>
> —I love this country. I shall die here, clearing up debris to sow seed. It is not the time for Zen yet, but I am the first of the Zen school to come to New York and bring the teaching. I will not see the end.[60]

Sokei-an was less interested in the theory of Zen than he was in its practice. He respected D. T. Suzuki but insisted that Zen could no more be learned from reading about it than boxing could be learned through a correspondence course. He recognized, however, that Western students, in contrast to Japanese students, needed some understanding of the theory before they would willingly undertake the practice. So, he invited them to consider the wonder of the process of awareness, that in the "darkness without beginning...unconscious creative activity" should arise. Then this "creative activity becomes aware of its own activity" through human self-awareness. Until a human child is about four years old, this awareness is pure, unsoiled by what Suzuki had called the "bifurcation of subject and object." As the child develops a sense of being an independent self, however, he acquires habits of thought conditioned by a particular social environment and forms opinions and beliefs—all of which contribute to a growing sense of separateness. This state of duality is characteristic of what Buddhism designates the "sleeping mind" which differs from the awakened mind.

> It is as though you are sleeping in the broad daylight under the sun. You look at the sun with your eyes, but you are snoring. That is life. Your wisdom gate must awaken.[61]

Sokei-an noted that Americans, in particular, had little discipline in their thought processes. "When I came to America, I realized that people here…don't care what thoughts run about in their brains. Their minds are really in a primitive state."[62]

The practice of Zen is intended to awaken the sleeping mind and transcend this illusion of duality. It accomplishes this through concentrative absorption and meditation, the subject of which was "mind" itself. Buddhism, Sokei-an asserted, was founded upon samadhi. When the Buddha sat in meditation, the subject of his zazen was not anything external to him but rather his own mind

> —from which had been extracted every thought, every image, every concept. He paid no attention either to the outside or the inside. Perhaps we should say mind exercised zazen upon itself. In true Buddhist zazen, mind by itself is the meditator and is at the same the object of the meditator's zazen.[63]

The role of the teacher in Zen differs significantly from the concept, common in the west, of the teacher as an individual with certain knowledge and information it is his responsibility to convey to the student. The Zen teacher—as Nyogen Senzaki told his students on the West Coast—"has" nothing to give to the student. The student needs to come to discovery—to awakening—by examining his own mind. "The whole law is written in your mind, in your body. The key to the mystery of the cosmos is really already in your possession."[64]

Some students were frustrated by this approach and complained that Sokei-an was not teaching them, not answering their questions or revealing "secret doctrines" such as were promised in the Theosophical school and Tibetan lore. He remained unapologetic:

> It is not a secret doctrine if I can teach it to you. It is secret because you must teach yourself. All knowledge is written in your own soul. I cannot put any secret doctrine on your mind.[65]

While a novice at Ryomokyokai, Sokei-an had been assigned the task of standing at the gate of the temple in order to greet visitors. As was the custom when indoors, he was either barefoot or wearing *tabi*, the socks with a separate sleeve for the big toe so they can be worn with sandals. In this manner, he was always able to feel the floor or the ground beneath his feet.

One rainy day, he also donned a pair of the sandals—called *geta*—with wooden slats on their bottoms. He had a sudden realization that the *geta* did not feel the wet ground. "I don't understand Zen," he thought. "But my shoes do!"

He took this insight into his next face-to-face meeting with Sokatsu, whose response was: "Shigetsu, don't talk so much!"

On the wall of the room in Sokei-an's apartment, where his students met, there was a framed motto which declared in bold print: "Those who come are received. Those who go are not pursued."

Many of Sokei-an's students felt that his talent as a teacher was best displayed in his Dharma talks. He spoke slowly and in labored English punctuated by periods of silence which could be disconcertingly long. Some of his listeners found his accent distracting and difficult to understand; others found it charming. Alan Watts provided this sample:

> One evening he was giving a formal lecture on the *Sutra of Perfect Awakening*, dressed in robes of brown and gold brocade and seated in his chair of estate at a small table-altar with candles and incense. He would pause from time to time, and drop powdered sandalwood or aloeswood on the hot brick of charcoal in the *karo*, or incense burner. He came to a passage where the sutra spoke of the importance of living without purpose, and, true to his accent, commented: "In Buddhism pahposeressness is fundamentar'. No pahpose anywhere in rife itser'f. When you drop fart you do not say, 'At nine o'crock I drop fart.' It just happens."[66]

When students in sanzen offered wordy explanations of the koans on which they were working, Sokei-an would tell them, "I've heard your words; I understand what you are saying. But I'm from Missouri. You have to *show* me your understanding!"

A group of Christian ministers paid Sokei-an a visit. They asked him how he prayed, and he told them that he did so by meditating.

"And on what do you meditate?"

"On emptiness."

"Emptiness? But what does that mean?"

"If it meant anything, it would not be emptiness."

"Well, it seems to us that if all you are doing is meditating on emptiness you're simply wasting your time."

"Not at all," Sokei-an rejoined. "If I did anything other than meditate on emptiness, *then* I would be wasting my time!"

Sokei-an's physical condition continued to deteriorate after his release from internment, and he recognized that he did not have long to live. He was prepared for death, remarking, "I have always taken Nature's orders; I will do so now." Still, he was concerned that he had no heir. He tasked Ruth with the responsibility of ensuring that a formally trained Rinzai teacher be found to work with the Buddhist Society. He also encouraged her to return to Japan after his death to complete her own training.

On May 17, 1945, after less than half a year of marriage, Sokei-an died. His last words were: "I go.... I die...won't die...live forever!"

After his death, the Buddhist Society was renamed the First Zen Institute of America and committed itself to preserving Sokei-an's teachings.

2

As Sokei-an had hoped, Ruth returned to Japan after his death in order to continue her training. She approached Zuigan Goto, who had been a member of the group that had taken part in the feckless California farming venture with Sokatsu. Goto was teaching at Daitokuji, where Ruth was accepted as a lay student and given a small house within the temple grounds, separate from the monks who were all male and Japanese.

Sokei-an had also asked her to identify a qualified teacher to carry on his work in America, and, in 1955, after six years at Daitokuji, Ruth returned to New York with Isshu Miura.

As a young man, Miura had studied with Nanshinken Roshi, who had introduced Ruth to Zen practice during her first visit to Japan. Nanshinken was known for his rigorous training methods, in particular his liberal use of the *kyosaku*—something Ruth wholly approved of.

After Nanshinken's death, Miura continued to study with Taiyu Nakamura at Koonji. Eventually he received *inka* from that teacher, after which he became the abbot of Erinji.

Erinji was famed for the beauty of its grounds and gardens as well as its treasury of art works. During the war, however, like many other temples, it fell into disrepair. After the Japanese surrendered in 1945, Miura focused his energies on trying to restore Erinji to something of its former beauty. He discovered that the most effective way to rid the grounds of the weeds which had taken over was to pour kettles of boiling water over them. When Ruth extended the invitation for Miura to come to America, she told him that all he would need to bring with him was his stick. "Oh, no!" Miura responded. "The kyosaku is too soft. I will bring my kettle!"

In New York, Miura gave a series of talks on koans with Ruth acting as translator. These became the basis of a book they co-authored entitled *The Zen Koan: Its History and Use in Rinzai Zen*.

In 1957, Ruth returned to Daitokuji, where Goto allowed her to add a small zendo to the side of her house. This was the first zendo in Japan specifically intended to receive Western students. The following year, she became both the first woman and the first Westerner to be ordained in the Daitokuji temple system.

After Ruth's return to Japan, Miura stayed with the First Zen Institute for a while, but he was not comfortable with the predominantly female board of directors. In 1963, he resigned his position, although he stayed in New York and maintained a small number of private students with whom he worked until his death sixteen years later.

One of the features distinguishing North American Zen from its Asian antecedents is the active participation of women in the sangha. Ruth Fuller Sasaki was the first of these, but she was not an easy person to work with. She was strong-willed, confident of her own opinions, and often inflexible. When she informed Zuigan Goto that she intended to add a dormitory to her small zendo, he told her he would rather she did not. She ignored his request and went ahead with the construction. In Japanese culture, it was unheard of for a student to disregard a teacher in this manner. It caused a rift between the two, and Goto disavowed her as one of his disciples.

Ruth gathered together a group of scholars in Kyoto to continue Sokei-an's work of making Chinese and Japanese texts available in English. Several of these—including Philip Yampolsky and Burton Watson—later would become significant figures in the academic world. Working for Ruth provided these young men with an unparalleled access to rare documents, but they often felt that the specific tasks she assigned them were tedious and of questionable value. She was also quick to get rid of people with whom she disagreed or of whom, for whatever reason, she became suspicious. At one point, for example, she unjustly accused Yampolsky of stealing a manuscript on which they were working. He was able to demonstrate that he had not done so, but she still found grounds to dismiss him.

Simple projects could balloon out of control under her direction. She began annotating the slim *Zen Koan* published with Miura, eventually adding over 150 pages of footnotes—in a smaller typeface—in addition to bibliographies, maps, genealogical charts and a "Zen Phrase Anthology." By the time it was re-released as *Zen Dust*, shortly after Ruth's death in 1967, it had swollen to a 574 page tome.

To the end, she remained a formidable personality, and often a generous one. Through her efforts, and those of the First Zen Institute, several Americans—including Walter Nowick and Gary Snyder—were able to travel to Japan in order to study Zen. In her way, she made as significant a contribution to the process of bringing Zen to North America as had her husband.

Chapter Four
"Beat" Zen

By the 1940s, information about Zen was plentiful and accessible outside of Asia. The number of actual practitioners in North America was small, but there were active communities on both coasts. It might have remained a minor religious and intellectual curiosity, however, had there not been an audience which found something compelling about this very foreign tradition. The circumstances which would come together to make Zen a cultural phenomenon in the United States began with an unlikely group of writers who first met in New York in 1943.

Jack Kerouac coined the term "Beat" to refer to a small cadre of poets and prose writers which included himself and friends like Allen Ginsberg, Gregory Corso, and William Burroughs. He was inconsistent about what he meant by the term. At times, it referred to being "beat down" by the circumstances of their lives and the difficulties they had with contemporary culture; at others, it referred to the "beat" of jazz music and the spontaneous improvisations which the writers emulated in their own work; and at times he suggested it referred to "beatitude," to an effort to develop a spiritual basis in one's life.

By the 1950s, many of the Beats had relocated to San Francisco where Ginsberg was enrolled in classes at the Berkeley campus of the University of California. He also attended the poetry *soirées* of established poet, Kenneth Rexroth, who introduced him to a few young West Coast poets, including Gary Snyder. None of the younger poets were yet published, but Rexroth admired their work and had confidence in them.

These writers were the harbingers of the counter-culture movement of the 60's, railing against contemporary mores and standards. Ginsberg began his most famous work, *Howl*, with the lament that he had seen "the best minds of my generation destroyed by madness." They were deeply aware of the injustices they saw in America and the disenfranchisement of marginalized members of society—homosexuals, racial minorities, or people whose ideas were considered socially or politically suspect. They were sexually adventurous; they flaunted their use of alcohol and experimented with drugs, including peyote. Their books and poems inspired a generation of young readers to question the structures of previous generations—institutionalized and legal racism, conservative Christian moral and religious values, an assumption that the natural role of women was that of being sexual partners and helpmates for the men in their lives, the belief that homosexuality was a psychological aberration, the unquestioning acceptance of what was generally referred to as the American Way of Life. It was a generation which would be receptive to new ideas from distant cultures.

Kerouac became interested in Buddhism by accident. He was tracking down some references to Hinduism he had come upon while reading Thoreau, and, searching the library, he found a biography of the Buddha. He was struck by the first of the Buddha's Four Noble Truths—that "life is suffering."[67] This led him to peruse other Buddhist literature, including the works of D. T. Suzuki. Kerouac never became a formal practitioner of Buddhism, nor did he renounce his French-Canadian Catholicism; instead, he developed a personal spiritual perspective in which Buddhism and Catholicism were mixed.

When Kerouac first tried to share his enthusiasm about Buddhism with Ginsberg, who had also read Suzuki, the poet's response was lukewarm. In 1948, when he was living in Harlem, Ginsberg had had a vision of William Blake reciting "Ah! Sun-Flower" and revealing the underlying interconnectedness of all things. The experience had struck him as being similar to Suzuki's description of satori, but when he visited the First Zen Institute in New York he did not find the atmosphere welcoming . It seemed to him to be very much like a university faculty club. When, years later, Ginsberg did develop a Buddhist practice, the flamboyant Tibetan tradition was more to his taste than the austerity of Zen.

Kerouac was especially impressed by Suzuki's descriptions of the Tang Dynasty Zen Poets, Hanshan and Shide[68]—Zen lunatics, as Kerouac would dub them, the original "Dharma Bums" who flaunted the conventions of their day and inscribed their poems on rock faces and the bark of trees. They reminded him of his Beat friends and some of the hobos he met in his journeys between New York, Mexico City, and the West Coast.

In 1954, Kerouac came upon a copy of Dwight Goddard's *Buddhist Bible* in a library and was so impressed by it that he stole it and carried it with him on his journeys, eventually having it covered in leather to protect it. He read the *Diamond Sutra* over and over again, and, when in Mexico City the following year, he composed a poetry cycle based on his understanding of Buddhism and modeled on the blues improvisations of saxophonist Charlie Parker. He called his collection *Mexico City Blues*. He fantasized about becoming a Buddhist hermit living on a mountain top.

That autumn, he went up to San Francisco to visit Ginsberg, who introduced him to Gary Snyder. In Snyder, Kerouac found an American Hanshan who did live like a hermit and was familiar with the mountains of the Pacific Northwest. Snyder was also, at that time, preparing to go to Japan to work with an authentic Zen Master. He became the inspiration for the character Japhy Ryder in *The Dharma*

Bums, the book Kerouac released after the success of *On the Road* and which he dedicated to Hanshan.

There is a note of prophetic melancholy struck early in the book. As in his other works, the narrator is a Kerouac himself, in this case under the pseudonym of "Ray Smith." Smith looks back on a time in his life when he believed in things in which he no longer has much faith. He observes: "I was very devout in those days and was practicing my religious devotions almost to perfection. Since then I've become a little hypocritical about my lip-service and a little tired and cynical."[69] But the portrait of Japhy Ryder is exuberant and appealing—a Zen practitioner, an outdoorsman and poet; a scholar, in addition to being both sexually accomplished and wise in the ways of the natural world of the wild. He did not look like a Bohemian at all, Smith noted; instead he was vigorous and athletic. It was a portrait which would intrigue and inspire many young readers.

One day at a Chinatown restaurant, Kerouac saw one of the cooks taking a smoke break. "Why did Bodhidharma come east?" Kerouac asked him.

The cook looked at him for a moment, then said: "I'm not interested."

Kerouac enjoyed the response so much that he related the encounter in *The Dharma Bums*.

Kerouac, Ginsberg, and Ginsberg's lover, Peter Orlovsky, were on their way to a party celebrating the publication of *The Dharma Bums* when Kerouac had the idea of dropping in on D. T. Suzuki. The three writers went to a phone booth and found Suzuki's number in the directory. The phone was answered by Mihoko Okamura, who reluctantly informed Suzuki of the call. Suzuki knew about *On the Road* and agreed to see them.

Half an hour later, they showed up at his doorstep, already a little drunk. Suzuki invited them in and listened politely as they talked about haiku and their understanding of Zen philosophy. After a while, Suzuki stood and said, "You young men remain here and write some haiku. I will go make tea."

He returned with the appropriate implements and served them whisked green tea. Kerouac later wrote that he and the others then got high on it. He described his meditation experiences to which Suzuki attended without comment. Finally, when Suzuki suggested it was time for them to leave, Kerouac burst out: "I would like to spend the rest of my life with you!"

"Someday," Suzuki replied, deftly maneuvering them to the door.
As they went out onto the step, Suzuki said, "Don't forget the tea."
"The key?" Kerouac asked.
"The tea," the Japanese scholar said. Then he gently shut the door.

As they are climbing in the Sierra Nevada, Japhy Ryder explains to Ray Smith that the

> —secret of this kind of climbing…is like Zen. Don't think. Just dance along. It's the easiest thing in the world, actually easier than walking on flat ground that is monotonous. The cute little problems present themselves at each step and yet you never hesitate and you find yourself on some other boulder you picked out for no special reason at all, just like Zen.[70]

Fame was not kind to Kerouac. He was disappointed by the way in which *The Dharma Bums* was received by both literary critics and the current spokespersons for Buddhism in America. The latter dismissed his understanding of Buddhism as naive; even Snyder was critical of the book, telling Kerouac that his interpretations of Buddhist doctrine were personal rather than accurate. Further, Kerouac—who was politically conservative in many ways and had attended Columbia University on a football scholarship—had little in common with the hippies of the 1960s who came to revere his novels, in particular *The Dharma Bums*.

Although he had hoped to become respected for his writing, he had never been comfortable performing in public. He was hurt by the virulence of some of the attacks on both him personally and on what were now termed "beatniks" (because, like the Russian Sputnik, they were "far out there"). After being beaten up by three men outside a Bleecker Street bar in New York, he became nervous about appearing in public at all.

He spent much of his later years withdrawn from even his old friends, living with and caring for his mother, and drinking too much. When he died in 1969, he was only 47 years old.

2

Kerouac, Ginsberg and their friends had met in New York City and shared an urban East Coast perspective. Gary Snyder came from a very different background. He was twenty-five years old when he met Ginsberg and Kerouac, but he had already been a seaman, had worked as a timber scaler at a mill on the Warm Springs Indian Reserve, had cleared forest trails, and had worked as a fire-lookout in deep isolation in the North Cascades.

He was raised on a small dairy farm outside Seattle. His parents were depression era socialists with little sympathy for religion in any form. The region was populated by left-thinking individuals, the descendants of the Wobblies, the Industrial Workers of the World who had been suppressed by government intervention during the "Red Scare" of 1924. The ideological views of his parents and neighbors contributed to forming Snyder's later political perspective.

When he was seven years old, he was laid up for four months because of an accident sustained during a brush fire, and his parents brought him books from the Seattle Public Library to keep him amused. This began a lifelong interest in reading and learning. His mother, Lois, expected him to do well in school and once forbade him from going on a planned camping trip because he failed to get an A on a Latin quiz.

In 1942, when he was twelve, Snyder's parents divorced, and he and his sister moved to Portland, Oregon, with their mother. Throughout his formative years in both Washington State and Oregon, he was curious about the physical environment around him. He hiked and explored the countryside and, as soon as his parents were confident he could look after himself, went on solo camping expeditions. He was an experienced mountaineer by the time he was twenty. He was also intrigued by the native peoples of the Pacific Northwest and admired their way of relating to the natural world. From them, he developed the idea of a "sense of place"—a sense of belonging to a particular region and being a participant in a complex ecological pattern that included both the human and the nonhuman. It was a point of view similar to the Zen teaching that all things had Buddha-nature, all things had inherent value and were connected with all other things.

He lived up to his mother's expectations that he be a good student and received a scholarship to attend Reed College in Portland, where he met Philip Whalen and another future Beat poet, Lew Welch. For a while, the three lived in the same communal apartment building where Snyder had a room in the basement. Whalen and Snyder, in addition to their interest in poetry, shared an interest in Asian studies. Whalen, who was older and had been in the armed forces during the war, had investigated Hindu Vedanta after his time in the military was over. Snyder had become curious about Asia after viewing Chinese landscape scrolls in the Seattle Art Museum.

He was struck by how similar the mountains portrayed in them were to the Northwest ranges with which he was familiar. The scrolls held his interest in a way that European landscapes in another gallery of the museum failed to do.

After his first year at Reed, Snyder lost his scholarship because of poor academic performance, so he joined the Marine Cooks and Stewards union and went to sea for the summer, earning enough money to return to college without the scholarship funds. A sign in the Union Hall, when he applied for membership, declared: "No Red-baiting; no queer-baiting; no race-baiting. First offence, $100 fine. Second offence, dismissal from the union." It was a strong position even for a labor union to take in 1947.

The early influences in Snyder's life—his interest in Native American and Asian cultures, his love of wilderness areas, and the political leanings of his parents—all wove together during his college years and were reflected in his poetry. He majored in anthropology and literature and did field work on the Warm Springs Indian Reservation; his senior thesis was a study of Haida folklore. At the same time, he was reading a lot of Asian and Buddhist literature and even taught himself meditation by studying the posture of the statues of Buddha in museums.

His academic performance improved, and he was offered a scholarship to attend Indiana University in Bloomington in order to continue work in linguistics and folklore. Before he left for Indiana, he and Whalen had a farewell dinner in San Francisco after which they trolled a local bookshop where Snyder picked up a couple of books by D. T. Suzuki, whom he had heard of but had not yet read. These included the first volume of *Essays in Zen Buddhism* and the *Manual of Zen Buddhism*. The books were stored in his backpack when he set out to hitchhike to Bloomington. During a lull between drives, he started to read the *Essays* and there, unexpectedly, found something to which he was deeply drawn. The Zen tradition, with its emphasis on personal realization and physical labor rather than academic study, made sense to him as did its inclusive view of nature not as something "fallen" but as something with which humankind was ecologically bound up. Snyder had been drawn to a similar perspective in the spiritual traditions of Native Americans but recognized that they were closed to him. One had to be born a Hopi, for example, in order to follow the Hopi way. But Zen, with its emphasis on personal experience, appeared to be a tradition open to anyone who was willing to undertake the training.

Suzuki's book redirected Snyder's life. He remained at Indiana University for a single semester, then returned to San Francisco in order, as he put it, to pursue the Dharma. He decided he needed to go to Japan to work with a Zen master, and, in order to prepare, he enrolled in courses on Asian languages and cultures at the University of California at Berkeley and attended seminars at the American Academy of Asian Studies. The director of the Academy at the time was Alan Watts.

He and Snyder formed a lifelong friendship. Watts admired the younger man so much that, in his autobiography, he expressed the wish that he could claim Snyder as his heir.

When Ruth Sasaki visited San Francisco to speak at the Academy, Watts introduced her to Snyder, and she encouraged his interest in traveling to Japan. In a letter, she suggested that he should consider making a three year commitment, the first to be spent learning the language and becoming acculturated and the next two working with a transmitted Zen master. If he applied himself, she wrote, he should "reasonably well expect" to pass his first koan in that time.

During this period, he spent his summers working as a fire-lookout for the US Forestry Service in the North Cascades. Lookouts were virtual hermits, living in small shacks deep in the mountain ranges. For many, the solitude was difficult to cope with. The job suited Snyder, however, allowing him time to meditate, practice Chinese calligraphy, study, and try his hand at composing haiku. Snyder later encouraged Jack Kerouac to work for the Forestry Service as well, but, in spite of his fantasies of living like a mountain hermit, Kerouac found the reality difficult and frightening.

In San Francisco, Snyder regularly attended the poetry readings and discussions held by Rexroth, through whom he met Ginsberg. Ginsberg immediately liked Snyder and invited him to take part in an up-coming poetry reading. Snyder convinced Ginsberg to extend the invitation to Philip Whalen.

That reading at Six Gallery, where Ginsberg presented an early draft of *Howl*, is considered the beginning of the San Francisco Renaissance. Kerouac was in attendance as well but was too shy to be one of the readers. Lawrence Ferlinghetti, the publisher of City Lights Books, was in the audience, and it was in large part through his efforts that the five poets who read that evening—including Michael McClure and Philip Lamantia—began to gain literary recognition.

Snyder read "A Berry Festival," a poem based on the Warm Springs Berry Festival and influenced by his reading in Native American and Asian folklore. Ginsberg's reading of *Howl*—proclaimed like an Old Testament prophet calling down the wrath of Yahweh—was a hard act to follow, but Snyder was equal to the task. Wearing heavy work boots and casually dressed, he looked more like a woodsman than a poet. The poem demonstrated his skill at translating his experiences into a virile and masculine verse, nothing at all like the poetry high school students were assigned in literature classes.

At the time, as Kerouac described in *The Dharma Bums*, Snyder was trying to emulate the Zen lifestyle described in the books he was reading—studying

Buddhism and meditation. He also experimented with poetic techniques based on Asian models and set himself the task of translating the Cold Mountain poems of Hanshan into English.[71]

In the summer of 1954, he was looking forward to returning to the stillness of the Fire Watcher's lookout in the Cascades but was informed that the Forestry Service was unable to take him on again because, as a member of the Maritime Cooks and Stewards Union, his name had been added to the list of suspected Communist sympathizers drawn up by McCarthy-era federal authorities. He spent the season, instead, working on a trail crew in Yosemite National Park. His difficulties continued the following year when he tried to finalize his preparations to travel to Japan. He was refused a passport because, he was informed, the State Department "believed that it is not in the best interests of the United States for you to travel abroad at this time." The refusal was only reversed when Ruth Sasaki intervened on his behalf and arranged for him to come to Japan as an employee on her translation project.

What first struck Snyder about post-war Japan was the poverty he saw everywhere. Reconstruction was still going on, and conditions both among the general populace and in the monasteries were hard. Life was also more expensive than he had anticipated. Ruth had assured him that he should be able to survive on $50 a month; so he was unprepared when one of his first expenses turned out to be a $30 "appropriate sitting cushion." He also quickly realized that the portrait of Zen presented by Suzuki had been an idealized one; there was often a "snobbish aristocratic and insular self-esteem"[72] in the monks he met. Zen was no longer a popular pursuit in Japan; many contemporary Japanese youth viewed it as a remnant of feudalism and the militarism which had resulted in the war that had ended so disastrously. Snyder came to believe that one of Suzuki's most important contributions to Zen was to revitalize the tradition by bringing it away from Japan and presenting it to an American audience which had no knowledge of its political past.

Ruth Sasaki had arranged for Snyder to share quarters with another American student, Walter Nowick, and to be accepted as a lay student at Shokokuji where he would study with and serve as an English tutor for Isshu Miura, who was then preparing to move to New York. Snyder formally became a Buddhist by taking the refuge vows[73] from Miura, and, once his knowledge of the Japanese language improved, he began koan study. He was given a Dharma name, Chofu ("Listen to the Wind"), but remained a layman and knew that he would eventually return to America. He recognized that monastic life in Japan was elitist and that it removed monks from the mainstream life of the community. While monks dedicated themselves to their meditation practice, as Snyder put it, someone else had to grow the tomatoes.

Zen training turned out to be arduous. It was very different from the *laissez-faire* Buddhism imagined by Kerouac. In an article later published in the *Chicago Review*, Snyder noted: "Zen aims at freedom but its practice is disciplined."[74] He was, however, better prepared than many who followed him to Japan. In addition to having some knowledge of the language, he was inured to hardship and privation from his childhood experiences and from his work with the Forestry Service and on the Warm Springs Reservation.

In 1958, he made a return visit to America by working as a crewman in the engine room of an oil tanker. He was proud of the fact that none of his fellow crewmen suspected he had been to college. He arrived back in California just before the release of *The Dharma Bums*, about which he had mixed feelings. In a letter to Philip Whalen he expressed his hope that the book did not result in them all being arrested as Neal Cassady—the model for Dean Moriarty in *On the Road*—had been.

Snyder's first major publications had come out before he left Japan. "A Berry Feast" and the Cold Mountain poems had been published in the *Evergreen Review* and "Spring Sesshin at Shokoku-ji" was included in the spring issue of *The Chicago Review* along with Alan Watts' article, "Beat Zen, Square Zen, and Zen," and an excerpt from Kerouac's yet-to-be released *Dharma Bums*. The following year, Snyder's first book of poems, *Riprap*, was published in Kyoto by Origin Press. Later editions would include the Hanshan Cold Mountain Poems.

When he returned to Japan in 1959, he was joined there by the poet Joanne Kyger. Ruth Sasaki insisted, for reasons of propriety, that the two should be married, so Kyger became Snyder's second wife (he had been briefly married in the 1950s).

Miura was now in New York, and he suggested that Snyder continue his studies at Daitokuji with Oda Sesso, with whom the Dutch writer, Janwillem van de Wetering, also studied.[75] Oda Sesso assigned Snyder the koan "Show me your face before your parents were born."

"Don't explain it to me," the master instructed him. "Don't give me a philosophical interpretation of it. Don't talk about it that way at all. Show it to me."[76]

Although he passed the koan after eighteen months, he had come to Japan not so much to achieve satori as to find training in a way of life which appealed to him. Zen practice cultivates an awareness of the interrelatedness of things—interdependence—and thus fosters a respect for life in all its forms. In Japan, this awareness is cultivated in a monastic environment, but Snyder and others would demonstrate that it was a perspective which could be taken out of the cloister and made the basis for an effective politically and socially engaged lay life.

During his last years in Japan, he was surprised to learn from letters he received that others were pursuing similar training in San Francisco with a Japanese Soto Zen master, Shunryu Suzuki, who provided meditation instruction in the Bay Area.

In 1964, Snyder returned home and, the following year, joined with Allen Ginsberg, Richard Baker (then a senior student of Shunryu Suzuki), and Swami Kriyananda (a student of the Indian yogi, Paramahansa Yogananda) in buying 100 acres in the Sierra foothills. Baker was looking for property on which to build a retreat center for Suzuki's San Francisco Zen Center, and Kriyananda, who held the largest portion of the territory, was looking for a location where he could establish his "World Brotherhood Colony."

Baker's and Ginsberg's lots remained undeveloped, but Snyder gathered a team of volunteers to help build a house which later became his primary residence. The house was called Kitkitdizze, the Native American term for a local shrub also known as Bearclover. The ten volunteer carpenters included four women who, at times, worked shirtless along with the men. Snyder wrote a poem in which he compared the color and shape of their breasts as they worked.

Every morning before work began, the crew gathered to sit zazen in a nearby meadow. After the house was finished, regular sitting continued to be held inside, then was moved to the barn—which participants referred to as the "Barndo." Eventually a traditional zendo, named Ring of Bone after a line in a poem by Lew Welch, was built.

Isshu Miura visited Kitkitdizze "shortly before his death; he looked at the pines surrounding the house, ate and drank sake, and before he left the next morning took a deep breath of the pine-fresh air, and said, 'Very good.'"[77] Like the Native peoples of the Northwest whom he admired, Snyder had found his place.

Growing up on a farm, Snyder had learned to be practical about work. When he arrived at Daitokuji, part of the training consisted in spending a certain amount of time on work assignments—*samu*—in the garden and on the grounds. Snyder noted that many of the techniques employed were not particularly efficient, and, from time to time, he would suggest ways in which they could be improved, saving both time and effort. The monks listened politely but did not implement any of the suggested changes. Eventually one of them took Snyder aside and told him, "We don't want to do things any better or any faster, because that's not the point—the point is that you live the whole life. If we speed up the work in the garden, we will just have to spend that much more time sitting in the zendo, and your legs will hurt more."[78]

Snyder encountered a group of ascetic monks in Japan, the Yamabushi, who lived in the mountains outside Kyoto. When he sought to join them, they had him climb a particular cliff face while chanting the Heart Sutra. At the top, they tied ropes around his ankles and threw him off the cliff leaving him hanging upside down. Warning him that they would let go of the ropes if he lied to them, they proceeded to ask him a series of personal questions.

In that way, he was initiated into membership.

When Snyder invited Joanne Kyger to join him in Japan and take up Zen practice, she asked, "What will happen if I do?"

"You might lose yourself," he told her.

"But why would I want to do that?" she asked. "I've only just finally got a self!"

One day in the '80s, during a phone call to a friend, Jim Dodge, Snyder mentioned an up-coming event at the Ring of Bone Zendo. Dodge

> —couldn't resist asking, "Are you still sitting on your ass trying to get totally and perfectly enlightened?" "Yes," Gary said. Then, lowering his voice, he confided, "But you know, Jim, I've been doing it so long now that when I sit I can fall asleep almost instantly; and no one can tell."[79]

In spite of his friendship with Ginsberg and Kerouac, Snyder did not consider himself a "Beat writer," and certainly his work went on to become more varied and successful than any of the other writers of that milieu. He would win the Pulitzer Prize, and his work would begin an unprecedented school of environmental writing. Throughout it all, however, there remains a profound Zen perspective. In writings and in his own life, Snyder made Zen something less fantastic and exotic. Perhaps his most important contribution to North American Zen was to demonstrate not only that westerners were capable of undertaking formal Zen practice but were also capable of integrating the benefits of that practice in their broader careers.

3

Philip Whalen and Gary Snyder met at Reed College, which Whalen attended on the GI Bill. He had served in the Army during the war. Poor eyesight had kept him from going overseas, but he was trained to be a radio mechanic and instructor. Like Snyder, he was already writing poetry when he arrived at Reed and was reading Asian literature and philosophy—although at the time Whalen's interest was with Vedanta rather than Buddhism. When Snyder came to San Francisco after dropping out of graduate school at Indiana University, Whalen joined him and, through Snyder's intervention, became one of the poets who took part in the Six Gallery reading. He appears in *The Dharma Bums* as Warren Coughlin, whom Kerouac described as a "big fat bespectacled quiet booboo."[80] Japhy Ryder, however, tells Ray Smith that there is more to Coughlin than meets the eye.

Whalen was a physical contrast to Snyder. He was, if not fat, hefty and not naturally athletic. His two favorite activities were eating and reading. Although he was seven years older than Snyder, Whalen often followed the younger man's lead. Snyder, for example, was able to convince him to apply to be a fire lookout for the Forest Service, and Whalen proved better able to handle the position than Kerouac would. It provided him solitude and time to read and write. He spent three seasons in the Cascades. The Forest Service managers were particularly happy to have him because of his skills as a radio operator.

He also practiced a desultory form of self-taught meditation while on lookout, based on his reading of Patanjali's *Yoga Aphorisms*. He dipped into Tibetan Buddhism but found the complex hierarchies of bodhisattvas and deities—which would fascinate Ginsberg—bewildering and off-putting. While staying with Snyder in San Francisco, he read his friend's copies of Suzuki, and, while this was more to his taste, he did not yet see it as a path appropriate for him.

Another way in which Whalen followed Snyder's lead was in using peyote. The hallucinogenic cactus buds were easily available in San Francisco, and many of the Beat writers used them. Snyder respected peyote as a traditional Native American aid to developing spiritual insight; Ginsberg included a reference to peyote in the litany that forms the first part of *Howl*. Whalen, however, remained cautious until 1955. When he did try it in the spring of that year, he reported that it acted on "my spirit and mind and body and everything else as a great cure."[81] He had visions which drew upon his interest in Vedanta, and he found himself identifying with the gods Vishnu and Ganesh. He used it again in June and still felt energized by the effects of the drug and the insights he derived from that second trip when he returned to the Cascades to take up his Forestry Service responsibilities.

The journey to his lookout on Sourdough Mountain was made on horseback accompanied by pack mules to carry the supplies. These animals, however, first had to be ferried by raft across Ross Lake. In order to accustom them to the raft, they were corralled on it the night before departure. During that night, one of the horses fell off the raft, waking everyone with its frantic splashing. Whalen was the first of the crew members to reach the horse, and he hooked his arm under its neck, keeping its head above water while another crew member went to fetch a boat to tow the animal ashore. As he struggled there, Whalen saw the moon rising over Jack Mountain. The tableau had as strong an effect on him as the dead horse in the New York street had had on Sokei-an:

> I was kneeling over the edge of this raft in my underwear, holding this horse under the chin. It was two o'clock in the morning and it was a beautiful summer night, and the mountains were all around, and the lake, and this horse, and me—and I suddenly had a great weird kind of *satori*, a sort of feeling about the absolute connection between me, and the horse, and the mountains, and everything else. And you can't describe it very well—the feeling—because the feeling is a feeling. But it was…a big *take* of some kind.[82]

The event seemed particularly significant because his given name, Philip, meant "lover of horses" in Greek. The "horse in the water" became, for him, a kind of totem animal and its significance was confirmed to him when he discovered that the old Chinese Zen Master, Mazu Daoyi,[83] was known as "Master Horse."

That summer he came to think of his experiences on peyote not so much as "visions" but as what he called "identifications." Peyote was like the finger pointing to the moon in the frequently quoted Zen admonition that if one paid too much attention to the finger, one would miss what it was pointing to. Whalen found himself becoming more interested in what the peyote "identification" was indicating.

In 1966 Whalen followed Snyder's lead once again, joining him in Japan where he found work teaching English at the YMCA of Kyoto. Here, at last, he discovered his own way. He was oddly at home in the spiritual capital of Japan and spent long periods of time wandering the city absorbing the atmosphere of the temples, gardens and shrines he came upon. The Japanese, likewise, responded warmly to his open and friendly manner. A man who knew Whalen in Japan at the time described him as "the kindest looking man I ever met."[84]

Kenneth Rexroth, who visited Whalen and Snyder in Japan, noted that when

> —Philip Whalen, in his red whiskers, looking like a happy Ainu bear-god, walks down Omiya-dori in Kyoto's weavers' quarters, every face lights up with that old-time Buddhist joy, even though most of the inhabitants are Left Communists, militant atheists, Koreans and Untouchables.... I have in fact seen Philip ambling past the market stalls and running into a march of demonstrating strikers, and everyone smiled and waved and he waved back.[85]

He still resisted taking up formal Zen practice with a teacher, but he learned the fundamentals of zazen from, and occasionally sat with, another American, Richard Baker, who was also living in Kyoto at the time. Morning zazen became part of his daily routine; no matter how late he had stayed up the night before, no matter how much alcohol he had consumed, he rose early enough the next morning to sit.

By the time Whalen returned to the US, Baker had been installed as Shunryu Suzuki's successor as abbot of the San Francisco Zen Center, and he invited Whalen to live there. The only demand put upon him was that he should join the rest of the community in morning zazen practice. Since this was already Whalen's habit, it was not a difficult condition to meet.

Baker admired Whalen as a poet and, as Whalen later discovered, had arranged for him to gain residence at Zen Center ahead of a number of people who had earlier applied to stay there. Whalen found his living circumstances pleasant; they afforded him ample opportunity to write and pursue his own interests. Over the next ten years, while Snyder attained respectability as a member of the Board of the California Arts Council and was awarded the Pulitzer Prize for Poetry, Whalen almost inadvertently underwent ordination and training in the Soto Zen Tradition.

When a former drag-queen and drug addict, Issan Dorsey—who was also living at Zen Center—moved out to establish a hospice and practice center for AIDS victims, Whalen joined him with Baker's encouragement. In 1987, Dorsey and Whalen became the first individuals to whom Baker gave "Dharma transmission," and, when Dorsey himself succumbed to AIDS, Whalen became his successor as abbot of the Hartford Street Zendo.

Helen Tworkov reported that Whalen's first intensive sitting at the San Francisco Zen Center's practice center at Tassajara

> —reminded him of being back in the army. "It took me several training periods to see that they weren't trying to kill you. All you had to do was follow the schedule and you wouldn't have to argue with anybody, not even yourself."[86]

While researching his book, *One Bird, One Stone*, Sean Murphy made a number of unsuccessful attempts to arrange an interview with Philip Whalen, who was then abbot of the Hartford Street Zendo. Finally, Murphy determined to visit the center without an appointment on the chance that he might be able to meet Whalen. When he arrived, a ceremony was in progress marking the tenth anniversary of Isan Dorsey's death. The organizers assumed Murphy had come to mark the occasion, and he was conscripted to take part in a ritual procession.

During the ceremony, Murphy was able to identify the elderly Whalen who by then was very nearly blind and had to be accompanied by an attendant. At the reception that followed, Murphy took the opportunity to approach Whalen. He pulled up a chair beside Whalen and introduced himself as the writer who had been trying to arrange an interview.

> "Ah, yes," said Whalen. "I haven't called you back." He sighed an old man's raspy sigh. "I've done so many interviews, you know," he said, reaching moodily for a stuffed mushroom h'ors d'oeuvre. "I find them terribly irritating."[87]

Philip Whalen died in 2002 at the age of 78.

4

When Gary Snyder returned to California in 1964, he found a very different social environment than the one Kerouac had described in *The Dharma Bums*. The short-lived Beat movement was already *passé*; beatniks had been supplanted by hippies. Two years later, Ginsberg and Snyder both took part in the Human Be-In at Golden Gate Park which ushered in the "Summer of Love."

This new generation was more flamboyant than the dour Beats had been; they listened to a different type of music and were more politically engaged. And many were pursuing a "higher consciousness" through the use of psychedelic drugs, including mescaline—which was synthesized peyote and had the advantage of not inducing nausea before inducing visions, as the natural cactus buds often did. As they had for Philip Whalen, the experiences these youths attained by using psychedelics seemed to make more sense in terms of Eastern rather than traditional Western traditions. As a consequence of their drug experiences, young people were reading classical Asian texts such as the *Upanishads* and the *Bhagavad Gita*.

They also read the books of an expatriate Englishman and former Episcopalian Priest and listened to his broadcasts about Zen and related topics on the radio.

CHAPTER FIVE
Alan Watts

THE LEAD ARTICLE IN THE 1958 ISSUE of the *Chicago Review* in which Gary Snyder's "Spring Sesshin at Shokoku-ji" appeared was "Beat Zen, Square Zen, and Zen" by Alan Watts. Much to Ruth Sasaki's amusement, her former son-in-law had become an acknowledged media expert on Zen. Her own opinion on the matter is probably best revealed in a remark she made about the "misinformation being spread about...by those professed exponents of Zen in the west" who had not actually undergone Zen training.[88]

In the *Chicago Review* article, Watts contrasted the popular Beat use of Zen as justification for what he considered often mediocre art and a lifestyle flaunting traditional values with the Square Zen of those, like Ruth, who were trying to establish formal Japanese Zen training and discipline in America. Neither, in Watts' opinion, were true to the spirit of Zen as he understood it:

> For Zen is above all the liberation of the mind from conventional thought, and this is something utterly different from rebellion against convention, on the one hand, or adapting foreign conventions, on the other.[89]

As Square Zen became more established in North America, Watts' credibility as an expert on Zen diminished, but—whether he intended it or not—his contribution to the development of American Zen was as significant as that of Suzuki or any of the early teachers to come to the United States.

Watts was born during the First World War in the English village of Chislehurst in Kent. It was a pretty village with extensive common areas and nearby woods. His mother, Emily, came from a staunch Evangelical Protestant family. She was loving, but strict, and was the family disciplinarian. Watts' father, Lawrence, on the other hand, was a more gentle and tolerant figure. Emily had been raised to believe that human life was a testing ground during which it was determined whether one was worthy of salvation or was to be condemned to eternal damnation, and she was as concerned about her only child's spiritual well-being as she was his physical. Religious instruction took place in a gloomy, unheated second-floor bathroom. In this bleak environment, Watts' nanny read him Bible stories, and his mother taught him his first prayers and spanked him when she deemed it necessary. It was also the room where he was quizzed every morning about the state of his bowel movements. He hated the room.

In contrast to the disagreeable bathroom was the first floor Sitting Room, reserved for use on special occasions only. Before she was married, Emily had taught at a school for the daughters of missionaries to foreign lands, and, in the Sitting Room, she kept exotic presents given her by the families of those girls: Chinese and Korean vases, a Japanese tapestry and cushions, and a brass coffee table from India. Here Watts first acquired his love for the mystique of the Orient.

Watts suffered through the brutalities of the British boarding school system, where he received what he later described as a "Brahmin's education." The preparatory school to which he was sent was expensive, and his parents had to struggle to make the fees, but they were willing to do so in order to ensure their son received the type of education they believed would serve him well in the future. The all-male boarding school, however, was not the type of environment for which Watts was suited; among other things, even as a young boy he preferred the company of girls and women. The curriculum focused on the history of the British Empire, militarism, and low church theology. Watts sought escape from the dreariness of this course of study by reading the novels of Sax Rohmer, in which he identified more with the Asian villains, like Dr. Fu Manchu, than with the square-jawed British heroes, such as Nayland Smith.

He decorated his room at home with the type of inexpensive Asian ornaments a school boy could afford, including a small reproduction of the Kamakura Daibutsu.[90] Eventually his mother—who had good taste in such matters—supplemented these with better pieces, as well as presenting him with a copy of the New Testament written in Chinese, which roused a lifelong interest in Chinese calligraphy. Once more—as in the contrast between the awful bathroom where Bible stories were told and the Sitting Room—the brightly colored exotica of the Orient provided an alternative to the drabness of all things British and Protestant.

He was intellectually gifted and earned a scholarship to King's College in Canterbury, a public (that is to say, private) school to which otherwise his parents would not have been able to send him. The rich history of Canterbury, its elaborate Gothic architecture, and the pageantry of High Church Anglicanism provided a more stimulating environment for Watts than his preparatory school had. On the other hand, he was well aware that he was not of the same class as the majority of his fellow students. In order to counter a bourgeoning sense of social inferiority, he developed a persona which allowed him to feel intellectually superior to his classmates.

He may not have belonged to the gentility, but his tastes ran in that direction. He was precocious enough, while still a young teen, to be able to cultivate adult friendships which permitted him to share in a lifestyle beyond his family's reach. His appreciation of Asian art and aesthetics led him to search for books on Japan and China. One of his adult friends loaned him a number of these, including a pamphlet by Christmas Humphreys, then President of the Buddhist Lodge in London. In the overview of Buddhism provided by Humphreys—and in the work of other writers such as Lafcadio Hearn—Watts found a view of life which struck him as more reasonable than Christianity, so, at the age of 15, he boldly announced to his classmates that he was a Buddhist. He also initiated a correspondence with Humphreys in which he expressed himself so maturely that Humphreys assumed the writer from King's College was a member of staff and was later surprised to discover, when Watts attended his first Lodge meeting during the holidays, that his correspondent was in fact a sixth form student.

Humphreys was the type of adult Watts admired and sought to befriend, a wealthy and sophisticated man, a barrister who was to become a well-respected judge. Humphreys and his wife, who were childless, admired the young Watts and came almost to look upon him as a son. Watts' actual parents, perhaps hoping his interest in Buddhism was a youthful enthusiasm he would outgrow, supported his inquiries and even attended Lodge meetings with him. Lawrence eventually became a Buddhist and the Lodge treasurer. Emily remained reserved, noting that Humphreys ran Lodge meetings much like a Sunday School class. It was Humphreys who introduced Watts to the books of D. T. Suzuki.

When he was head boy of his house at King's College, Watts had the freedom to use a certain Elizabethan room after hours, and there he experimented with meditation guided by clues he had found in his reading, although he was not clear about what the writers meant by *satori, moksha, samadhi,* or enlightenment. He was considering this problem in the fall of 1932, wondering what the experience was that Asian teachers were talking about:

> The different ideas of it which I had in mind seemed to be approaching me like little dogs wanting to be petted, and suddenly I shouted at all of them to go away. I annihilated and bawled out every theory and concept of what should be my properly spiritual state of mind, or of what should be meant by ME. And instantly my weight vanished. I owned nothing. All hang-ups disappeared.[91]

Watts' masters at King's College—and his relatives—felt that he should easily be able to earn a scholarship to Oxford, but he did poorly on the examination, and the scholarship did not materialize. Once he completed public school, his formal education came to an end. His prospects were not good, and he was fortunate to have the friendship of Humphreys at a time when his mother's family, in particular, let him know how disappointed they were with him. Without a university degree, the professions were closed to him, and it was not clear how he was going to support himself financially.

With Humphreys' help and guidance, he continued his independent studies. He met a number of people who shared his interest in esoteric religions and the occult, among whom was Dmitrije Mitrinovic, who was rumored to practice black magic. Mitrinovic introduced him to the study of psychology, which would remain one of his abiding interests. He also read the *Upanishads*, the *Diamond Sutra*, and the *Daodejing*. Humphreys—whose Buddhism was liberally laced with Theosophy—introduced him to Blavatsky, but their greatest shared interest remained Suzuki whose works they continued to study and discuss.

Lawrence was able to help his son get employment at the foundation where he worked raising funds for London hospitals. The job was not difficult, and it gave Watts, still only 19, time in the evening to work on an attempt to clarify Suzuki's writings. At the end of a month of effort in 1935, he had a manuscript entitled *The Spirit of Zen*. Humphreys contributed a foreword, and the book was released by John Murray the following year.

It was a small work, less than 40,000 words, which was essentially a reader's guide to Suzuki, but it already demonstrated a skill, which Watts would hone throughout his life, of being able to describe spiritual issues in a clear and intriguing manner. A second book, *The Legacy of Asia and Western Man*, was released in 1937. Watts' literary career was launched, although it remained to be seen if he could earn a living from it.

The year after *The Spirit of Zen* came out, Watts met Suzuki, who was in London to attend the World Congress of Faith and, as the guest of the Buddhist Lodge, made a greater impression on his hosts than they had anticipated. Here, they found, was someone who not only understood Zen but embodied it; Suzuki struck Watts as a man wholly at home and at ease in whatever environment in which he found himself. His presence alone validated Zen.

In 1937, Ruth Everett was in London and showed up at a Buddhist Lodge meeting accompanied by her daughter, Eleanor. Watts was overwhelmed by the mother—who, after her time in a Japanese monastery, knew more about Zen than he—and was smitten with the daughter. She had an American vivaciousness and freedom of behavior unlike anything he had encountered in the few girls he had been with prior, and she enjoyed trying to tease him out of his British reserve, although it would take many years of living in the United States before he wholly shed that aspect of his persona. When Ruth returned to America, Eleanor stayed behind.

She loved music, and she and Watts attended concerts and the ballet together. She taught him to dance using his hips rather than in the stiff manner of polite ballroom dancing. She was also able to sit in full lotus posture during the meditation sessions at the Buddhist Lodge and, in spite of his status as a published author on such matters, she proved to have greater insight into Buddhist practice than he. As they walked home one evening, after a session of meditation, Watts mused aloud on the methods of concentrating on the present moment. Eleanor asked:

> "Why try to concentrate on it? What else *is* there to be aware of? Your memories are all in the present, just as much as the trees over there. Your thoughts about the future are also in the present, and anyhow I just love to think about the future. The present is just a constant flow, like the Tao, and there's simply no way of getting out of it." With that remark my whole sense of weight vanished. You could have knocked me down with a feather. I realized that when the Hindus said *Tat tvam asi,* "YOU ARE THAT," they meant just what they said.[92]

Looking back on that moment in his autobiography, he referred to it as a "premature *satori*" for which he remained "perpetually grateful to Eleanor."

> I was unable to resist the temptation to write, think, and intellectualize about it. Yet when I am in my right mind I still know that this is the true way of life, at least for me. Conscious thoughts, reflections, analysis, cultivation, and intention are simply using the mind's radar or scanning beam for purposes which the mind as a whole can do of itself, and on its own, with far more intelligence and less effort.[93]

Eleanor and Watts were married in April 1938. Although they both professed to be Buddhists, it was a traditional Anglican ceremony. Watts was 23. Eleanor was 18 and pregnant. She was also wealthy. The young couple moved to New York where Ruth had arranged an apartment for them next door to hers.

Through Ruth, Watts met Sokei-an. He made an effort to work with the Zen master but discovered—as he would realize throughout his life—that he preferred being the teacher to being the student. After their brief formal relationship ended, Watts continued to observe Sokei-an in order to learn how a Zen master lived his life, something which became easier to do when Sokei-an began his courtship of Ruth after her husband's death.

Possibly because she was having difficulties as a young mother, possibly because she still lived closer to her own mother and her mother's influence than she would have liked, Eleanor did not fare as well in New York as her husband. She became increasingly unhappy and depressed. Then one day she stopped in at Saint Patrick's Cathedral, looking for a place to rest during a trying day, and there she had a vision of Jesus so vivid that she could describe in detail everything he was wearing.

This vision came to her around the same time that Watts had become interested in Christian mysticism and was wondering whether—as long as it shed its claim to be the only true religion—Christianity might also be an effective means to achieve that sense of union with God/Tao/Ultimate Reality which in his most recent book, *The Meaning of Happiness*, Watts had asserted was the purpose of religion and the route to happiness.

Ruth was not surprised when Eleanor and Watts suddenly dropped their purported Buddhism—she had apparently not thought it very deep to begin with—and began attending services at St. Mary the Virgin Episcopalian Church. Not long after this, Watts approached the curate to inquire how he could become a priest.

In his autobiography, he struggles to rationalize this decision, explaining that if he were to help Western people understand the "perennial philosophy" underlying all genuine religious traditions, he could best do so within the prevailing tradition of the West. His biographer, Monica Furlong, posits that it might have been simply a way to earn a living and become less dependent upon Eleanor's family; his daughter, Joan, later speculated that, as the United States was drawn into the war, her father may have sought to become an ordained minister in order to avoid military conscription.

Whatever his motives, Watts and his family moved to Evanston, Illinois, where he entered Seabury-Western Theological Seminary; after which, for six years, the now Reverend Alan Watts served as a chaplain on the campus of Northwestern University. He published another book, *Behold the Spirit*, in which he compared Christian mysticism with Zen and other Asian traditions. It was well received in church circles.

His clerical career came to an end in 1950, when Eleanor informed his bishop that she and her husband had become estranged in large part because of his sexual need to be beaten—a taste he may have acquired during boarding school—and his affairs with women who satisfied desires she was unwilling to fulfill. Nor was

Eleanor entirely innocent, having taken a lover ten years younger than she, who—with Watts' complicity—lived in their house with them. When Eleanor, already the mother of two daughters, became pregnant with her lover's child, the situation was something that could no longer be concealed.

Watts resigned his priesthood and affiliation with the Episcopal Church before he could be dismissed, writing a long and self-justifying letter to the bishop in which he asserted that church doctrine had become so out of touch with the realities of contemporary culture that he could no longer, in conscience, continue as its spokesman. It was, at best, a disingenuous argument.

Eleanor procured an annulment, and Watts—behaving almost like a caricature of an adulterous husband—married Dorothy DeWitt, one of his students and his daughters' sometime babysitter. He retained custody of his children—Eleanor was content with her new son—but no longer had the financial security his former wife's wealth had provided him. His income from writing was inadequate to support his new family, so he accepted an invitation to move to San Francisco in order to help Frederic Spiegelberg establish the American Academy of Asian Studies. He shed his nominal Christianity and returned to nominal Buddhism without compunction.

Watts immediately loved California and immersed himself in the burgeoning cultural scene although he still came across as a little square. Kerouac portrays him as Arthur Whane in *The Dharma Bums*:

> Arthur Whane was sitting on a log, well dressed, necktie and suit, and I went over and asked him "Well what is Buddhism? Is it fantastic imagination magic of the lightning flash, is it plays, dreams, not even plays dreams?"
>
> "No, to me Buddhism is getting to know as many people as possible." And there he was going around the party real affable shaking hands with everybody and chatting, a regular cocktail party.[94]

He still had a restrained British manner and dressed formally, and he had what sounded to Americans like a very cultured accent. He came across with authority, and it was natural for him to assume the position of Director of the Academy when Spiegelberg stepped down in order to teach at Stanford.

Watts arranged for a number of interesting guest lecturers to visit the Academy including both D. T. Suzuki and his former mother-in-law with whom he appeared to have been able to retain a civil relationship. At any rate, she loved her granddaughters, and they lived with their father.

California had long attracted people with an interest in Asian philosophies. Krishnamurti, the Vedandist, Swami Prabhavananda, and other credible spiritual teachers were well established in the state. A Soto Zen master, Shunryu Suzuki, had recently arrived. Watts fit in easily. In addition to his work at the Academy, he became a frequent guest on educational radio and television. Then in 1956, he published the book for which he would become best known, *The Way of Zen*. He dedicated it to the three children he had now had with Dorothy (a fourth was on its way).

D. T. Suzuki's books had appealed to a broad but relatively small and well-educated readership. The membership of Nyogen Senzaki's Floating Zendo and the First Zen Institute in New York came to no more than a few hundreds. Watts was a much clearer writer and easier to read than Suzuki, and his book introduced Zen to an even wider audience. To some extent it was a matter of timing; the book came out when interest in Zen, in part because of the Beats, was on the rise. In the Preface, Watts suggests this might be the case because people in the West had lost faith in traditions which no longer seemed viable in the light of advances in the physical sciences and psychology:

> Familiar concepts of space, time, and motion, of nature and natural law, of history and social change itself have dissolved, and we find ourselves adrift without landmarks in a universe which more and more resembles the Buddhist principle of the "Great Void."[95]

Under these circumstances, it was natural that some people would feel attracted to

> —a culturally productive way of life which, for some fifteen hundred years, has felt thoroughly at home in "the Void," and which not only feels no terror for it but rather a positive delight.[96]

Watts, however, warns that he is not in favor of importing Zen wholesale from Japan

> —for it has become deeply involved with cultural institutions which are quite foreign to us. But there is no doubt there are things which we can learn, or unlearn, from it and apply in our own way.[97]

He begins his analysis of Zen with a point to which he frequently returns in his work: that what one perceives as one's Self is an arbitrary social convention. It is not only that one tends to see oneself in light of the way in which others perceive and define one (one's social role, personality, even physical appearance); one also tends to view the Self as what he described elsewhere as "an ego encapsulated in a bag of skin"—a soul separate from and animating a physical body, both of which (soul and body) are cut off and distinct from the environment about one.

Zen is a "way of liberation" through which the individual can realize the restrictions and limitations of social conventions and come to identify the "self" as part of a larger ecological whole which is all of Being. This is not a matter of rejecting or rebelling against other perspectives. It is rather a matter of seeing through the illusion of separation or dualism. For Watts, this is something which must occur spontaneously; it cannot be achieved by effort which inevitably only substitutes one set of conventions for another.

He presents Zen as a matter of cultivating a particular attitude towards life rather than being a training which brings about a change in one's manner of experiencing. Seated meditation, zazen, is just a natural way to sit and be; it had not been intended, he suggests, to become the strained and sustained practice it had evolved into in Japanese monasteries. Perhaps, he proposes, it had become so because

> —of the conversion of the Zen monastery into a boy's training school. To have them sit still for hours on end under the watchful eye of monitors with sticks is certainly a sure method of keeping them out of mischief.[98]

To support this contention, he quotes a conversation between the Tang dynasty Zen figure Baso[99] and his teacher, Nangaku.[100] Nangaku came upon Baso sitting in zazen and asked, "What is it that you're trying to accomplish by sitting like this?" Baso replied that he wanted to attain Buddhahood. Nangaku sat down beside him, picked up a piece of broken tile, and began to rub it vigorously. When Baso asked what he was doing, Nangaku said that he was polishing the tile to make it into a mirror.

"But no amount of polishing will turn a tile into a mirror!" Baso complained.

"Neither will any amount of meditation, as you practice it, make you into a Buddha," Nangaku shot back.

Watts ends the passage at this point.[101] D. T. Suzuki, Philip Kapleau and later Zen practitioners would complain that by doing so he distorted the intent of the story. To present it as a condemnation of zazen

> —is to do violence to the whole spirit of the koan. Nangaku, far from implying that sitting in zazen is as useless as trying to polish

a roof tile into a mirror—though it is easy for one who has never practiced Zen to come to such a conclusion—is in fact trying to teach Baso that Buddhahood does not exist outside himself as an object to strive for, since we are all Buddhas from the very first.[102]

The criticism was just, but, in fairness to Watts, he had specifically denied being a spokesperson for traditional Zen in his book and did not intend it to be an instruction manual. What it did do was present the Zen perspective as an appealing orientation towards life from which Western readers could learn to develop a more healthy relationship with their fellows and their environment than currently found in contemporary North American society.

The book became, as Watts put it, a "minor bestseller," and its publication allowed him to resign his position as Director of the Academy—which was in a hopeless financial situation—and earn his way as a writer and lecturer.

Watts' reputation was on the rise. He received invitations to give lectures and seminars from as far away as Zurich; tens of thousands of people attended these and read his books. Ironically, his personal life was a mess. He had become a heavy drinker and proved to be no more capable of fidelity to Dorothy than he had been to Eleanor.

In 1960, Watts left Dorothy, then pregnant with their fifth child, and entered into a relationship with the woman with whom he believed at last he was genuinely in love and with whom he remained for the remainder of his life—Mary Jane (Jano) Yates. His desertion of his family shocked many of his friends, as well as his parents, and several gave up on him. He would not be the last individual associated with North American Zen whose personal life would become an issue.

On another level, however, Watts finally broke free of his British reserve. He entitles the chapter in his autobiography which deals with this period, "Breakthrough." He gave up suits for kimonos and other exotic apparel; he let his hair grow long and grew a beard; he developed friendships with uninhibited personalities with whom he could engage in exuberant activities like all night drumming festivals. He experimented with and wrote about LSD. He at last broke free of those inhibitions which—in spite of the fact that he had lauded freedom and spontaneity in his books—still restrained him.

James Ford was one of many future serious practitioners whose initial introduction to Zen was Watts' book. He relates that, as a consequence, he was pleased to have a chance to meet Watts when he was serving on the

—guest staff of the Zen monastery in Oakland led by Roshi Jiyu Kennett. I was enormously excited to actually meet this famous man, the great interpreter of the Zen way. Wearing my very best robes, I waited for him to show up—and waited and waited. Nearly an hour later, Watts arrived dressed in a kimono, accompanied by a fawning young woman and an equally fawning young man. It was hard not to notice his interest in the young woman who—as a monk, I was embarrassed to observe—seemed not to be wearing any underwear. I was also awkwardly aware that Watts seemed intoxicated.[103]

Watts was riding the crest of a wave which was swelling nationally. A new youth generation had arisen in which many young people were exploring "alternative consciousnesses." Watts may not have sought it, may not have been entirely comfortable with it, but he found himself in a new role—that of a guru to the hippies. His talks on public radio reached record audiences. He was more relaxed in his personal life, which was reflected in his public persona. He tried to downplay his authority and described himself as a performer, a "philosophical entertainer," but the performances were brilliant.

As his fame grew, so did the number of his detractors. Academics dismissed him as a popularizer, and some members of the growing Zen community dismissed him because of his lack of formal training (and for consorting with young women who did not wear underwear). Shunryu Suzuki, however, when overhearing his students criticize Watts, told them that they should respect what he had accomplished and consider him a great Bodhisattva.

Young people flocked to him and sought to become his disciples; the fact that he did not accept any of them only increased his allure. Monica Furlong reports that, for instance, on one occasion while he was dining at a restaurant, a young woman came in and knelt at his feet. At the Human Be-In of January 1967, Watts was present with Ginsberg and Snyder; Shunryu Suzuki was there as well. In the counter-culture, Watts had become mainstream.

The "Summer of Love," however, was short lived, and, as the original innocence of the first hippies dissipated, a few began serious spiritual quests. Richard Alpert, who with Timothy Leary at Harvard had introduced hundreds of students—and celebrities—to LSD and psilocybin, went to India and remade himself as a Hindu mystic named Baba Ram Dass. Zen centers, now located in places as unlikely as Minneapolis, were filling up. The total number of practitioners was not large compared to the general population, but it was large enough to have been unthinkable in 1958 when Kerouac, in *The Dharma Bums,* had predicted a generation of Zen practitioners across the land.

In his 50s, Watts was able to mend his relationships with Ruth Sasaki and with his father; his mother had died in 1961. But his lifestyle was destroying his health. He was a heavy smoker and drank as much as a bottle of vodka a day. On top of this, he was a workaholic, rising early each morning—no matter how late he had stayed up carousing the night before—to maintain his daily writing regime. He accepted more speaking engagements (as Gary Snyder put it) "than anybody in their right mind would want to do just earning money."[104] But the reality was that he needed the money; he had seven children to support, plus a personal staff, as well as a succession of girl friends. He may have loved Jano, but he still had affairs, and soon she was drinking almost as much as he.

There was never any doubt about the sincerity of his interest in Zen and other Asian spiritual traditions, but he was too much the sybarite to adhere to any of their disciplines or to benefit from them. His importance historically rests on the ability he had to inspire others.

For example, the Jesuit, Robert Kennedy—who eventually became a Zen teacher while remaining a Catholic priest—first became interested in Zen when he heard Watts over his car radio pointing out "nothing in nature is symmetrical." "I don't know why that statement hit me with the strength that it did," Father Kennedy later said, "but I had to stop the car and think. It was an extraordinary moment."[105] He went back to his rooms, took a blanket off the bed, folded it to make a cushion, and began to sit.

Father Kennedy is only one member of the wide and eclectic audience Watts was able to reach with his compelling portrait of Zen. The following passage was originally published in *Playboy* magazine:

> —Zen meditation is a trickily simple affair, for it consists only in watching everything that is happening, including your own thoughts and your breathing, without comment. After a while thinking, or talking to yourself, drops away and you find that there is no "yourself" other than everything which is going on, both inside and outside the skin. Your consciousness, your breathing, and your feelings are all the same process as the wind, the trees growing, the insects buzzing, the water flowing, and the distant prattle of the city. All this is a single many-featured "happening," a perpetual *now*

without either past or future, and you are aware of it with the rapt fascination of a child dropping pebbles into a stream.[106]

Eventually his lifestyle took its toll. He died in his sleep on November 16, 1973 at the age of 58. Both his father and Christmas Humphreys outlived him.

Richard Baker, then Shunryu Suzuki's heir at the San Francisco Zen Center, presided at a ceremony during which a portion of Watts' ashes were interred beneath a stupa on the grounds of the Center's Green Gulch Farm. In the Japanese fashion, Baker bestowed on Watts a posthumous name, Yu Zen Myo Ko, "Profound Mountain, Subtle Light," as well as the title, Dai Yu Jo Mon, "Great Founder, Opener of the Gate of Samadhi."

CHAPTER SIX
Robert Aitken

WHILE NYOGEN SENZAKI AND SOKEI-AN SASAKI WERE in internment camps in the United States, Robert Aitken was a prisoner-of-war in a Japanese camp at Kobe on the south coast of Honshu, the principal island of Japan.

Aitken had grown up in Honolulu, not far from Pearl Harbor. In 1941 he dropped out of university, where he had not been doing well, and found work with a construction crew on Guam. There was a general feeling that war with Japan was inevitable, so, in addition to the naval personnel stationed there, there was a small contingent of Marines; however, when Japanese warships encircled the island the day after the attack on Pearl Harbor, the American troops surrendered without a fight.

Aitken and the other members of the construction crew were classified as "Military-Civilian Prisoners of War." As such, they were kept separate from military prisoners and were spared the harsh treatment to which those prisoners were at times subjected. On the whole, Aitken had greater liberty than Senzaki and Sokei-an had in the United States.

He was first incarcerated in the old British Seaman's Mission and then later at Marks House, the former residence of a British banker. There was a library at the Mission to which the detainees were allowed access; they were also allowed brief excursions into the town for medical appointments and to purchase books. Aitken decided to make the best use he could of his imprisonment by improving his general literacy.

The book that redirected his life, however, did not come from the library but was loaned to him by one of the guards. It was *Zen in English Literature and Oriental Classics* by Reginald Horace Blyth, who had taught English at the high school the guard had attended before the war.

Blyth had been imprisoned in England during the First World War for declaring himself a conscientious objector and, after release, had abandoned the British Isles to explore Asia. He eventually met and married a Japanese woman in Korea, then returned to Japan with her and settled in the port city of Kanazawa. Like Senzaki and Sokei-an, he was more at ease in his adopted country than in his homeland; however, his sympathies did not extend to its current government. He began the process of becoming a Japanese citizen before the war erupted and planned to complete the procedure after the war only if Japan lost.

Blyth's Zen was literary. He did not practice zazen but valued Zen insight which he believed was universal.

> Zen is the most precious possession of Asia. With its beginnings in India, development in China, and final practical application in Japan, it is today the strongest power in the world. It is a world-power, for in so far as men *live* at all, they live by Zen. Wherever

there is a poetical action, a religious aspiration, a heroic thought, a union of the nature within a man and the Nature without, there is Zen.[107]

In his book, he sought to demonstrate that Zen themes—such as the quest for enlightenment—were common throughout world literature. Zen, as he understood it, was found not only in China and Japan but as well "in Christ; in Eckehart [sic], and in the music of Bach; in Shakespeare and Wordsworth."[108]

It was an unorthodox approach to the subject, but it was an ideal introduction for Aitken, who had already read some haiku and admired the poetry of Basho.[109] Blyth's book helped him gain a better understanding not only of Japanese poets but of Shakespeare as well. He reread the book so often that the guard, fearing the binding would break, took it back.

Coincidentally, Blyth was not far away in a camp for civilian prisoners where, in spite of his Japanese wife, he was detained as an "enemy alien." In 1944, the prison camps in the area were combined, and both Blyth and Aitken were housed in a complex which had previously been a reform school.

Although Blyth was at first nonplussed by the young Aitken's admiration, gradually the two developed a friendship. They shared a common attitude to their imprisonment, turning it into something like a monastic opportunity for study. Aitken now had someone to guide his reading. Blyth, in addition to acting as Aitken's tutor, used the time to work on an ambitious project to translate haiku into English; these translations would fill four volumes when eventually published.

Blyth taught Aitken some rudimentary Japanese and introduced him to Suzuki's *Essays in Zen Buddhism*. From his reading, Aitken developed a desire to investigate Zen further after the war, but he had no desire to remain in Japan. Conditions in the camp deteriorated as the war dragged on. The food was poor, and Aitken, who had never been robust, struggled with asthma in the damp, unheated rooms. He was physically emaciated and frail when finally released, and it took a while for him to recover his health back in Hawaii.

After the war, he returned to the University of Hawaii and graduated with an English degree in 1947. From there, he and his wife, Mary, left for California where he planned to do graduate studies in Japanese literature and language. He was still interested in Zen. Since, however, there appeared to be no appropriate Zen teachers available, he tried, unsuccessfully, to visit the Indian-born mystic and teacher Krishnamurti who many Theosophists believed to be an incarnation of the Buddha. Later, Aitken heard about Nyogen Senzaki in Los Angeles, and he and Mary relocated there in order to be near him.

The first meetings between Senzaki and Aitken were discussions about philosophy and literature. Eventually, drawn by Senzaki's personal manner and kindness, Aitken realized that what he wanted was not information about Zen but a way to develop the insight which animated Senzaki.

Aitken and Mary joined Senzaki's meditation group. Instead of cushions, they used chairs which Senzaki felt was a more normal way for Americans to sit. Aitken later remarked that Senzaki, then 78 years old, had grown so stout it had probably become difficult for him to sit on cushions. Senzaki gave Aitken a Buddhist name, Chotan, which meant "deep pool" and, aware of Aitken's literary background, assigned him as a koan Eckhart's "the eye with which I see God is the same eye with which God sees me." "Show me that eye," Senzaki commanded Aitken.

In 1950, the Aitkens returned to Hawaii, and he completed his master's degree at the University of Hawaii. His thesis was on Zen and the haiku of Matsuo Basho. He also helped organize the East-West Philosopher's Conference which D. T. Suzuki attended. When Aitken expressed a desire to return to Japan in order to pursue further Zen training, Suzuki was able to help him obtain a fellowship to do so. Mary had recently given birth to their son, Thomas, and she chose to remain in Hawaii.

Back in Japan, Aitken renewed his acquaintance with Blyth, who arranged for him to take part in a week long sesshin at Engakuji in Kamakura under the direction of Asahina Sogen. This was Aitken's first experience of extended zazen. Although he was thirty-three years old and not very flexible, he was expected to sit in traditional cross-legged posture for ten to twelve hours a day. There was no formal instruction given the participants, although the monk seated beside Aitken in the zendo was given the responsibility of showing Aitken zendo protocols. When they were introduced, the monk said, "How do you do? The world is very broad, don't you think?" Aitken admitted later that he had no idea what the monk meant, but he was charmed nonetheless.

Eagerly, Aitken took his place on the *tan* (platform) where the monks were seated. The atmosphere in the zendo was all he had imagined it would be—incense burning, black-robed monks steeling themselves for the ordeal ahead, the sounds of the various clackers, drums, and bells, even the staccato chanting of the opening ceremonies. Then the teacher got down from the tan and prostrated himself before the altar and image of Manjusri, the Bodhisattva who oversees sesshin. Not once, but a total of nine times, Asahina Roshi lowered himself to his knees, bent forward until his forehead touched the floor, then brought his hands beside his head and made a lifting motion, as if receiving the feet of the Buddha. Aitken was appalled when he realized that he, too, would be expected to prostrate himself before the statue. His western sense of dignity and a cultural aversion to idol worship rose up in protest. He had not fully comprehended until that moment that Zen was more than a psychological practice; it was a religion. He continued with the sesshin but with new reservations about Zen or what he had imagined Zen to be.

In sanzen, he informed Asahina Roshi that Senzaki had assigned him the Eckhart statement as a koan, and Asahina told him, instead, to meditate on Huineng's "Original Face" which, he explained, had the same intent. It was difficult to remain focused on the koan, however, as he struggled with the pain in his legs and rising doubts about the ritual elements of the sesshin.

In spite of these challenges, he persisted and, in December, returned to Engakuji to take part in the Rohatsu sesshin. Still unused to cross-legged sitting postures, Aitken found the ordeal even more excruciating than the November sesshin had been and was left dispirited by the experience. He doubted his ability to continue Zen training.

Nyogen Senzaki had spoken of his friendship with the Zen teacher and poet, Soen Nakagawa, and Aitken wrote to him, receiving in return an invitation to visit Ryutakuji. The men shared an interest in haiku among other things and got along well. Nakagawa explained that it was not unusual for Zen students to attend sesshin at a number of temples and with different teachers until they found the one best suited to them. He suggested Aitken take part in the January sesshin at Ryutakuji.

The teacher at Ryutakuji, Gempo Yamamoto, felt that Aitken's approach to the "Original Face" koan was too intellectual. He assigned him Joshu's Mu, which allowed no room for rational analysis.

> I felt a little resistance to this change, but on returning to my cushions, I discovered what zazen really is. No longer was I aware that the cracks in the tile floor formed a weird pattern. I could sink at last beneath the surface of my mind.[110]

Aitken stayed at Ryutakuji for the remainder of his time in Japan, but the physical demands of monastic life were ruinous to his health. His knees and legs ached constantly, and the drafts in the zendo, especially in the winter months, exacerbated his respiratory problems. Then in June he was hospitalized with dysentery.

He returned to Hawaii in August, disappointed by what he considered his lack of progress and looking and feeling almost as physically worn down as he had upon being released from the prisoner of war camp.

Just before he departed, he and Nakagawa were walking in Tokyo, and Nakagawa saw a statue of Bodhidharma in the window of a bookstore. He insisted on purchasing the statue and presenting it to Aitken, telling him that he should use it as the central figure in the Zen temple he would eventually found in Hawaii. Aitken, uncertain about his ability to continue Zen training at all, thought the possibility that he might establish a temple highly unlikely, but he accepted the gift and brought it back to Hawaii.

After his return, he became preoccupied with the responsibilities of earning a living and supporting a family, but things did not work out well. His marriage unravelled and, after his divorce, he left Hawaii to return to Los Angeles so he could continue to train with Nyogen Senzaki. He found a job in a bookstore where he earned so little that all he could afford for housing was a room at the YMCA.

In 1956, another of Senzaki's students told him that Krishnamurti's Happy Valley School in Ojai was in need of an English teacher. Aitken applied for the position and was accepted. Within a year he was married to the school's assistant director, Anne Hopkins. It proved to be an auspicious union. Anne's personality complemented Aitken's. His Dharma heir, John Tarrant, described Aitken as a "real beatnik, bohemian kind of character who was very pissed off with authority all the time and, really, with everybody all the time, especially society."[111] He was not comfortable in social situations, and his manner was often stiff and formal. In contrast, Anne was "very gracious and floaty, with flowing clothes and the ability to drift through smiling...full of warmth and generosity and feeling."

Their wedding trip to Japan was not what most newlyweds would have considered a honeymoon. The day after they arrived, Aitken abandoned the marriage bed to attend sesshin at Ryotakuji, where Nakagawa had been installed as abbot and principal teacher.

Anne supported her new husband's desire to take part in the sesshin but had no intention herself of spending seven days sitting immobile with aching knees. Nakagawa made one of the monastery's guest rooms available to her. It had a fine view of the temple garden and fish pond, and, while Aitken struggled with Mu, Anne passed the time reading the few English books available in the temple library. Nothing she read changed her mind about the practice of zazen. In fact, she responded to the books much as Aitken had to the prostrations at Engakuji.

After the sesshin, Nakagawa served as a tour guide for the newlyweds, taking them, among other places, to Mount Fuji. He also introduced them to Eido Shimano, known by his given name, Tai-san. He was a young monk who spoke excellent English and who Nakagawa hoped to send to Los Angeles to assist Senzaki. The Aitkens' first impression of the young man was very positive.

Then, in August, they went with Nakagawa to a small temple in Tokorozawa outside Tokyo where Nakagawa—although a Rinzai Zen Master in own right—was going to flaunt established protocols by attending a sesshin and serving as assistant to a teacher from the rival Soto tradition. This teacher was Haku'un Yasutani. Yasutani had been the student of Daiun Sogaku Harada, a Soto priest who—dissatisfied with the level of understanding he had acquired through Soto practice—undertook koan study with a Rinzai teacher and came to awakening. Yasutani, in turn, did koan practice with Harada Roshi and achieved kensho in 1927. Afterwards, he continued to work with Harada, deepening his insight, until 1943 when he was authorized to teach. He broke with the official Soto tradition and established an independent school he called Sanbo Kyodan.[112] He also broke with tradition by chosing to work with lay practitioners rather than monks.

Although Anne had not intended to take part in the sesshin, there was little else for her to do. Yasutani provided her a western-style easy chair not in the zendo proper but on the verandah where she was free to sit when she chose; it was the same accommodation that Nanshinken had made for Ruth Fuller Everett years earlier. Anne did not care where she sat; she was just filling time. Yasutani also told her she could attend dokusan if she wished. It was those private meetings with Yasutani which finally broke down her resistance to zazen, and by the end of the sesshin she was making a serious effort.

Two of the participants attained kensho during the sesshin, and, while Aitken had not done so himself, he was now convinced, in a way he had not been before, that awakening was achievable.

Before going to Japan, the Aitkens had decided to move to Hawaii so Robert could be nearer his son. But they were still under contract at the Happy Valley School and had to return there to fulfill their obligations.

That May, Nyogen Senzaki died, and Soen Nakagawa came to Los Angeles to perform the funeral rites and to hold a memorial sesshin in Senzaki's honor. It was the first full seven day sesshin to be conducted on the US mainland. Both Aitken and Anne participated.

In Honolulu, the Aitkens opened a second-hand bookstore specializing in books on Asian spirituality. They kept a record of customers who purchased books on Buddhism and, when they received authorization from Nakagawa to organize a zazenkai (a sitting group), invited those customers to join them for regular Zen practice at their home. Although only two others joined them in their first sitting, the statue of Bodhidharma which Nakagawa had bought was set up on a make-shift altar in the Aitkens' living room. The opening and closing of the meditation periods were marked by striking a Pyrex bowl with a wooden spoon.

The number of attendees increased steadily, and the group came to refer to themselves as the Diamond Sangha, an allusion to both the Diamond Sutra and the nearby Diamond Head peak. Shimano was sent from Japan to assist them. Eventually, there was not enough room in the house to accommodate the people who wanted to participate, so the Aitkens moved to a larger one near the University. When Soen Nakagawa visited it, he named it Koko An. As with Diamond Sangha, the name had a dual reference, suggesting Koko Head crater, and meaning, in Japanese, "Small Temple Right Here."

In 1961, Nakagawa led a sesshin at Koko An which Aitken approached with determination. He put as much vigor into his sitting as he was able to muster and continued late into the night after the formal meditation periods had ended. One evening he had what the Japanese call *makyo*—a hallucination or vision—in which he imagined himself seated on the stone floor of an ancient temple with tall monks circumambulating him and chanting sutras. The vision further energized him.

Then, on the fifth day of the sesshin

> —Nakagawa Roshi gave a great "*Katsu!*"[113] in the zendo, and I found my voice uniting with his, "Aaaah!" In the next dokusan, he asked me…a checking question. I could not answer, and he simply terminated the interview. In a later dokusan, he said that I had experienced a little bit of light and that I should be very careful.[114]

Shimano enrolled at the University of Hawaii, where he was more socially active than the Aitkens believed appropriate; however, his presence at Koko An provided them an opportunity to take leave of the community and go to Japan for seven months to do intensive practice with Yasutani. During this visit they met Philip Kapleau who had studied with Soen Nakagawa for a while and was now working with Yasutani, sometimes functioning as his translator. The three of them discussed the possibility of arranging for Yasutani to come to the US to lead sesshin.

When they returned to Honolulu, Aitken accepted an administrative post at the University of Hawaii. The United States was just being drawn into the Vietnam war, and Aitken became active on campus as a vocal and aggressive critic of US foreign policy in Southeast Asia. He was a member of the American Friends' (Quaker) Service Committee and counseled young men who sought to avoid military conscription.

The membership of the Diamond Sangha was also undergoing a change. The earlier, older, members had belonged to the generation which had been drawn to Buddhism through their interest in Theosophy and the occult. The new, younger, members had largely been drawn to meditation as a result of their drug experiences.

Between 1962 and 1969, Yasutani made a series of regular visits to the United States and conducted sesshin in Hawaii, Los Angeles, and on the East Coast. Aitken took part in as many of these as he could and was now considered a senior student but, except for the "little bit of light," still not had achieved kensho.

In 1964, two of the female students at Koko An were hospitalized with breakdowns. A social worker informed Aitken that, in both cases, a factor contributing to their conditions was that they had been involved in sexual relationships with Shimano. Aitken, unsure how to respond to these allegations, flew to Japan to discuss the situation with Nakagawa. Nakagawa and Haku'un Yasutani both down played the matter, and Aitken returned to Hawaii dissatisfied and unclear about the appropriate way to respond. The matter was taken out of hands, however, because when Shimano learned that Aitken had gone to Japan, he left Koko An and moved to New York.

In 1967, Aitken turned 50. Anne was 56. They began to think about their eventual retirement and purchased a former hotel, rumored to have once been a geisha house, on the island of Maui. It had previously been rented to a succession of young social drop-outs. Hippies had arrived in Hawaii, and Maui had become a popular destination. The island was under-populated and had large public beaches. There was ample space to built make-shift shelters, fresh fruit in abundance, and a climate suitable for clothing-optional lifestyles. Drugs were also easily accessible. Before the Aitkens moved to their new property, they allowed young people to stay there in exchange for looking after the grounds. It turned out to be a one-sided arrangement.

People kept showing up even after the Aitkens were in residence, and Aitken recognized that some of them, at least, were genuinely engaged in a spiritual quest. So, although they had not originally intended to do so, the Aitkens once more opened their home to people interested in practicing Zen. The response was even greater than it had been in the city, and the new Maui Zendo became an official center of the Sanbo Kyodan Zen School. Although it remained a center for lay practice, Aitken established a formal schedule centering around zazen and manual labor which was almost monastic; he decided that the young people with whom he was now working needed structure in their lives.

In Honolulu, the Koko An Sangha was firmly enough established to continue without the Aitkens' daily supervision, although Robert still returned regularly to sit with the group. Now that Shimano was gone, Nakagawa arranged for one of his lay students, Katsuki Sekida, to move to Hawaii to assist the two communities there.

Not all awakening experiences are dramatic, and, after a time with the Diamond Sangha, Sekida came to believe that Aitken had attained realization without being aware of it. He expressed his opinion to Yasutani, who had come to conduct the first sesshin at the Maui Zendo in October 1969. Yasutani tested Aitken, who found—as he put it—that he "could make sense of some koans." Yasutani agreed that Aitken had had kensho, but Aitken himself remained unsure and was still unclear what Yasutani meant when he demanded that he *demonstrate* the significance of the koans he was assigned.

After Yasutani retired, his successor, Yamada Koun, came in his stead to Hawaii to lead sesshin, and it was Yamada Roshi who gave Aitken *inka* in 1974, making him the first North American to receive transmission in the Sanbo Kyodan tradition. Still doubtful of his qualifications, Aitken went to California to do further training under Taizan Maezumi. There he finally gained confidence and, with Maezumi's and Yamada's encouragement and guidance, took on the responsibilities of a teacher and became the first American to be given the title *Roshi*.[115]

During the transmission ceremony, Aitken also "took the precepts"—*jukai*. *Jukai* has been described as "lay ordination" by some North American practitioners, but Aitken objected to that terminology. He continued to think of himself as a layman and, to his mind, ordination suggested something else. Now that he was an authorized teacher, he needed to determine how that role should be defined in a lay western—as opposed to a monastic Japanese—context.

For example, on a personal level Aitken's Zen practice was intimately connected to social and political activism. That type of engagement was unknown in Japan; nor would it be a priority for most of those who came to the Maui and Koko An Sanghas. Aitken was one of the founders of the Buddhist Peace Fellowship, and he and Anne risked arrest for refusing to pay that percentage of their taxes which would be used for military purposes. He was also committed to environmental issues, pointing out that one of the fundamental teachings—and realizations—of the Zen school was the interconnectedness of all things. He further challenged tradition by actively encouraging his female students to examine the role of women in what remained a male-dominated practice not only in Asia but in North America as well. They established *Kahawai: A Journal of Women and Zen* in which they published their reflections.

Aitken's spiritual practice was not a retreat from the world and its challenges, as it could be for persons entering monasteries whether Buddhist or otherwise; for him, practice included being deeply engaged in the world. Not many of the members of the Koko An and Maui communities, however, shared his views. The majority of them had come to Zen seeking ways of dealing with personal rather than global concerns. And while no one was required to adopt Aitken's views, at times members felt he was disappointed in them for not doing so.

The Maui Center had been communal from its beginning. It was not a monastery; members were not celibate. The question of what shape that community should take was a complex one. With transmission, Aitken had gone from being a senior student (a first among peers, as it were) to being the teacher, and while he did not view himself as an authority figure, others started to see him that way.

He was aware that many of the traditional structures of Zen practice were cultural rather than intrinsic. The question was which of these to retain and which to dispense with. John Tarrant compared the early days at Maui to a Cargo Cult:

> We had a great Japanese temple bell, a big bell that you banged at 4:30 in the morning, and everyone would run about wearing robes, homemade *faux* monastic Japanese robes. People would say things like "Hai!" when you said things to them. And they'd bow and gassho and do full prostrations when you went in to see the teacher. It was like a cargo cult. The idea was if you could just clear some land in the jungle and make some plywood airplanes, the other airplanes will be attracted. If you followed the forms, no doubt you'd become a Zen master.

Over time it became clear that the many of the forms could be moderated. Japanese behaviours fell away, although students still bowed—rather than prostrated—when presenting themselves at dokusan. Experiments were made in coming to community decisions through consensus.

There were things, however, about which Aitken was inflexible, such as prohibiting the use of marijuana which most of the students considered harmless. Some members drifted away, feeling the rules were too strict. On the other hand, Yamada Roshi, a gentle and humble man by Japanese standards, was uncomfortable with what he considered the degree of informality he found at the Maui Zendo.

The process of developing appropriate Zen structures and traditions for North Americans was going to be a long and difficult one played out over and over again in Maui, San Francisco, Rochester, and elsewhere.

As Aitken grew in confidence, he became an accomplished and generous teacher. Recognizing that most Americans had no access to a genuine Zen teacher, he included his postal address with his early publications and invited people to write to him. One of his most important contributions to American Zen was working with Yamada to develop a koan curriculum which transcended culture and was effective with non-Asian students.

It was the emphasis on the practice of zazen that distinguished the Zen of the emerging training centers, such as Aitken's, from the literary Zen of Alan Watts and D. T. Suzuki. The goal of Zen, Aitken taught, was to realize "the nature of being, and zazen has proved empirically to be the practical way to settle down to where such realization is possible."[116] He quoted Yamada Roshi's statement that the practice of Zen "is forgetting the self in the act of uniting with something." "Forgetting the self is the act of just doing the task, with no self-consciousness sticking to the action."[117]

He compared it to riding a bicycle. When one is first learning to do so, there are many things one has to think about and one is awkward trying to keep them all in mind. But eventually there comes a point when one stops thinking and, in effect, becomes one with the vehicle. When this happens, one no longer has to struggle to keep the bike balanced; it balances itself.

Formal Zen practice begins with taking a proper seated position. Once the correct posture is assumed, beginning students are instructed to simply count their breaths from one to ten, a practice called *susokkan*. By doing so one-pointedly, keeping the attention on each number and bringing it back over and over again to the count when the mind drifts off, one develops the "power to invest in something."[118] It is more than focusing on the breath; one strives to become one with the breath and the count

> —if you merely sit with a focus, you tend to close off your potential. You and your object remain two things. Become each point, each number, in the sequence of counting. You and the count and the breath are all of a piece in *this* moment. Invest yourself in each number. There is only "one" in the whole universe, only "two" in the whole universe, just that single point. Everything else is dark.

At first, as a beginner, you will be conscious of each step in the procedure, but eventually you will become the procedure itself. The practice will do the practice.[119]

It was a point to which Aitken would frequently return: The way to learn zazen was to do zazen. In sesshin, he told the students not to worry about how they were progressing. "It is natural to wonder, 'How am I doing?' Let me reassure you. You're doing fine."[120]

In the prison camp in Japan, Blyth had introduced Aitken to basic Buddhist teachings, including the Four Vows—to save (liberate) all beings without number, to eliminate endless blind passions, to pass innumerable Dharma Gates, and to achieve the great way of Buddha.

"How can one vow to save all beings?" Aitken objected. "How is that even possible?"

"It's possible by including them," Blyth told him.

When first working on "The eye with which I see God is the eye with which God sees me," Aitken's attempts to answer the koan during dokusan were verbal, and Nyogen Senzaki rejected them all.

"You are not listening," Senzaki complained. "Show me that eye! Don't tell me about it!"

Aitken struggled a while longer, then one day an answer occurred to him. When he next met with Senzaki, Aitken simply closed his eyes.

"Oh, ho!" Senzaki said. "Very well then, where does it go when you're asleep?"

Aitken did not know how to respond.

There may have been disagreements about the rules pertaining to personal behavior at the Maui Zendo, but no one questioned that it was essentially a training center. People came there to learn Zen. Helen Tworkov relates the story of a young man

> —who arrived at the Maui airport, walked up to the information desk, and asked, "Can you show me the way to the monastery?" The

information clerk was clearly baffled, but a man standing nearby directed the newcomer to the Maui Zendo. He was led into the house to meet Aitken, who was standing next to a beautiful young woman wearing a flimsy summer dress. Aitken recalls this man saying in a very solemn manner, "'Greetings! I have come to enter the monastery,' one huge suitcase in each hand, all the while looking out the tail of his eye at the young woman. I [Aitken] said, 'I'm sorry, this isn't a monastery, but come in anyway.'"[121]

The young man chose to stay.

Although Aitken was a vegetarian, on one occasion he was invited to a dinner party at which meat dishes were served. Later one of his students asked him why he had chosen to eat the meal. "The cow was already dead," Aitken told her. "But my hostess wasn't."

Aitken led several sesshin at the Ring of Bone zendo established by Gary Snyder. During the first of these, one of Snyder's friends, Dale Pendell, wondered how Snyder would react to having

> —a real full-blown roshi at the center of what he had patiently sat by, sat with, watered, labored for, encouraged in countless ways that most people never even saw. I wondered how it would be for him.
>
> I got my answer. At our first *sesshin,* and all of us beginners with Aitken's style, discipline was a bit lax.... We were using a tent as the hojo, and the most level surface, and not so very level, was so close to the barn that the people in the *dokusan* line could hear little bits and pieces of conversation in the tent from time to time. One time Gary had been in line in front of me, and had gone in. I remember hearing some kind of rush, or sudden movement, from inside the tent. Later, in the house, Gary had this dazed smile. Shaking his head, he said, "Man, he's good!"[122]

After he received transmission, Aitken led sesshin not only in Hawaii but elsewhere in the United States and Australia. He also accepted an invitation to lead sesshin at a Catholic retreat center in Tacoma, Washington, and one of his Dharma heirs was an ordained Catholic priest, Father Patrick Hawk. Aitken was respected throughout the Zen community in North America in which he was recognized as a pioneer and first patriarch (he preferred the gender-neutral term "ancestor"). The Diamond Sangha helped provide teachers and establish Zen Centers in California and the US Southwest, Germany, Argentina, and Australia.

Robert Aitken died in 2010 at the age of 93. Anne had died before him in 1994.

Chapter Seven
Shunryu Suzuki

THE FIRST ZEN TEACHERS IN NORTH AMERICA—Soyen Shaku, Nyogen Senzaki, Sokei-an Sasaki—were all members of the Rinzai School. The form of Zen described in the books of D. T. Suzuki and Alan Watts was almost exclusively Rinzai. Shokokuji, where Gary Snyder studied in Japan, was a Rinzai temple. Even though Harada Roshi and Yasutani Roshi were ordained in the Soto priesthood, the Sanbo Kyodan school—which derives from their teaching and in which Robert Aitken received transmission—was more closely aligned with Rinzai practice.

In Japan, the Soto school is much larger than the Rinzai and in the years between the two world wars was actively engaged in missionary work. The Zenshuji Mission for Japanese immigrants and their descendents in Los Angles was established in 1922, and the Sokoji Zen Mission in San Franciso was inaugurated in 1934. The membership of both was almost exclusively ethnic Japanese who had little interest in Zen meditation or training but who wanted a religious establishment which would meet their ritual needs and help them retain their traditions and a sense of cultural identity.

Soto meditation practice differs from Rinzai in several significant ways. There is less emphasis on achievement. In Rinzai practice, the need to attain kensho—or awakening—is stressed, after which there remains the specter of hundreds of koans students are expected to resolve in order to deepen their insight and integrate it into their lives. The practice is difficult for Japanese; it is often brutal and frustrating for Western students. North American meditators can spend years working on Mu without resolving it; the few who do pass Mu can continue to struggle with and be stymied by koans which draw imagery from Chinese and Japanese folklore or literature with which they are unfamiliar. Instead of koan study, Soto practice centers on *shikan taza* or "just sitting" and "silent illumination." It is a subjectless meditation in which the practitioner sits with an alert mind not focused on anything in particular.

The teacher responsible for introducing Soto meditation practice to North Americans seldom referred to enlightenment as something to be attained. Instead, like Dogen, the founder of the Soto School in Japan,[123] he taught that awakening and practice were one. It is not necessarily an easier practice than working with koans, but for many North American inquirers it proved to be a more accessible practice.

The teacher was Shunryu Suzuki. To distinguish himself from D. T. Suzuki, he jestingly referred to himself as the "small Suzuki." He was born in 1904 and died in 1971, at the age of 67. For all but twelve of those years, he lived in Japan. Only the last dozen years of his life were spent in the country where his teaching would have its greatest impact.

Suzuki's father, Sogaku, was a Soto priest who had married late in life and then only because of reforms brought about by the Meiji government in an attempt to reduce the political power of the Buddhist clergy. His rural temple was not a wealthy one, and the family was poor. There was a stream in front of the temple into which farmers and vendors threw vegetables which had been discarded because they were old or misshapen. Sogaku would retrieve these vegetables for the family's meal, pointing out that all things have Buddha-nature and therefore nothing should be wasted.

His parents could not afford to have young Shunryu's hair clipped in the short style favored by schoolboys of the time, so his father shaved his head, which drew the derision of his classmates. They also teased him about being the son of a priest and expressed contempt for the Buddhist clergy. To ease his son's unhappiness, Sogaku explained that the boys were only mimicking what they had heard their elders say. He told Shunryu of the persecution of Buddhism during the early years of the Meiji Restoration, when the powers of the emperor had finally been wrested from the shoguns and native Shintoism had been declared the National Religion. His stories about the spiritual and secular accomplishments of Zen Masters of preceding generations fostered in the boy a desire to follow in their footsteps and become a priest.

At the age of 11, Shunryu left home and entered Zoun-in Temple in the village of Mori. The abbot there was his father's adopted son, Gyokujun So-on Suzuki. So-on was a strict and demanding teacher who taught traditionally, not by verbal instruction but by example. For instance, the only meditation instruction Shunryu received when he arrived was the command to sit in full lotus posture and keep still. So-on considered all aspects of temple life opportunities for Zen practice. Students were expected to observe the master and older students and, by following their example, bring full attention to whatever activity in which they were engaged—whether this was daily meditation, cleaning the fish pond, polishing the wooden corridors, or scraping soot off cooking pots.

Shunryu was ordained at age 13 and formally became So-on's disciple. He was given a Buddhist name, Shogaku, which means "Auspicious Peak," but So-on generally referred to him as "you crooked cucumber!" A crooked cucumber was one which farmers discarded as unsalable, the type of vegetable likely to end up in the stream before Shunryu's childhood home. There may have been some affection in the name, but it also expressed So-on's early doubts about his step-brother's abilities.

So-on had eight students at the time, all young boys who were expected to surrender their individualist inclinations and follow the model of their teacher. Suzuki later referred to this process as "acknowledging" one's teacher. It was difficult training, and none of the other boys were ultimately able to endure it. By the time Shunryu was fourteen, he was the only disciple remaining with So-on; the others had returned to their homes.

In 1918, So-on was given charge of a second, much larger, temple in a coastal town fifty miles away. This temple, Rinso-in, had been neglected during the Meiji years and had fallen into disrepair. The Soto hierarchy charged So-on with restoring it. He brought his only disciple with him.

So-on met the expectations of his superiors. He looked after the physical repairs the temple structures needed, and he won the support of the surrounding lay community, many of whom had drifted away taking their financial support with them. Under So-on's leadership, they returned their allegiance to Rinso-in, and some families sent their sons there for training. Shunryu had companions again and seniority.

To broaden their training, So-on arranged for his young novices to spend a period of time practicing with a Rinzai master. Before they departed, he instructed them to maintain *shoshin*, or "beginner's mind." It was a term from Dogen's *Shobogenzo* which Shunryu would later make famous in English. So-on warned his disciples against becoming attached to any particular practice; when they were at a Rinzai Temple they should follow Rinzai forms and when at a Soto Temple, Soto forms. Regardless, they should always think of themselves as beginning students. As Suzuki put it to his American students much later:

> The goal of practice is always to keep our beginner's mind. Suppose you recite the Prajna Paramita Sutra only once. It might be a very good recitation. But what would happen to you if you recited it twice, three times, four times, or more? You might easily lose your original attitude towards it....
>
> Our "original mind" includes everything within itself. It is always rich and sufficient within itself. You should not lose your self-sufficient state of mind. This does not mean a closed mind, but actually an empty mind and a ready mind. If your mind is empty, it is always ready for anything; it is open to everything. In the beginner's mind there are many possibilities; in the expert's mind there are few.[124]

The boys were assigned a koan while at the Rinzai temple, and, one by one, the other students passed it. Only Shunryu failed to do so. On the final day at the temple, he went for a last sanzen and blurted out an answer which the teacher accepted. Shunryu suspected that the teacher had passed him out of sympathy rather than because he actually understood the koan, which left him with a life-long reservation about koan practice.

At age twenty, Suzuki attended a Soto school in Tokyo. Because he came from a rural community where there had been few educational opportunities, he needed to take a number of upgrading courses in order to catch up with his classmates, many of whom were younger than he. He applied himself and was particularly fond of his English lessons.

One summer day, he snuck into the school's basement storage room. He had a sweet-tooth and had often snuck into his mother's larder to steal sugar; at Zoun-in he had become adept at finding where So-on hid the treats lay people brought to the temple. This time his quarry was a melon.

Once he found the melon, he heard someone calling from the cellar door to inquire if anyone was down there. Suzuki remained still, and the investigator left, closing the door behind him, leaving the basement in total darkness. Still clutching his melon, Suzuki carefully made his way forward, then he felt a sharp pain in his left eye. He had caught himself on a hook hanging from the rafters. The metal pierced his eyelid and came out above his eyebrow. Any move he made increased the pain; he was stuck where he was, bleeding profusely. He had no choice but to wait patiently for someone to rescue him. He controlled his panicked breathing and stood as still as possible for over an hour before he was found. During that time, a calmness gradually came over him, and he had what he considered a profound experience of awakening. Afterwards, the event remained significant to him.

Suzuki received Dharma Transmission from So-on in 1926, when he was 22 years old. He realized that it was essentially a formality which had taken place so he could inherit responsibility for Zoun-in. His father and mother joined him there, and Sogaku—who had served at Zoun-in before So-on—was recognized as *inkyo*, or retired master. Two years later, Shunryu was installed as the 28th abbot of the temple, and his name was recorded in the temple records as such.

Sogaku looked after the day-to-day operations of the temple while his son continued his studies in Tokyo. There he resided in the western-style house of his English teacher, a British woman named Nona Ransom who had previously lived in China and had been a tutor in the imperial household before the revolution. Miss Ransom did not speak Japanese, and, in exchange for room and board, Suzuki acted as her translator and houseboy.

Nona Ransom knew little about Buddhism, which struck her as a primitive form of idol worship, and she was surprised that her houseboy, who otherwise seemed a reasonable young man, paid so much reverence to a statue of the Buddha displayed in her home. The statue had been given to her by the Chinese imperial family and, as far as Miss Ranson was concerned, was merely decorative, but Suzuki treated it almost as if it were sentient. He bowed before it every morning and brought it tea and incense offerings. To her mind, it was bizarre behavior.

Eventually she asked him about it, and he explained that in honoring the image of the Buddha one was not offering it worship but was rather acknowledging one's own true—or Buddha—nature. She slowly acquired a greater respect for the religion under Suzuki's tutelage and eventually practiced zazen with him.

Nona Ransom was the first Westerner to whom Suzuki tried to explain Buddhism, and he found it a rewarding experience. He believed it was precisely her unfamiliarity with Buddhism—her beginner's mind, the fact that she admitted she knew nothing about Buddhism—which made her a receptive student. He felt he now knew what he was called to do. There were, after all, Christian missionaries in Japan; he would be a Buddhist missionary to the west.

It would be a while, however, before he was able to realize that ambition.

Even after Suzuki was installed as abbot of Zoun-in, there was further training to undergo. He was sent to Eiheiji and Sojiji, the two principal temples of the Soto school, and in both he was once more treated as a novice. The training was much as it had been under So-on. Things were not explained, rather students were expected to observe and work things out for themselves. Activities were undertaken for their own sakes rather than to achieve a particular end. There was a strict formality about every endeavor—how one took one's place on the meditation mat, how one dressed, how one ate. In this way students learned through experience that everything they did was part of their practice.

When his formal training came to an end, Suzuki returned to Zoun-in and took over the duties Sogaku had been carrying out in his stead. A priest's duty centered on care for the dead—conducting funerals and memorial services—and carrying out ritual activities such as weddings or chanting sutras on behalf of the community. The routine was dull and repetitive and Shunryu had been happy to leave it to Sogaku. Now he had full responsibility for the temple. Few of the students sent to him to begin their training as monks had any serious interest in the Dharma. Suzuki was beginning to recognize that the Soto Zen tradition had grown stale and that something needed to be done to revitalize it.

When Sogaku died in 1933, Shunryu became head of the family. He was briefly married to a woman who was then diagnosed with tuberculosis and left him to return to her own family which was better able to look after her needs. Then So-on died. The loss of his wife and the deaths of his father and his teacher emphasized the basic Buddhist teaching that nothing is permanent; all things are transitory. The first of the Buddha's four noble truths declared that suffering is inherent in life. The second noble truth identified the cause of suffering to be desire—in particular the desire for things to be other than they are, for things to remain constant when it is not in their nature to be so. Suzuki's understanding of Buddhism continued to deepen.

He inherited So-on's position at Rinso-in and married again, this time to Chie Muramatsu. Within a year, the first of their four children was born, a daughter they named Yasuko; she was followed four years later by a son, Hoitsu.

Suzuki was critical of the expansionist policies of the Japanese government but was careful to express his opinions guardedly. Japan had already occupied Formosa and Mongolia, and war with the west appeared inevitable. Suzuki's point of view was not a popular one within the Soto hierarchy which officially advocated patriotism and devotion to the Emperor.

Ironically, the day of the attack on Pearl Harbor was December 8 (December 7 east of the International Date Line), the day recognized in Japan as the anniversary of the Buddha's enlightenment. Japan was now officially at war with the country to which Suzuki still hoped someday to carry the Dharma.

The military commandeered Rinso-in at first in order to house troops and, later, Korean slave-labor. The temple bells were melted down on behalf of the war effort. Amid the chaos, Suzuki maintained a sitting group of young men called the High Grass Mountain Group. The members came to Rinso-in early each morning to sit in zazen and to discuss current affairs, but one by one they were conscripted and—like the temple bells—disappeared into the war effort.

Suzuki published a number of articles warning that Japan's military action would inevitably have dire consequences, but no one foresaw the devastation that the atomic bomb would cause in Hiroshima and Nagasaki.

During the war, propagandists warned that American soldiers, if they successfully invaded Japan, would engage in wholesale slaughter and mass rape. So the populace was surprised and relieved when the occupying forces behaved with unexpected restraint and even demonstrated respect for Japanese culture and traditions. It had been expected that the Emperor might be executed; instead, under the terms of the new constitution , the Emperor retained his throne but lost his claim to divinity. Many Zen teachers, however, had their licenses revoked because of their support for government policies; the articles Suzuki had written were enough to allow him to retain his.

The nation was in tatters, and reconstruction was long and difficult. Suzuki felt that the most important contribution he could make to rebuilding the nation was to re-establish local schools. His first step was to reopen the kindergarten at Yaizu. Mitsu Matsuno, who—throughout the war—had been able to retain classes at a kindergarten in a community some thirty miles away, was recruited to head up the project. She was a widow with a young daughter. The two of them took up residence in Rinso-in along with Suzuki, Chie, Chie's mother, and the children.

In 1952, the household expanded once more with the addition of an odd and often unsettling monk named Otsubo. He had been sent to Rinso-in by Ian Kishizawa, who had been Suzuki's teacher at Eiheiji. Otsubo was awkward around other people and kept to himself, which suited the others at the temple. It was thought he may have been driven mad as a result of his experiences during the war. Chie told her husband that the monk was a disruptive presence, but, out of loyalty to Kishizawa, Suzuki permitted him to stay and reprimanded his wife and children whenever they complained about him.

One day, Otsubo was chopping firewood. Chie apparently heard him tormenting the household dog, which he was wont to do. She intervened, and Otsubo struck her seven times in the face with his ax. Chie's death was a shattering experience for Suzuki, who blamed himself for allowing Otsubo into the household. Prior to Chie's death, Suzuki had been formal and distant with his children in a manner considered appropriate for Japanese males and priests in particular. After her death, he made an effort to be more overtly affectionate and less demanding. These traits did not come easily to him, and Yasuko, in particular, continued to find him distant.

He had never lost the desire to carry the Dharma to America, and the opportunity finally arose in 1959 when he was asked by Soto Headquarters to take charge of Sokoji, the mission temple in San Francisco. The duties would be much as they were at Rinso-in—fulfilling the ritual needs of the Japanese population of the city. The temple board, however, had specifically asked for a married priest. So Suzuki asked his mother-in-law to assist him in finding a new wife. She suggested Mitsu.

Yasuko's husband was assigned to look after Rinso-in until Suzuki's three year appointment in America was up. The younger daughter, Omi, had never recovered from her mother's death and was institutionalized in a mental hospital where she would commit suicide in 1964. Hoitsu, who was expected eventually to become Suzuki's successor at Rinso-in, was in university, after which he would still have further training to undergo at Eiheiji. The youngest son, Otohiro, was to join his father in San Francisco later with his step-mother. Mitsu was ill at the time and unable to travel, so Suzuki left for America without her. She was not happy about the arrangement and felt abandoned.

Sokoji served about sixty Japanese families in the San Francisco area. The entire congregation had been interred during the war, and they had lost most of their possessions and wealth. The war had been over for a while, but resentments lingered. The temple was the center of community life, somewhere the members were not out of place, where traditional Japanese values were retained and respected.

The building was a former synagogue built in Sephardic style, three stories high, with a wide, columned balcony on the second floor and turrets on either side of the third. Outwardly, nothing about its architecture looked Japanese, much less like a Zen Temple. Indoors, the walls were a garish red. Pews were set up in an auditorium before an altar as in a Christian church. Here there were regular Sunday services at which the temple priest—addressed as "Reverend"—was expected to preach a sermon. Suzuki would not be addressed as "roshi" until, several years later, Alan Watts suggested it was a more appropriate term than "reverend." The head of the Soto missions to California, located in Los Angeles, was called a "bishop." Although there was a shrine room, traditionally furnished except for the use of chairs, there was no zendo or meditation hall. Zen might be the "meditation school" of Buddhism, but, like most Japanese, the temple members considered zazen something that monks—not lay people—did.

The membership tended to be middle-aged or elderly and traditional; many were farmers who spoke little English. They welcomed Suzuki warmly but expected him to carry out his duties without fuss.

While temple members probably did not listen to Alan Watts' popular local radio broadcasts about Zen, many other people did, and some began to look for a teacher to introduce them to Zen. A few took courses at Watts' American Academy for Asian Studies, where Watts invited the new Japanese Zen priest to speak. Suzuki told the students that he sat zazen in the shrine room of Sokoji every morning at 5:45. None of the temple members sat with him, but gradually a handful of non-Japanese started to show up.

The American students were a pleasant surprise to Suzuki. They were much more excited and curious about Zen than the laity in Japan had been. Specifically they wanted instruction in the proper way to practice Zen. They had—he realized—

that beginner's mind which had made Nona Ransom so receptive to learning about Buddhism. They were clean slates.

There were teachers and housewives, people who had attended programs at the American Academy for Asian Studies, artists, and beatniks, to be followed later by hippies and even some street people. There were serious and intent youth who used terminology they had picked up through reading D. T. Suzuki and Alan Watts. They were searching for a "Zen Master"—someone who had attained "satori" and had achieved "enlightenment." Shunryu Suzuki used none of these terms. Many came to Sokoji expecting to be challenged as Hakuin had been by Shoju Rojin;[125] instead what they found was a very small man (even by Japanese standards) with a shaved head who invited them to sit zazen with him, nothing more. A surprising number accepted the invitation.

The western students remained distinct from, and not always welcomed by, the temple congregation. Slowly the Shrine Room was transformed into a room for meditation practice, a zendo with tatami mats and cushions called zafus (Buddha seats). The Japanese congregation continued to use the pews in the auditorium.

Over time, the sitting became more formal. Suzuki introduced the kyosaku, which frightened some first-time sitters into not returning. The group chanted the Heart Sutra[126] in Japanese accompanied by the rhythmic beat of a fish-shaped drum called a *mokugyo*. Prostrations were introduced, and, when Suzuki's students reacted as Aitken had at Engakuji, his response was to increase the number of prostrations at the beginning and end of morning meditation sessions from three to nine. Americans, he told the sitters, were stubborn, so needed more prostrations.

There was no talk of enlightenment, no koans or obscure remarks. Suzuki's instruction focused almost exclusively on how to sit, how to place the hands, how to focus the attention on the breath. Occasionally a student would come with questions about theory or philosophy; Suzuki became deft at side-stepping these, explaining that if he were to give them an answer they would only think they understood something they did not. Over and over, he directed them back to practice.

When Suzuki had been in the United States for two years, Mitsu and Otohiro, then seventeen, joined him. One of the presents he bought for her before she arrived was an American style ironing board and iron. She was welcomed by both the temple congregation and the zazen students, who were beginning to coalesce into a community—a sangha—of their own.

It was important to Suzuki that the expenses associated with the zazen group be kept apart from those of the temple itself. He did not believe that the donations of the congregation should support the American students; the students needed to cover their own costs. So in 1961, the sitting group was incorporated as Zen Center. The first president was a young Englishman named Grahame Petchey. Both he and his wife were members as were their friends, Richard and Virginia Baker.

When another year passed, Suzuki completed the three year term to which he had originally agreed, and Mitsu hoped that they would return to Japan. Suzuki, however, chose to remain in San Francisco. In Japan he had only been a rural priest with no stature in the Soto hierarchy; in America, he had disciples. It was a surprise to his students who did go to Japan to discover that he was not held in the same esteem there as he was in California. In May 1962, a traditional "Mountain Seat" ceremony took place by which Suzuki was formally installed as the abbot of Sokoji. It was a momentous occasion not just for the temple congregation but for the entire Japanese community, and the auditorium was full. The occidental Zen Center members unobtrusively took seats in the back.

The following August, after the Zen Center's first seven day sesshin, fifteen members took part in a ceremony that came to be called "Lay Ordination" in which they accepted the precepts of Buddhism and were given Buddhist names. Richard Baker and Grahame Petchey were among them.

The Mountain Seat Ceremony and the lay ordination ceremony were conducted in Japanese and made use of traditional Japanese forms. These were the forms Suzuki knew. He told his students that American forms might eventually evolve, but until then they should use the forms he could teach them.

Zen Center was undergoing a major change. It was no longer just a place where people came to practice zazen as one element among many in their lives. Suzuki began to see it as a training center based on Japanese models—in effect, a monastery. Trained priests from Japan were recruited to work with both the Sokoji congregation and the zazen students. Dainin Katagiri was sent from Japan to work with the Los Angeles mission in 1963 but relocated to San Francisco soon afterwards to act as Suzuki's assistant. Senior students, starting with Grahame Petchey, were ordained as Zen priests by Suzuki and sent to Japan for formal training. They were not always inspired by what they found there. The Japanese authorities made no accommodations for their foreign novices; Grahame Petchey, who was six foot four, was expected to sleep on his 30 inch square zabuton or meditation mat. Every activity, other than zazen which was done in a cross-legged posture, was done seated in seiza—the traditional Japanese form of sitting on one's heels. In Japan, this was the natural way to sit; people were accustomed to it from the time they were toddlers. For Western student, used to chairs, it could be excruciating. There was a lot of popular superstition still associated with Buddhism, hungry ghosts, for example, which needed to be propitiated. The behavior of Japanese novices was often petty. Careerism and rivalries were still common in the Soto training centers. Suzuki was well aware of the problems in Japan and even harbored the hope that his American students might eventually reform the stagnant Soto School in Japan. He did not like his students to complain, however, and told them to persevere and to write stories focusing on the positive elements of their time in Japan for the Zen Center newsletter.

Zen Center sponsored a number of satellite centers where regular zazen was practiced under the supervision of senior students: Bill Kwong in Mill Valley, Mel Weitsman in Berkeley, and Marian Derby in Los Altos. Like an itinerate preacher, Suzuki visited each in turn to give a short talk and supervise the sitting. The group in Los Altos met in Marian Derby's converted garage. It was called the Haiku Zendo because there were places for seventeen to practice (traditional Japanese haiku consist of seventeen syllables).

Certain students were given more responsibility than others; the student of whom Suzuki had the highest expectation was Richard Baker, who became President of Zen Center when Grahame Petchey returned to Japan for a second training period.

Baker was put in charge of looking for a place outside the city where a traditional practice center could be established. Eventually the place decided upon was an abandoned resort at the Tassajara Hot Springs which Baker had first visited while on a camping trip with Petchey. Suzuki loved the place, and Baker determined to raise the funds necessary to purchase it. The budget of Zen Center at that time was less than $5500, and they had $2,304.24 in the bank; but Baker undertook to raise $150,000. In the end, the price was double that. It seemed an impossible task to many Zen Center members, but Baker had exceptional organizational skills and was able to get support for a fund-raising campaign from a number of prominent people friendly to the idea, including Alan Watts, Allen Ginsberg, and Gary Snyder. The Grateful Dead and Big Brother and the Holding Company held a "Zenefit Concert." The impossible started to become probable.

As Baker's status within Zen Center rose, there were jealousies and rivalries. Members who had been with Suzuki for a longer than Baker resented the preference he was shown, but Suzuki recognized and admired the fact that Baker had the energy and confidence to get things done. On July 2, 1967, Baker was ordained a priest in the first public ordination Suzuki conducted and was installed as head monk at Tassajara. This was a break with Soto tradition because there were others who had been ordained, although privately, before him. It was obvious that he was now Suzuki's primary disciple.

Tassajara Zen Mountain Center was the first Buddhist monastery ever established outside of Asia. Here, Suzuki believed, American students would be trained not only to spread the Dharma in America but eventually to revitalize the tradition in Japan. The Tassajara practice schedule was monastic and grueling. A wake-up bell rang at 4:00 am; there were two rounds of zazen and a chanting service before breakfast, which was eaten in formal oryoki style, using chop sticks and a set of three nested bowls tied together with a cloth. Then followed samu, a three-hour work period. After lunch, again eaten oryoki style, was a study period and another work period, as well as rest periods and bath time. More ritual services preceded the evening meal. The day ended with a lecture given by Suzuki followed by two more rounds of zazen.

Learning how to use the *oryoki* bowls was a challenge in itself. It was, of course, a Japanese tradition, as were the shaved heads and other formalities. The chants were in archaic Sino-Chinese which no one understood. Suzuki had little patience with those who questioned the practices. Zen students in Japan, he pointed out, did not question their teacher; they did what they were told. Rules were necessary, and these were the rules he had decided upon. Zen students in the city waited for lights to change before crossing the street even when there was no traffic.

As the membership of Zen Center expanded, the congregation at Sokoji felt overwhelmed and overlooked. They believed that Suzuki was spending too much time with his zazen students. Eventually they pressured him into resigning his post at the temple, and Zen Center was forced to look for new quarters.

The new location was a former women's residence on the corner of Page and Laguna Streets. It could house 75 students who, as in Japan, would live in a residential monastic Zen community. There were four periods of zazen every day, as well as chanting and ritual services, communal vegetarian meals, and work assignments. The training regime for new students was what it had been in Japan; instead of being told what to do, new members were expected to observe senior students and follow their example.

Where Aitken and Senzaki had sought to develop a lay Zen practice in America, Suzuki was establishing a highly disciplined and structured monastic practice. What made it truly astonishing was that more anti-authoritarian, counter-culture hippies sought to reside at Zen Center than it had room for. Many of those not able to live in the residence found apartments and rooms nearby in order to be close to it.

The new neighborhood was largely African-American and did not immediately welcome the newcomers. It was also an area with one of the highest crime rates in the city. Some years later, Chris Pirsig—whose motorcycle trip with his father was recorded in *Zen and the Art of Motorcyle Maintenance*—was stabbed and killed in a mugging just two blocks from the Zen Center's front door.

A new generation of students was practicing at Zen Center on Page street. Some of the original members at Sokoji had fallen away, many finding the new Center too large and institutional. Tassajara was under the direction of a Japanese novice master—Sotan Tatsugami—whom Baker had recruited from Eiheiji, and under his direction the practice there was becoming even more ritualized and Japanese.

With Tassajara and Zen Center filled to capacity, all that Suzuki needed to ensure his legacy was to identify a successor, to give "transmission" to a worthy heir. There is evidence that he had intended to give transmission to several students, all of whom would then have equal authority. But in the end, only one student—Richard Baker—received transmission, and it was a controversial choice.

Part of the problem that would arise was that Suzuki's students understood transmission differently than he may have. The students had no doubt that their teacher was a fully enlightened and officially transmitted Zen Master, although Suzuki had not claimed to be either. For Suzuki, as was common in the Japanese Soto tradition, transmission was more a matter of authorizing another to teach. Often it was conferred as a matter of course to ensure that a son inherited his father's temple; Suzuki, for example, conferred transmission on the son of a friend during a visit to Japan even though the young man had not studied with him. Suzuki's students, on the other hand, saw transmission as an acknowledgement of achievement, a recognition that the recipient was also now a fully enlightened teacher. When Suzuki's chosen heir later exhibited what others considered unenlightened behavior, it became problematic.

The reason no other student received transmission was that Suzuki was dying. His heath had been poor during a visit to Japan in 1970, although he seemed to recover when back in San Francisco. In March of the following year when he had an operation to remove his gall bladder, a routine biopsy revealed that it was cancerous. He kept the information from his students. He spent as much time as he could during the summer of 1971 working in the gardens at Tassajara, which was now the place in all the world he most loved.

When the season was over, he returned to San Francisco and that October finally informed his students of his illness. By that time it was apparent to anyone who saw him how sick he was. He referred to his final illness as a "teaching opportunity." "So many young people," he told his physician, "are afraid of dying. I can show them that they do not need to be."

His daughter, Yasuko, and son, Hoitsu, came from Japan to see him in those last days. Both were astonished by what they found. They had loved their father, but they had seen him as little more than a small-town priest with only the rudimentary knowledge of Buddhism that clerics were expected to have. They were astonished to discover two thriving monastic communities and numerous disciples who obviously revered their father.

Among the many things which impressed Yasuko and Hoitsu was a book of their father's "informal talks" which was on its way to become one of the bestselling Buddhist books of all time—*Zen Mind, Beginner's Mind.*

Marian Derby, in Los Altos, had recorded several of the talks Suzuki had given during his visits to the Haiku Zendo. They were short, spontaneous discussions of whatever was on his mind at the time. He had not thought that they would be recorded. Once they had been, however, he agreed to having them transcribed and edited.

The book still provides readers with an overview of his teaching. It begins with the formal practice of zazen. He followed the teachings of Dogen, the founder of Japanese Soto Zen, stressing the importance of having a proper sitting posture:

> To take this posture itself is the purpose of our practice. When you have this posture, you have the right state of mind, so there is no need to try to attain some special state. When you try to attain something, your mind starts to wander about somewhere else. When you do not try to attain anything, you have your own body and mind right here.[127]

Unlike in the Rinzai tradition, enlightenment was not something to strive for:

> Enlightenment is not some good feeling or some particular state of mind. The state of mind that exists when you sit in the right posture is, itself, enlightenment.[128]

Therefore, one practices meditation without seeking anything from it:

> The most important thing is to forget all gaining ideas, all dualistic ideas. In other words, just practicing zazen in a certain posture. Do not think about anything. Just remain on your cushion without

expecting anything. Then eventually you will resume your own true nature. That is to say, your own true nature resumes itself.[129]

The focus of attention is the breath, either counting exhaled breaths repeatedly up to ten or just following the breath as it comes in and goes out like a "swinging door":

> When we practice zazen our mind always follows our breathing. When we inhale, the air comes into the inner world. When we exhale, the air goes out to the outer world. The inner world is limitless, and the outer world is also limitless. We say "inner world" or "outer world," but actually there is just one whole world. In this limitless world, our throat is like a swinging door. The air comes in and goes out like someone passing through a swinging door. If you think, "I breathe," the "I" is extra. There is no you to say "I." What we call "I" is just a swinging door which moves when we inhale and when we exhale. It just moves; that is all. When your mind is pure and calm enough to follow this movement, there is nothing: no "I," no world, no mind nor body; just a swinging door.[130]

If students complained that they did not feel enlightened while sitting and counting their breaths, Suzuki told them that the problem was not with the practice but with their desire to get something from it, the expectation that there was some special feeling they were supposed to get from sitting zazen.

In the same way that one sits zazen without seeking to gain anything from it, all other activities should be undertaken for their own sake, and thus all activity becomes part of one's practice. He uses Dogen's instructions to the *tenzo*, or monastery cook, as an example:

> To cook, or to fix some food, is not preparation…it is practice. To cook is not just to prepare food for someone or for yourself; it is to express your sincerity. So when you cook you should express yourself in your activity in the kitchen. You should allow yourself plenty of time; you should work on it with nothing in your mind, and without expecting anything. You should just cook![131]

One of Suzuki's students had a profound experience which he believed to be the *kensho*, or awakening, so assiduously sought by Rinzai students. He came to Suzuki and asked, "How can I maintain this insight?"

"Don't worry about it," Suzuki told him. "Just continue with your zazen; it will go away."

In spite of the instruction to sit zazen without expectation, students still came hoping to achieve enlightenment. On one occasion, when a student persisted in asking how to reach awakening, Suzuki asked him in turn: "Why do you want to be enlightened? You know, you may not like it at all."

Students came to Suzuki with questions about all aspects of their lives. In a frequently reported incident, one student asked about the precept forbidding sexual misconduct. What exactly, he asked, defined sexual misconduct? How much sexual activity, for example, is too much?

Suzuki told him, "Sex is like brushing your teeth. It's a good thing to do but not all of the time." He added that there was probably nothing wrong with having multiple partners as long as one was able to remember all of their names.

Elsie Mitchell, who had founded the Cambridge Buddhist Association in Massachusetts, invited Suzuki to visit their Center in 1964. Suzuki accepted and informed the group that he would arrive at the airport on a Wednesday evening. On Tuesday morning, several members of the Association met at Mitchell's house, where their meetings were held, and began to prepare the place for Suzuki's arrival.

> That evening the library-cum-meditation room was in the process of being scrubbed down when the doorbell rang. My husband climbed down a ladder and opened the front door. Suzuki Roshi was on our doorstep with a smile on his face. He was amused to find us amid preparations for his arrival. In spite of our protests, he immediately tied back his long kimono sleeves and insisted on joining in "all these preparations for the important day of my coming." The following morning, after breakfast and a meditation session, and after I had

left the house for shopping, he found himself a tall ladder, sponges, and pails. He then set to work scrubbing Cambridge grease, grime, and general pollution from the outside of the windows in the meditation room. When I returned with the groceries, I discovered him on the ladder, polishing with such undivided attention that he did not even hear my approach. He had removed his black silk kimono and was dressed only in his Japanese union suit. This is quite acceptable attire in Japan. Nevertheless, I could not help wondering how the sedate Cambridge ladies in the adjoining apartment house would react to the sight of a shaven-headed man in long underwear at work just outside their windows.[132]

When Zen Center moved to its new location on Page Street, they tried to leave the doors unlocked and welcoming as they had at Sokoji, but it was a different type of neighborhood and the young people in the area quickly determined that the shaved-head monks were easy marks. Children and teens wandered into the building, stealing things that looked valuable. One day three teenagers came in and began teasing the monks who, all young white liberals, tried to act unconcerned and accepting. Finally Suzuki came down the hall in his brown robes and with his *kotsu*—the spine-shaped baton carried by Zen teachers.

"Hey you!" one of the boys called out to him. "You know kung-fu, man?" he asked, making some *faux* martial arts moves.

Suzuki walked up to the young man. Although he was considerably shorter than the boy, he stood directly in front of him, not in a threatening manner, but blocking his way.

"What's that stick for?" the boy asked.

"I hit people with it!" Suzuki said, then very slowly brought it down to tap the boy's shoulder.

"Hey, man, don't get violent," the boys laughed. Suzuki escorted them to door. After that the front door was kept locked.

Shunryu Suzuki's presence often affected his students deeply, and they often spoke of the love they felt for their teacher. Issan Dorsey's most vivid memory of Suzuki was very simple. Dorsey, a monk at Tassajara, was ill for six weeks during one of the practice periods.

Suzuki-roshi was visiting, and he used to come from the baths at the same time every day. One day I looked out the window and I saw him. So then every day I knew what time, I'd look out my window at him. It just thrilled me to see him.

One day that I particularly remember, I saw him and he was carrying a teacup. That's the story. There's nothing else; just, he was carrying a teacup. For some reason it blew me away, to see that man, walking down the path, carrying a teacup. So I always say that's one of my memorable moments of Suzuki-roshi, and people are usually waiting for some great story. But I just end by saying, "He was carrying a teacup."[133]

A confluence of factors contributed to Suzuki's improbable success. As his own children recognized, in Japan he had been a simple, sincere country-priest, but that was enough to make him extraordinary in America. He arrived in San Francisco at a time when the initial interest in Zen was occurring; Alan Watts' talks on the radio intrigued people, as did Kerouac's novel. There were other Soto Zen temples and teachers in California, but the priests in those focused on ministering to the Japanese population; Suzuki was unique in welcoming non-Asian students. Then hippies arrived in San Francisco, many looking for spiritual guides who could help them attain the enlightenment experience they felt they had tasted on their drug trips. Others came seeking to deal with personal dissatisfaction in their lives. People who are content with their lives do not usually seek spiritual advisors. The unhappy, the confused, the lonely came searching for a Zen master, and this unassuming Japanese Zen priest invited them to practice zazen with him. He did not claim to be a Zen master as such, but they assumed that was exactly how a real Zen master would behave. And he was captivating. His students were not ashamed to admit that what they felt for their teacher was more than respect and admiration; they loved him. More than that, they invested their faith in him and therefore in the decisions he made.

Shunryu Suzuki died on December 4, just two weeks after Richard Baker had been formally installed as his successor and abbot of Zen Center. On the day of his death, the Rohatsu sesshin, marking the anniversary of the Buddha's enlightenment, was beginning at Zen Center. There were over 100 participants. It was a small example of what he had accomplished during his time in America.

CHAPTER EIGHT

Soen Nakagawa and Eido Tai Shimano

ALTHOUGH SOEN NAKAGAWA SPENT ONLY BRIEF PERIODS in the United States, he not only helped the Aitkens establish the Diamond Sangha in Hawaii, he was also the inspiration behind the International Dai Bosatsu Zendo in the Catskill Mountains—the first Rinzai Monastery to be established in North America. He was a complex person, renowned both for his prowess as a Zen master and as a poet; people in Japan who had little interest in Zen admired Nakagawa as the most accomplished haikuist of the 20th century.

According to his Dharma heir, Eido Tai Shimano, Nakagawa "had many faces":

> —he was a simple monk, a "crazy wisdom" Zen master, a genius in the arts, a spiritually realized being of the highest attainment, a dedicated student of the Dharma, a master manipulator, a troubled human being, a skillful politician, a tactful diplomat, a stupendous host, an inspired guest. He was refined yet could be wildly unpredictable; he was subtle yet could be exasperatingly vague.[134]

Soen Nakagawa was born in 1907 on the island of Formosa (now Taiwan), the eldest of three brothers. His given name was Motoi. His father, like D. T. Suzuki's, was a physician. Dr. Suketaro Nakagawa was attached to the armed forces, and, after his posting in Formosa, the family was relocated to Iwakune in the Yamaguchi Prefecture and then to Hiroshima. Again, like Suzuki, Motoi lost his father while still young; the death of a brother soon followed. His mother, Kazuko, had to work to support the family and ensure her first born an education.

His early training was that appropriate for one born to the samurai class, but he proved to be more interested in literary—than in martial—arts and showed early promise as a poet. In 1923, he and a close friend, Koun Yamada, enrolled at the First Academy, equivalent to High School, in Tokyo. They would both have significant impact upon the development of North American Zen.

In high school, Motoi sought for something meaningful to which he could dedicate his life. He found his direction after coming upon a passage by the German philosopher, Arthur Schopenhauer:

> In the *real* world, it is impossible to attain true happiness, final and eternal contentment. For these are visionary flowers in the air; mere fantasies. In truth, they can never be actualized. In fact, they must not be actualized. Why? If such ideals were to be actualized, the search for the real meaning of our existence would cease. If

that happened, it would be the spiritual end of our being, and life would seem too foolish to live.[135]

He began reading books on Zen, including the *Orategama* which Suzuki had taken with him on his visit to Setsumon Michizu at Kokutaiji. He passed the book onto Yamada, initiating his interest in Zen as well. The two attended Tokyo Imperial University together; at that time, Motoi resided in a dormitory attached to a Pure Land temple. He studied both classical and religious literature and continued to develop his skill as a poet. His graduation thesis was on the haiku master, Matsuo Basho.[136]

He formed a Zen sitting group at the university, but it was not until after graduation that he determined to become a monk, much to the disappointment of his family who felt he was wasting the education he had received. He took the precepts at Kogakuji, the monastery founded by Bassui[137] and was given the Buddhist name, Soen. The master at Kogakuji was Keigaku Katsube, and it was under his direction that Nakagawa began his formal Zen training.

Although now ordained, he did not feel at ease in the communal life of the monastery and chose to follow Bassui's example by going into solitary retreat on Dai Bosatsu Mountain. There he lived an ascetic life, foraging for wild food, practicing zazen, and writing poetry. He published a few poems in a journal dedicated to haiku and, in 1933, released a collection of poems that he had kept in draft form in a small wooden box; he entitled the volume *Shigan*, or *Coffin of Poems*. In San Francisco, Nyogen Senzaki's landlady came across some of Nakagawa's work in a magazine and showed it to Senzaki. He also admired the haiku and initiated a correspondence with the young poet.

Nakagawa developed a very personal practice while at Dai Bosatsu. He composed an original mantra—*Namu Dai Bosa*, "unity with the great bodhisattva"—which he chanted with fervor for hours. Aware of current global tensions, he dreamed of establishing an International Dai Bosatsu Zendo where people from all nations could come to practice Zen. He even took part in a feckless prospecting expedition to Sakhalin Island in Siberia in hopes of finding gold in order to fund the project.

In 1935, Nakagawa served as an attendant to Katsube at a sesshin held for students at the Imperial University. When they arrived, they discovered they had forgotten to bring a kyosaku. Katsube directed Nakagawa to go to a nearby temple, Hakusan Dojo, to borrow one. It happened that sesshin was taking place there as well under the direction of a visiting teacher, Gempo Yamamoto of Myoshinji in Kyoto. Nakagawa arrived while Yamamoto was giving a teisho. Nakagawa had heard many teisho before, but none had touched him as this one did, even though Yamamoto's rural accent was so thick that it was often difficult to understand him.

Not long after, Nakagawa found another opportunity to hear Yamamoto speak. This time he sat directly in front of the elderly and almost blind teacher, feeling as if he were being addressed personally. Yamamoto quoted Mumon's commentary on the fourth case in the *Mumonkan*: "If you want to practice Zen, it must be true practice. When you attain realization, it must be true realization."[138]

Nakagawa was deeply stirred by the statement and sought a private meeting with Yamamoto wherein he expressed his interest in working with him. It was a serious matter to go from one teacher to another, and, when Yamamoto accepted Nakagawa, Katsube is reported to have called him a thief.

Nakagawa began his studies with Yamamoto at Ryutakuji (Dragon Swamp Temple) and went on to accompany Yamamoto to Manchuria in 1937. The region had been occupied by the Japanese in 1931, and—following the example set by European colonizing powers—Buddhist missionaries followed in the wake of military forces.

Coincidentally Koun Yamada was in Manchuria as a labor supervisor for the infamous Manchurian Mining Company, and he and Nakagawa had the opportunity to resume their friendship. They took walks together during which Nakagawa described to Yamada his hope to found the International Dai Bosatsu Zendo separate from the current corrupted Zen establishments. Yamada, in turn, spoke about his own spiritual speculations and questions. Nakagawa listened for a time, then said, "Yamada, all you do is argue. Why don't you try sitting zazen?" The remark struck Yamada forcefully and motivated him to undertake serious Zen training.

Through their correspondence, Nakagawa and Nyogen Senzaki discovered they shared many opinions, and, although the political situation did not permit Nakagawa to visit Senzaki, as he had hoped to be able to do, they determined that they would meet in spirit. In 1938, Nakagawa wrote to Senzaki from Manchuria proposing that they set aside the 21st day of each month for a shared practice to be known as Spiritual Interrelationship Day. He envisioned a time when people all around the globe with an interest in the Dharma would sit for half an hour in zazen starting at 8:00 p.m. local time, then recite the twenty-fifth chapter of the Lotus Sutra followed by a period of chanting "Namu Dai Bosa." The evening would culminate with a "joyous gathering."

During the war years, Nakagawa remained with Yamamoto; however, to the annoyance of many other monks, he persisted in refusing to accommodate himself to the forms of monastic life. Several of them petitioned Yamamoto to expel him. Yamamoto not only refused to do so, he even had a small house built on the temple grounds for Nakagawa's mother so she could live near her son.

Yamamoto was respected throughout Japan for his wisdom and sound judgment, and, when it became clear that the Japanese would not be able to prevail in the War, the Prime Minister, Admiral Kantaro Suzuki, sought his advice. Yamamoto told him he must advocate a surrender. According to Eido Shimano, the words that the Emperor of Japan used in the radio broadcast which announced the end of the war were those Yamamoto had spoken to Admiral Suzuki: "we must endure the unendurable and suffer what is insufferable."

Once the war was over, Nakagawa was able to travel to San Francisco and meet Senzaki with whom he had been corresponding for fifteen years. He arrived in San Francisco on the 8th of April, the day recognized on the Japanese calendar as the Buddha's birthday. Nakagawa composed a haiku to mark the first meeting with his long-time correspondent:

> No matter how much I contemplate this tea bowl
> It is still—a tea bowl!
> Thus I arrive in San Francisco

He was delighted by the form of Zen practice he found in America, shorn of the more archaic Japanese traditions. Senzaki's relationship with his students was free of stilted formalities and even in sanzen there was a freer, more frank, communication between teacher and student.

Nakagawa's first formal presentation in America was given at the Theosophical Society Library where a number of Senzaki's students, as well as members of the local Theosophical Community, gathered to welcome him. Nakagawa chose to speak on the traditional objectives of the Theosophical movement,[139] although his approach to the subject may have mystified the Theosophists in attendance. He slapped the top of the table behind which he was seated and demanded, "Who is it who hears this sound?" The Master of Hearing, he went on, the one who hears, is without race, gender, or creed. To be able to hear that sound is the nucleus of a Universal Brotherhood of Humanity. However, in order to understand this, one needed to ask

> —and ask until you reach the Bottom. All of a sudden, when the bottom is broken through, you will realize what "the unexplained laws of nature" really are, and you will be able to acquire an understanding of "the powers latent in man."[140]

Senzaki had hoped that Nakagawa would remain in the United States and become his heir, but Nakagawa felt obligated to return to Ryutakuji, where he would later welcome Robert and Anne Aitken during their wedding trip to Japan.

In 1950, to the surprise of many—including Nakagawa—Yamamoto announced his retirement and appointed Nakagawa his successor. Inspired by Senzaki's example, Nakagawa relaxed many of the formalities associated with the abbot's position. He chose not to distinguish himself from other monks, wore the same robes they did, ate with them, and even shared the same bath house. His unconventionality was not admired by the Zen establishment, which saw it as a sign that he had not sufficiently matured into his responsibilities. It was this lack of convention, however, which enabled him to play a major role in the spread of the Dharma to North America.

Japanese society tends to be ethnocentric and little accommodation is made for people from other cultures. After the war, soldiers from America as well as from Japan made their way to Ryutakuji looking for a path which would help them deal with the traumas they had suffered. The monastery became known for being accessible to foreign students wanting to learn about Zen. Unconcerned about convention, Nakagawa was not disturbed when students were unfamiliar with the behavioral protocols and matters of etiquette upon which other Zen teachers insisted.

Although he had passed some 500 koans under Yamamoto's tutelage and was an abbot in his own right, Nakagawa approached Daiun Harada—with whom Yamada had studied—and continued training with him. After Harada's death, Nakagawa completed his koan work under the instruction of Harada's heir, Haku'un Yasutani, and did not consider himself a qualified teacher until he had done so.

In 1955, Nyogen Senzaki returned to Japan for the first time since his departure fifty years prior. Nakagawa noticed how his friend was aging and was so concerned that he suggested sending his disciple, Tai Shimano, to act as Senzaki's attendant in Los Angeles. Before Shimano could leave, however, Nakagawa received word that Senzaki had died.

Senzaki had appointed Nakagawa his executor, and Nakagawa went to California to preside at the funeral service and carry out those duties. Afterwards, attended by Aitken, he conducted the first formal sesshin to be held in the United States.

Nakagawa's mother, Kazuko, died in 1962, a year after Gempo Yamamoto's death. The deaths of Senzaki and then two more people who had played such important roles in his life sent Nakagawa into a depression he struggled to deal with. For a while he returned to his hermitage on Dai Bosatsu, but, by this time, his reputation was such that he received invitations from Zen communities around the world which he felt obligated to accept. In 1963, he led sesshin not only in the United States but also in England, Austria, Denmark, Egypt, Israel, and India.

In 1967, Nakagawa climbed a tree on the Ryutakuji grounds, possibly in order to gain a better view of the temple grounds. He slipped, fell, and lay on the ground, unconscious, for three days before he was found by the monks. He was rushed to hospital, where it was discovered that a sliver of bamboo had pierced his brain. Doctors advised surgery, but he refused it. The fall and his injuries had consequences on his health and personality for the remainder of his life. His sister-in-law, who looked after him during his time in hospital, overheard him one evening lamenting, "What a stupid thing I did!" But he never told anyone why he had climbed the tree.

He had a number of disciples in the United States, particularly in New York where Shimano had established the Shoboji Zendo. Nakagawa returned there several times between 1968 and 1971 to lead retreats. During the 1968 visit, he stopped in California to lead a sesshin, after which—accompanied by Tai Shimano and Haku'un Yasutani—he visited Shunryu Suzuki at the Tassajara Zen Mountain Center. There Nakagawa scattered a portion of Nyogen Senzaki's ashes on a mountain top.

The New York students who worked with Nakagawa in the late 1960s were largely unaware of the physical pain and psychological difficulties he continued to suffer as a result of his fall at Ryutakuji. What they saw and responded to was a man whom Peter Matthiessen described as "elfin, and merry, entirely at ease and entirely aware at the same time...."[141] He was a kind, jocular, mischievous man energized by enthusiasm and a "wild joy."

When you are in airplane, do not read a magazine! Look out! Won-derful! Everything is very important, in any event, in any moment, everything this MU! Everything is right-here-now! We are all Buddhas, all bodhisattvas, all mis-er-robble creatures—away with this mis-er-robble word *kensho*! If I wish to be a thief, I just steal! If I wish to be a buddha, I just *do* it! Be the Buddha! No need to be so serious. Be light, light, light—full of light!.[142]

His own moods after his fall, however, were difficult to control.

In 1973, after having conferred Dharma transmission on Shimano in New York, Nakagawa resigned as abbot of Ryutakuji. He joked that his resignation would now allow him time to act as a midwife to the International Dai Bosatsu Center which Shimano was building. He came back to the US for a while and stayed at the lakeside lodge at Beecher Lake on the Dai Bosatsu grounds. The house was unheated and without electricity, and Nakagawa foraged for wild plants to eat just as he had as a young man on the original Dai Bosatsu. Then he returned to Japan, where he may have expected to be asked to take on various duties at Ryutakuji in his capacity of former abbot; when that invitation did not come, he went into solitary retreat.

Nakagawa had a mischievous sense of humor which he used to deflate the somber seriousness of his American students who often approached their practice with a convert's zeal. On one occasion, he invited a number of them for a traditional tea ceremony which he then conducted using instant coffee and Styrofoam cups. During a sesshin, he once placed a large pumpkin on the teacher's seat in the dokusan room and hid behind a screen. When students came in and made their prostrations before the pumpkin without being aware of what they were doing, Nakagawa giggled, then rang the bell signaling their dismissal.

During a visit to Christmas Humphreys' Buddhist Lodge in London, Nakagawa looked around for a bathroom. As he was about to open the door, Humphreys happened to pass by and informed him that the room was occupied. Nakagawa waited outside the door but after a while knocked on the door politely. When no one answered, he opened the door and found the room vacant. "No one there!" he exclaimed in delight. "Wait as long as you like, never anyone there! From the beginning!"

Nakagawa was a great lover of music. As a young man, he and a group of friends once listened to a recording of Beethoven's *Ninth Symphony*, and the experience left him shaken for three days.

One evening he invited Robert and Anne Aitken to his mother's cottage at Ryutakuji to listen to a recording of Gregorian chants he had recently acquired. Before the music began, Nakagawa explained to his attendant, "This is the way Western monks recite their sutras."

In New York, he could often be heard humming tunes from the musical *Fiddler on the Roof* which he was particularly fond of. On one occasion, a student questioned why a particular ritual had to be carried out as it was, and Nakagawa replied by singing, *"Tradition!"*

Philip Kapleau frequently told this story: He and a friend paid a visit to Nakagawa at Ryutakuji. The friend was a professor of history then working in Japan who had read about the koan Mu. He wanted Nakagawa's advice about the best way to approach the koan. "How can I expedite my understanding of Mu?" he asked.

Nakagawa was engaged in preparing tea for his visitors and, without looking up from what he was doing, he asked, "What was it that Jesus said on the cross?"

"Jesus? I'm not sure what you mean."

"What did he say to God?"

"Do you mean, 'My God, my God, why have you forsaken me?'" Kapleau suggested.

Nakagawa served the tea and said no more. Kapleau's friend became irritated and remarked, "We have made considerable effort to come here to see you because we are very serious about learning something about Zen and had hoped that you could give us some direction."

"What was it that Jesus said on the cross?" Nakagawa asked again.

"'My God, my God, why have you forsaken me?'" the friend repeated impatiently.

"No," Nakagawa said. "That was not it."

"Well, then, what do you think he said?"

Nakagawa stretched his arms wide and screamed as if in agony, *"My God! My God! Why have you forsaken me!"*

During this same visit, Nakagawa gave Kapleau and the history professor a tour of the temple. The Americans were surprised by the amount of ritual activity taking place. As they came upon the various altars with their statues of the Buddha, sundry Bodhisattvas, and historical figures, Nakagawa lit incense and bowed before them. Kapleau, whose knowledge of Zen at that time was limited to what he had read, said, "I thought Zen masters were famous for burning Buddhist statues and spitting on them. Why do you bow before them?"

"If you want to spit," Nakagawa said, "spit. I prefer to bow."

2

According to the autobiographical sketch he wrote for a book published by the Zen Studies Society to coincide with the inauguration of Dai Bosatsu monastery, Tai Shimano's introduction to Buddhism occurred while he was still a school boy during the war. A teacher copied out the words of the *Heart Sutra* on the blackboard and taught the students to recite them. It was enough to stir his interest. After the war, Shimano entered Empukuji in Chichibu, where his family had moved to escape the bombing raids on Tokyo. The teacher there was Kengan Goto, from whom Shimano received his Buddhist name, Eido; it was derived from the first syllable of the names of the two monks who brought Rinzai and Soto Zen to Japan— Eisai and Dogen.[143] After acquiring the basics of monastic training from Goto, Shimano sought entrance to Heirinji outside Tokyo. As tradition required, he spent two days seated at the gate before gaining admittance.

In 1954, Zen Masters and abbots from throughout Japan came to Heirinji to attend the funeral of a former abbot. Shimano was one of the monks assigned to wait on these dignitaries, and, when they first gathered together, he brought them tea. Most accepted their cups without acknowledging the monk serving them. The youngest of the abbots, however, put his hands together in *gassho*, palm to palm, and bowed his thanks. Surprised to be recognized in this manner, Shimano returned the bow and, later, asked the other servers who the polite master had been. He was informed it was Soen Nakagawa, the recently appointed abbot of Ryutakuji.

Shimano went to Ryutakuji and—after spending another two days waiting at the gate—was accepted as a student. That October, in 1954, he took part in his first sesshin with Nakagawa. During his initial face-to-face meeting with his new teacher, he expected to be given a koan. Instead Nakagawa appeared to ask him a series of personal questions: "Where are you from?"

"Chichibu," Shimano replied.

"Where did you spend the last training period?"

"At Heirinji."

"When did you leave there?"

"Last summer."

At that point, Nakagawa rang his bell, signaling that the meeting was over, and Shimano left the dokusan room unclear about what had just occurred. It took him a while to realize that he had been given the fifteenth case in the *Mumonkan*.

Tozan came to study with Unmon. Unmon asked, "Where are you from?" "From Sato," Tozan replied. "Where were you during the summer?" "At Hozu, south of the lake." "When did you leave?" "August." "I spare you sixty blows," Unmon told him.

Shimano proved to be a committed and insightful practitioner, and, over time, master and disciple grew close. Shimano had great respect for Nakagawa and, one summer, made a pilgrimage to Dai Bosatsu Mountain where he located the cottage in which his teacher had stayed. The cottage, however, was no longer as isolated as it had been. Dai Bosatsu was becoming a tourist destination and would eventually become a popular resort area.

As he progressed in his training, Shimano was given a number of duties within the monastery. Because of his knowledge of English, he was assigned responsibility for explaining monastery procedures and etiquette to the European and American students who made their way to Ryutakuji. He was known to them by his familiar name, Tai-san.[144] He later wrote that he liked the Westerners he met but recognized that their to approach Zen practice was very different from that of Japanese students. Americans demanded explanations and clarifications and posed questions their Asian counterparts would have considered inappropriate. He also seems to have been attracted to the way in which many of these Western students challenged and flaunted those traditional values and mores which seemed, to them, no longer relevant.

Recognizing Shimano's ability to interact smoothly with Americans, Nakagawa intended to send him to Los Angeles to act as attendant to the aging Senzaki. When Senzaki died, Nakagawa instead sent him to Hawaii to assist the Aitkens. The Aitkens had met Shimano in Japan and had liked him, so were happy to sponsor his immigration to the US. Shimano arrived at Koko-an in 1958; he was 27 years old.

In 1962, Nakagawa and Haku'un Yasutani were scheduled to lead a number of sesshin in the US. Just prior to departure; however, Nakagawa's mother fell ill, and he decided to remain with her. He arranged for Shimano to act as Yasutani's attendant and translator. Because there were only the two of them, Shimano also had to carry out the duties of *jiki-jitsu*, the monk in charge of overseeing the running of sesshin, and *junkei,* monitor.

The first of these sesshin was held at Koko An in Hawaii, and, even though students needed Shimano's assistance to communicate with Yasutani during dokusan, five were acknowledged to have achieved some degree of kensho. Shimano accompanied Yasutani on other tours and stated that it was from assisting at these retreats that he learned how to work with students.

Over time, relations between Shimano and the Aitkens became strained. The young, polite, deferential monk they had met in Japan proved to be more problematic in Hawaii. While it was clear he was committed to Zen practice, he also insisted on little extravagances, like a motorcycle which he claimed to need in order to get around. Aitken may not have been happy with these requests, but a case could be made that most of them were reasonable. Then, in 1963, two women from Koko An were hospitalized with mental stress. Their social worker informed Aitken that in both cases they had been in sexual relationships with Shimano.

Aitken, uncertain how to proceed, travelled to Japan to discuss the situation with Nakagawa and Yasutani. Both admitted that it was possible that Shimano had had relationships with the women, but in Japan such matters do not carry the same weight as in North America as long as they are handled with discretion. It would not be the last time that Japanese and North American sexual mores would come into conflict.

Aitken was unhappy with the situation but—heeding legal advice he was given—decided to deal with it quietly in order to protect the still nascent Zen community. The day after Aitken returned from Japan, Shimano left Hawaii for New York. Later he would disingenuously tell Nakagawa that he left because "the Hawaiian climate is too good—it is a place for vacationers or retired people, but not for Zazen practice."[145]

Shimano arrived in New York on the last day of 1964. He was newly married to a Japanese woman who apparently granted him the latitude many Japanese husbands had as far as extra-marital relations were concerned. The following day—the first day of the New Year—he began his new life on the North American continent as a Zen teacher. Later, he would suggest that he attracted his first students by sheer force of personality just walking the streets of Manhattan in his Buddhist robes. In fact, however, a number of New York students who had attended Yasutani's sesshins provided him a base in the city. Although he had not yet received full transmission, he demonstrated skill as an insightful and inspiring teacher. He could be charming and was a sensitive and supportive friend. He could also turn stern and forceful if needed, showing little patience with half-hearted efforts in the zendo.

Annette Marks was one of the five persons who came to kensho during Yasutani's first sesshin at Koko An; her account of the event was included in Philip Kapleau's *The Three Pillars of Zen*:

> The third day everything changed. Our interpreter, the serenely smiling, "floating" Tai-san, became the angel of vengeance. "This is no tea party," his voice thundered, "but a sesshin! Today I will teach you the meaning of sesshin!" Whereupon he began cracking everyone with his kyosaku.[146]

The New York Zendo, as it was called, originally met in the living room of Shimano's small apartment. There were, as yet, no membership fees, and Shimano earned a small income by going through the Manhattan telephone directory culling Japanese names for a mailing list being compiled by the Bank of Tokyo.

As the number of students increased, programs and activities grew. At first there were only regular sittings at the apartment; then day-long sits were added and even weekend sesshin. When the living room zendo was no longer adquate, the sangha discussed ways in which to raise funds to purchase or rent a larger space. In order to do so, they needed to incorporate as a religious organization and acquire tax-exempt status. The expense associated with that process, however, was beyond their means. According to Shimano's account, it was for that reason that they approached the Zen Studies Society which had been established in the city some years prior to promote the work of D. T. Suzuki. Mark Oppenheimer, in his book, *The Zen Predator of the Upper East Side*, suggests that Aitken may have paved the way for the meeting between Shimano and the Society, hoping to transfer responsibility for Shimano's immigration sponsorship to them. The society was currently inactive and owned no property although it still existed as a legal entity. It was not in a position to assume responsibility for Shimano's immigration status, but the secretary of the society, George Yamaoka, assisted Shimano to become a board member, and the Society quietly merged with the New York Zendo. When Suzuki—then living in Japan—learned of the arrangement, he requested that his name be deleted from the Society's letterhead.

After the merger, fund-raising began in earnest, aided by a generous initial contribution of $10,000 from a Canadian student who was returning to home. Soon the group was able to move into new quarters on 81st Street, where Yasutani led their first sesshin in the summer of 1965. There was a growing interest in Zen practice throughout America, a surge never equaled since, and, before long, people were turned away from the zendo because there was not sufficient room for them.

A number of serendipitous events occurred during this period. On a visit to San Francisco, Shimano happened upon an antique shop where he found a large keisu—a bowl-shaped gong—which had been forged in 1555 for Daitokuji in Kyoto. In another antique shop, in New York City, he found a seated Buddha figure which had originally been made for a branch temple of Enpukuji, where he had begun his own training. Although the Zendo was still strapped for cash, money was found to purchase these treasures. Then, in 1968, Chester Carlson—founder of Xerox—donated funds for them to move to more suitable quarters in a former carriage house on East 67th Street. Carlson's wife, Dorris, was interested in Eastern spiritualities, and, through her intervention, Carlson anonymously assisted both Shimano and Philip Kapleau in establishing their communities.

That summer Yasutani and Nakagawa were in California to conduct the annual sesshin there, and Shimano joined them. Afterwards, in New York, Nakagawa presided at the ceremony officially inaugurating the New York Zendo Shobo Ji (Temple of True Dharma). He was declared the zendo's abbot, and Shimano was the teacher-in-residence.

Four days after the dedication, their benefactor, Chester Carlson, died of a heart attack.

The pioneers who brought Zen to North America were familiar with two models from Japan: the temple and the monastery. Temples served the devotional needs of local communities, as Sokoji served its Japanese congregation in San Francisco. Monasteries had several functions; they were facilities where temple priests were trained, but they were also increasingly—especially, in the Rinzai tradition—centers for the spiritual development of both ordained and lay practitioners. Practice centers, such as Shobo Ji, were a distinctly Western phenomenon. Despite its title, Shobo Ji was not a temple in the usual sense of the term; nor was it a training center. During his visit to California, Shimano had been particularly struck by Tassajara—a remote training center dedicated to practice and formation.

No sooner had Shobo Ji been opened than Shimano and his board began to consider opening an American Rinzai temple and training center with a residential program where traditional Buddhist devotional and training activities could take place. Its primary function would be to serve as a dedicated site for sesshin. Currently, even with Shobo Ji, it was necessary to rent facilities with adequate accommodations for sesshin participants. The necessary physical apparatus—zabutons, zafus, keisus, mokugyos, and so forth—had to be transported to and from the rented site; rooms needed to be rearranged to serve as the zendo and the dokusan chamber.

Shimano envisioned an actual temple, and, because Zen temples in Asia were usually in the mountains, he hoped to find a suitable mountain setting. A Building Committee was established which explored a number of potential sites, each of which proved inappropriate. Then the chair of the committee chanced upon an ad in the *New York Times* for 1400 acres in the Catskill Mountains. The property had belonged to the family of Harriet Beecher Stowe; the small lake—the highest in the Catskills—was known as Beecher Lake. There was a handsome fourteen room summer house—referred to as a "lodge"—located there, remote from all other habitations. It was an ideal spot, but the cost would have been prohibitively expensive had it not been for another generous donation from Dorris Carlson.

Nakagawa came to New York that summer, and Shimano took him to the site. The older man was entranced. As they walked about the property and along the shore of the lake, Nakagawa told his disciple of his youthful hope of establishing an International Zendo on Mount Dai Bosatsu. Shimano suggested that this new site, in what Nakagawa liked to call the Cut-kill Mountains,[147] be named the Dai Bosatsu Zendo. Nakagawa's dream would become a reality, not in Japan but in America.

The first sesshin was held in the lodge. A small tent—just large enough for two people to sit face-to-face—was set up to serve as the dokusan room. The New York community energized by the sesshin and its location took on the construction project with enthusiasm. A local architect, Davis Hamerstrom, was hired and traveled to Japan with Shimano to study temple architecture. They visited a number of temples before coming to Tofukuji, the largest Rinzai temple in the country and a designated National Treasure. They were struck by the resemblance of its setting to the Beecher Lake site. The abbot, Ekyo Hayashi, opened a presently unused building where, at one time, as many as a thousand monks had practiced. Shimano was impressed by the

> —practicality of its design. Its structure was that of a Zendo within a Zendo: A corridor extended entirely around the rectangular Zazen Hall. This corridor served two purposes: Between Zazen periods the monks used it for kinhin [walking meditation], and during Zazen noises from outside the building were diminished.[148]

Hamerstrom and Shimano had found the model they had been seeking.

In September 1972, Nakagawa formally gave Shimano transmission, making him abbot of both Dai Bosatsu and Shobo Ji. Following the installation, there was a "Mountain Opening" ceremony, dedicating the site to the construction of the proposed temple, and Nakagawa was declared Honorary Founder. A final portion of Nyogen Senzaki's ashes were interred at the site.

The following spring, work began on what was, arguably, the most significant Zen construction project to be undertaken in America. Deep in the mountains, approached by a narrow county road and then another two miles of gravel road from the formal entrance gate, a Japanese-style temple of classic design was built.

Its full formal name is Dai Bosatsu Zendo Kongo Ji (Diamond Temple), and it was officially inaugurated on America's bi-centennial—July 4, 1976. Rinzai dignitaries from Japan came for the occasion; teachers from throughout America were there, including Robert Aitken, Richard Baker, Taizan Maezumi, Philip Kapleau, the Tibetan teacher, Chogyam Trungpa, and the Korean Zen Master, Seung Sahn. American writer, naturalist, and Zen practitioner, Peter Mattiessen, struck the large temple bell beginning the ceremony.[149]

The person conspicuous by his absence was Soen Nakagawa.

3

After Nakagawa returned to Japan in 1973, he still suffered a great deal of physical pain and sought solace in saki rather than in western medicines, which he distrusted. The drinking only made him more morose. In retrospect, his students would come to realize that he was suffering from depression; he hid his condition so well, however, that his few visitors failed to see the signs. He was always able to feign a pleasant and even merry facade when necessary.

He became increasingly withdrawn with the passing years, remaining in his quarters at Ryutakuji without interacting with the other monks. He allowed his hair and beard to grow. He stopped writing poetry. His relationship with Shimano had ruptured when he learned that Shimano was still involved in serial sexual relationships with his female students. The loss of that friendship added to his unhappiness.

In 1975, he was invited to take part in a ceremony at the prestigious Myoshinji in Kyoto, the primary Rinzai temple in Japan. The ceremony would have made Nakagawa acting abbot for a day, an honor which usually led to permanent appointment. In the history of the temple, Nakagawa was the only individual to turn down this opportunity. He said that, instead, he was preparing to take on the position of abbot at Dai Bosatsu in America. As the date neared for those opening ceremonies, however, Nakagawa put off his departure and in the end did not attend.

An American Zen student, Genjo Marinello, happened to be studying at Ryutakuji in 1980, and although he knew Nakagawa was on the grounds, he suspected he would spend his entire time in Japan without having an opportunity to meet him.

> During sesshin, because my Japanese wasn't so fluent, I would go to a little side room during the teisho time and listen to cassette tapes of Soen Nakagawa Roshi. So I'm sitting in zazen, and I'm listening to a cassette tape of Soen Roshi, and he's so eloquent, and he's so sweet, and he's so poetic, and it's such a treasure. And I just felt honored to be listening to him. And I knew that he was only feet away from where I was listening, but he was such a recluse, I thought I might be in Japan the whole time and never see him. So I'm sitting in this little ante-room, sitting in zazen and listening to his teisho, and in walks this guy in a grubby white kimono, somewhat in tatters. Long white hair and a long white beard. And my mouth drops open. And he sees me, a young American in formal Zen robes, listening to a teisho of his. And he had raided the kitchen. That's what he was doing, he was raiding the kitchen and hoping no one would see him, because it was teisho time and so everyone was in the zendo. So he didn't expect to see me there at all, and he's startled, but he doesn't look startled. He's a roshi. So he just sees me, and my jaw drops open. Of course, I know who I'm looking at. It's not a mystery. And then he just says, "Gassho!" So I put my hands in gassho, and he walks on by, and that was our first encounter.[150]

After that meeting, Nakagawa frequently asked Marinello to take walks with him around the temple grounds. He shaved his head again, took better care of his appearance, left the hermitage, occasionally sat in the zendo, and once again joined the monks at meal times. He also made numerous long distance phone calls much, Marinello remembers, to the abbot's annoyance.

Nakagawa made a final visit to the United States in 1982 and, in his last teisho to his American students, said:

There are so many pleasures in life! Cooking, eating, sleeping, every deed of everyday life is nothing else but This Great Matter. Realize this! So we extend tender care with a worshipping heart even to such beings as beasts and birds—but not only to beasts, not only to birds, but to insects, too, okay? Even to grass, to one blade of grass, even to dust, to one speck of dust. Sometimes I bow to the dust.[151]

Two years later he died at Ryutakuji. His death poem was a haiku:

Mustard blossoms!
there is nothing left
to hurl away.

Soen Nakagawa's ashes were divided into three parts. One third was returned to the Nakagawa family; one third was buried with those of the former abbots of Ryutakji; and one third was buried along with Nyogen Senzaki's at Dai Bosatsu, where a stupa commemorates both men.

4

Many of Eido Shimano's students respected him as an effective and inspiring teacher, and, for some, that alone mattered; for others, his personal life eventually became an embarrassment and impediment to continue working with him.

Aitken had remained silent about what he knew of Shimano's early sexual improprieties, perhaps hoping the young man would mature out of such behavior. As time passed, however, further stories emerged. The inauguration at Dai Bosatsu was the last time Aitken and Shimano were together. Afterwards, Aitken refused to attend conferences if he knew Shimano would be attending and—according to Buddhist scholar Helen Baroni—he advised other Zen teachers to do so as well.[152]

Shortly before his death, Aitken turned over his personal papers to the University of Hawaii. Included in them were his records regarding Shimano. The release of those papers were part of a series of events which eventually forced Shimano to resign his position as abbot of Dai Bosatsu.

Within a decade of the inauguration of Dai Bosatsu, several of the most prestigious Zen Centers in America would be burdened by issues of teacher misconduct and the discrepancy between enlightened perception and unenlightened behavior.

CHAPTER NINE
Taizan Maezumi

Hakuyu Taizan Maezumi, who was raised and trained in the Soto tradition, later received transmission in the Rinzai and Sanbo Kyodan lineages as well. The Soto-shu, the central authority of the Soto school in Japan which sent Shunryu Suzuki to San Francisco in 1959, had sent Maezumi to Los Angeles three years earlier. Unlike Suzuki, this was Maezumi's first official posting; he was 25 years old at the time.

He was the third of eight brothers born to a priestly family in Otawara, a town in the eastern part of Tochigi Prefecture. His birth name was Hirotaka Kurodo but later—as was the habit with Zen priests—adopted the Sino-Japanese pronunciation of his given name, Hakuyu. Because there were no surviving males on his mother's side to continue that family's name, his maternal grandparents formally adopted him after which he went by the surname Maezumi.

His father, Hakujun (White Plum) Kurodo, was a prominent figure in the Soto school; he was the head of the Soto Supreme Court and a chief advisor at Sojiji. Four of his sons became Zen priests. By tradition, the eldest, Kojun, would inherit Hakujun's temple; the other brothers needed to find positions elsewhere.

Kurodo's temple was Koshinji, a 16th century complex which was in an advanced state of disrepair when he inherited it. In the years before the war, he expended a great deal of effort to rebuild it. The temple became his sons' playground. Young Hirotaka ran up and down the long, enclosed corridors and liked to climb onto the roofs of the buildings to the consternation of his mother, who referred to her son as a "gangster."

At the age of 11, he formally became his father's disciple and was ordained a monk. He was given the Buddhist name, Taizan, meaning "Great Mountain."

He was 14 years old when the war ended. During the American occupation, Koshinji was commandeered by US troops, and Maezumi was intrigued by the soldiers he met, who proved to be very different from the monsters Japanese propagandists had portrayed them to be. They were often friendly and could be surprisingly generous. Maezumi picked up some English from them; they also introduced him to cigarettes, beer, and swearing.

Post-war conditions in Japan were harsh. While Maezumi's family was better off than many, they were not immune to hardship, and the death of his infant brother may have been due, in part, to the straitened conditions in which they lived. The country as a whole was experiencing the reality of Buddha's First Noble Truth.

When Maezumi was 16 years old, his father sent him to study with a Rinzai master, Koryu Osaka, who had survived the atomic blast at Hiroshima. Osaka's own teacher had been disappointed by the wide-spread corruption within the Rinzai priesthood and advised his disciple to remain a layman. Osaka did so, and most of his students were also lay. His teaching methods and his approach to lay formation provided Maezumi with models which would profit him when he later worked with students in America.

Osaka introduced Maezumi to koan study; it took him three years to resolve the koan Mu and achieve his first kensho. After remaining with Osaka for four years, Maezumi underwent traditional Soto training at Eiheiji and at Sojiji, where he had a second kensho experience. He received formal transmission from his father at the age of 24.

Soto authorities in Kyoto sent Maezumi to Zenshuji, their regional headquarters in California, because he had some knowledge of English. His duties there were much the same as those Shunryu Suzuki would have in San Francisco: to conduct traditional ceremonies and otherwise minister to the needs of the local Japanese congregation. The mission was not wealthy, and Maezumi had to take a series of part-time jobs outside the temple in order to cover his living expenses. He worked as a gardener and, for a time, composed texts for Chinese fortune cookies.

The Los Angeles congregation was no more interested in zazen than the congregation at Sokoji in San Francisco would be, but Maezumi was committed to deepening his own practice. He studied Dogen's *Shobogenzo* with the Soto bishop, Reirin Yamada, and he studied koans with Nyogen Senzaki. Maezumi was surprised to find that Senzaki had a number of non-Japanese students. It had not occurred to him that Americans, whom he assumed were all Christians, might also be interested in Buddhism.

Eventually, Maezumi recognized that if he were going to remain in the United States he needed to improve his spoken English. He enrolled in courses at the San Francisco State College, and, while in San Francisco, met Shunryu Suzuki and occasionally attended ceremonies at Sokoji. Maezumi was a sociable young man and had a number of American girl friends. He married twice. The first marriage was short lived; the second, with an American anthropology student, produced three children.

Maezumi met Haku'un Yasutani during one of that teacher's visits to the United States. He undertook to study with Yasutani and served as his translator on subsequent visits. Maezumi admired the way that Yasutani and his teacher, Daiun Harada, had combined elements of the Soto and Rinzai traditions.

When he returned to Los Angeles, Maezumi hosted a weekly zazen gathering at Zenshuji. As in San Francisco, the people who showed up were not of Japanese descent but were rather young Western students who had read Watts and D. T. Suzuki. Maezumi was a much younger man than Shunryu Suzuki and more social. His American students were drawn to him by their sense of his deep spiritual understanding but also by his obvious concern for them as individuals and his friendly, open manner.

The members of his Japanese congregation, however, were not happy about having to share him with the zazen students, and, by 1967, Maezumi realized he needed to find separate quarters for his meditation group. He located a house in what had been a Hispanic area of the city but was gradually transitioning to a Korean neighborhood. Here he established the Los Angeles Zendo, later to be renamed the Zen Center of Los Angeles or ZCLA. Maezumi declared his father, Hakujun Kuroda, the honorary founder of the zendo, and it was officially registered with Soto-shu in Japan.

American interest in Zen was at its height, and impressive things were taking place in San Francisco. Maezumi was invited to take part in the inauguration of Shunryu Suzuki's training center at Tassajara and came away inspired by what he saw. The Los Angeles Zendo hosted Haku'un Yasutani when he was in the city as part of his tour of the US, and even Maezumi was struck by the number of applicants these sesshin drew.

Although he was already an authorized teacher, Maezumi felt the need to deepen his practice in order to better serve his students. So in 1969, he left his senior disciple, Bernie Tetsugen Glassman, in charge of the Zendo and returned to Japan to continue koan study with Yasutani. He received *inka* the following year, after which he resumed work with Koryu Osaka, who offered to come to Los Angeles to complete his training. Over a period of three years, Maezumi went through 400 koans with Osaka and received transmission from him in the Rinzai tradition in 1973.

With authorization in the Soto, Rinzai, and Sanbo Kyodan schools, there was no other teacher in America whose credentials rivaled Maezumi's.

In Japan, zazen was largely a monastic practice. Lay people, including foreigners, could take it up but did so, in most cases, at cloistered temples. In Los Angeles and San Francisco, Maezumi and Suzuki were developing a new model suitable for the young American students who made their way to those centers. What they came up with bore a lot of similarity to secular communes being established elsewhere in the country.

Zen practice at ZCLA followed orthodox Japanese Soto guidelines augmented by koan study. Maezumi's insistence on correct ritual behavior, including formal prostrations, was a sticking point for some students, as it had been for Aitken in Japan and for Shunryu Suzuki's students in California. Maezumi knew and expected that the first generation of American-born Zen teachers would make changes to these structures. His principal dharma heir, Bernie Tetsugen Glassman, noted:

Over and over he said to me that I should take whatever I can from him—in terms of Zen—and then spit out what I think won't work in this country. He said, "I'm not an American. I'm Japanese. And I can't present the American Zen." He said, "You've got to do that."[153]

But before Glassman or others made those accommodations, Maezumi wanted to ensure they were grounded in the traditional forms.

In spite of its strictness, ZCLA went through a period of rapid growth in the 1970s. The communal atmosphere of the Center proved to be a draw; more young people than had been expected were attracted by the idea of living in a community focused on a formal spiritual practice. When John and Joan Loori (now Joan Yushin Derrick) first came to the center, there were 27 residents, including Glassman and his wife. The Looris and their four year old son were given a single room. Soon the number of residents was approaching 200, and space needed to be found to accommodate people.

In addition to the hippies then swarming to California in search of spiritual guidance, ZCLA also attracted a number of well-educated professionals. Glassman was an aeronautical engineer; Jan Chozen Bays (then Jan Soulé) was a pediatrician; John Daido Loori, a professional photographer; Gerry Shishin Wick was an atomic physicist and oceanographer. Maezumi ordained nearly thirty priests from among his senior students to provide leadership to the inquirers who continued to show up at the door, and, by the 1980s, he had given transmission to twelve individuals, some of whom went on to become significant teachers in their own right. In addition to Glassman, Bays, Loori, and Wick there were Charlotte Joko Beck, Dennis Genpo Merzel, and six others. Unlike Shunryu Suzuki, Maezumi was able to have his successors' names included in the official rolls at Soto-shu in Japan.

Two hundred people living together inevitably presented challenges. There were families with young children for whom childcare needed to be provided. Parents were torn between family responsibilities and the desire to commit as much time as possible to their quest for Enlightenment. On top of which most also had to earn a living. It became easy to understand why Zen practice in Japan took place under monastic conditions.

The situation was exacerbated by the fact that the neighborhood was not a good one in which to raise children. People in the area had mixed feelings about the relatively well-off outsiders who came to the center, and participants could be harassed as they made their way to morning or evening sits. There were also tensions between resident and non-resident students. The non-residents recognized that the resident students had greater access to the teacher than they did; the residents felt that non-residents did not contribute as much to the maintenance of the center as the residents did.

The Center purchased buildings and apartment complexes on their block as they became available; these were prudent investments but required initial funding. Glassman proved to be a natural entrepreneur and—as Richard Baker was doing in San Francisco—he established a number of businesses to help meet rising expenses. ZCLA ran landscaping, carpentry, house-painting, and even plumbing operations. Partly to establish good will with the surrounding community, he encouraged Chozen Bays to open a medical clinic. Services at the clinic expanded as new students came to Zen Center bringing with them expertise in alternative therapies such as chiropractics, acupuncture, and homeopathy. Originally intended to serve the neighborhood, the clinic began to draw clients from other parts of the city as well. Jan Chozen Bays remembers:

> We had a combination of Western and alternative medicine which was very unique at that time. And so people from wealthy areas, Hollywood and Rodeo Drive, would come to the clinic. So we had this weird waiting room where we had Sikhs and people with Gucci bags and very, very poor Hispanic patients, all together in the same waiting room.[154]

Satellite zendos were established, and a network of practice centers—the White Plum Sangha, named after Maezumi's father—was envisioned. Senior students expanded beyond Los Angeles with Maezumi's encouragement. Charlotte Beck opened a Zendo in San Diego. Glassman founded the Zen Community of New York, and Daido Loori established Zen Mountain Monastery in the Catskill Mountains. Each of the new centers was registered with Soto-shu.

By 1982, ZCLA and its associated centers was one of the most vibrant Zen programs in America.

Throughout the period of expansion, Maezumi's students were aware of his fondness for alcohol. To some extent, they enabled his drinking because, when tipsy, he became quick witted and acted and spoke more like the Zen masters in the stories D. T. Suzuki, Nyogen Senzaki, and others had made popular.

Chozen recalls:

> He was also funny when he got drunk, which was unfortunate because then people would encourage him to get drunk, because another side came out. He would do this imitation geisha which was really very funny. But he would also tell you the truth. The Japanese don't usually tell you the truth because they don't want people to lose face. For example, if Maezumi Roshi had something he wanted to tell me that was difficult, he would tell one of my Dharma brothers, and then they were expected to come tell me, because then I wouldn't lose face by being confronted by Maezumi Roshi directly. And vice versa. He would tell me something that I had to tell them. That's the way it's done in Japan. So it took a while to learn that. But when he was drunk, he would be very honest. In Japan, if you're drunk, you can be forthright, and it's all forgiven the next day. So you could tell your boss—because everybody goes out drinking after work; that's standard in Japan—so you could say something rude to your boss and the next morning it would be totally forgiven. It's the one time that that very tightly contained society can let go. It's an alcoholic nation essentially. So, when he was drinking, he would tell you what he thought of you. And you wanted to hear that, and you didn't want to hear that. But the temptation was very strong to hear that.

At first, Maezumi's drinking was not seen as a problem. He did not allow it, for example, to interfere with his commitment to practice. Peter Mathiessen relates an occasion, during a trip to Japan, when he and Glassman stayed up late into the night drinking with Maezumi. The next day, the Americans rose too late to attend morning zazen, and Maezumi reprimanded them.

> When I murmured that our sluggishness might be accounted for by all that drink, Maezumi snapped, "Saki is one thing, and zazen is another! They have nothing to do with each other!"[155]

On the other hand, when he had been drinking, he would at times flirt with female students, even during dokusan. Joan Derrick was married to one of his senior students and their son had recently been diagnosed with a malignant brain tumor, so she was both surprised and angry when she realized what Maezumi was doing.

> I went into dokusan, and he [Maezumi] was particularly loving, and so sweet, and he tilted his head, and he was smiling at me, no matter what I was presenting to him. He was flirting with me! And I said, "Don't be flirting with me! I don't want to know anything about that!" And that was the end of that. He straightened his head up, and he never did that again.[156]

Then in 1983, when it became clear that Maezumi had done more than flirt with other students, his wife left, taking their younger children with her. Joan Derrick points out:

> There was an *amazing* amount of drinking, and it was always started by the roshi. And all of us just jumped right in. We figured, you're sitting hard in sesshin, and it's a tortuous week, and then let's party when it's over.
>
> So there was a lot of craziness going on at that place, and I'm not really sure why. I think we American women are extremely selfish and very dominating, and we want what we want. Not just women; men too. But, for sure, the womanizing thing had two folds to it. There were women who propositioned him, as much as he took advantage.

It was natural for students to want to be closer to their teacher, and this was one way in which female students, at least, could get close. Although her affair with Maezumi contributed to the break-up of her own marriage, Chozen Bays believes that the sexual aspect of her relationship with Maezumi was minor.

> We had this very strange mix of hippie-commune and monastery, and not a terribly clear understanding of our own psychology. I think there is some spiritual-by-passing that often happens in Zen. Dick Baker's an example. Lots of examples. So what happened with me was that I fell in love with Roshi. In retrospect, after doing a lot of study and reading, I would say I fell in love with the Dharma through Roshi, as embodied by Roshi. In a way, what you're falling in love with isn't the Dharma in that person but your own

potential. So, it's like a mirror. You're falling in love with your own potential to become what this person embodies for you, or your version of it. Then you want to become more and more intimate with it, but because our human understanding of intimacy is so limited and involves sexuality, you think, 'Oh, this must be sexual. That's a way to become more intimate.'

Maezumi made a full confession after his wife left and admitted that the lack of judgment he had demonstrated in the affairs was due, at least in part, to his drinking. He acknowledged that he was an alcoholic and voluntarily entered the Betty Ford Rehabilitation Clinic. His students were stunned. Outside counselors were called in, and the community confronted the fact that they had, to a large degree, been complicit in enabling Maezumi's behavior.

While Maezumi underwent treatment, much of what he had accomplished in Los Angeles began to unravel. Students reacted in a number of ways. Some insisted that, at least as far as the sexual affairs were concerned, his private life should be no one else's concern. Some even tried to argue that the behavior of enlightened individuals should not be judged by ordinary standards. Others, however, questioned his credibility as a teacher, and many left the center. Joko Beck, who by this time had established her own center, renounced her affiliation with Maezumi and ZCLA. Chozen Bays, although she was Maezumi's transmitted Dharma heir, left ZCLA, moved to Oregon, and dropped out of Zen practice for a while.

In the midst of the trauma, a film crew, which had earlier arranged to do a documentary about the center, arrived. The instinct of many of the members was to cancel the shoot, but Maezumi insisted that the filmmakers be allowed to stay and complete the project. He agreed to be interviewed and, in the released film, frankly discussed his alcoholism without excuses and accepted full responsibility for his actions. He lamented that behavior he now characterized as "outrageous" and "scandalous" had harmed his family, his reputation, and, possibly, the Dharma as a whole.

Shishin Wick was the chief administrator of ZCLA at the time and was well aware of the impact the Maezumi's behavior had had on the center; however, Wick noted, "If he were my father, I wouldn't abandon him, and he was my spiritual father. So I stayed there and helped right the ship."[157] ZCLA survived and a period of reconciliation followed. However, the reduced membership meant that it had to divest itself of many of the properties which had been purchased during the period of expansion.

For the next twelve years, Maezumi dedicated his energies to ensuring that the Zen tradition would continue in America after the initial Japanese teachers gave way to a new generation of American-born teachers. He saw himself as a "stepping stone" in a process by which Zen would become fully Americanized. The realization of the White Plum Sangha and his one dozen transmitted heirs were measures of his success. In addition to the centers established by Glassman and Loori, Chozen Bays established the Zen Community of Oregon, Genpo Merzel established the Kanzeon Zen Center in Salt Lake City, and Shishin Wick, the Great Mountain Zen Center outside Denver. Other centers would be established in Mexico, New Zealand, Great Britain, Switzerland, Belgium, the Netherlands, France, Germany, and Poland. Maezumi also founded the Kuroda Institute for the Study of Buddhism and Human Values at the University of Hawaii in order to ensure an appropriate academic foundation for Zen studies.

While, at times, Maezumi broke with established Japanese customs, at his core he retained a traditional attitude to the Dharma. On one occasion, he invited another respected teacher, Gengo Akiba, to conduct a sesshin with him. In the opening remarks on the first day of the sesshin, Maezumi stated that although he himself was seen as a liberal and even radical teacher, Akiba was noted for his conservatism. Perhaps between the two of them, he said, they might be able to help students accomplish something during the retreat. Akiba, who had only a little English, then added, "Let me say that while I seem very traditional outwardly, inside, I, too, am radical." Maezumi nodded, then said, "And although I outwardly seem very liberal, inside I am very traditional and conservative."

Maezumi posited that people were drawn to Zen by a desire to discover their true nature, to understand the significance of birth and death. Anton Tenkel Coppens edited several of Maezumi's teishos for publication and chose to present them in poetic form in order to capture the slow, careful cadence of Maezumi's manner of speaking:

> Who are you?
> How come you are there?
> That is the question.
> What is there?
> Where did you come from
> standing there?
> If I present anything in particular
> as the answer,
> it is not it.[158]

These are universal concerns, but Zen students are unique because they are not satisfied with theoretical answers. Instead, they seek "the direct experience of what Shakyamuni Buddha realized over 2,500 years ago."[159]

In orthodox Soto fashion, Maezumi asserted that all persons are endowed with Buddha-nature; however, without practice and realization this Buddha-nature cannot be perceived. The wisdom, or understanding, Zen students strive for is

> —our life itself. We not only have that wisdom; we are constantly using it. When it's cold, we put on more clothing. When it's hot, we take some clothes off. When hungry, we eat. When sad, we cry. Being happy, we laugh. That's perfect wisdom.
>
> And this perfect wisdom doesn't only pertain to humans, but to anything and everything. Birds chirp, dogs run, mountains are high, valleys low. It's all perfect wisdom! The seasons change, the stars shine in the heavens; it's perfect wisdom! Regardless of whether we realize it or not, we are always in the midst of the Way. Or, more strictly speaking, we are nothing but the Way itself.[160]

The basis of Zen practice is zazen, which he presented much as Dogen had in the *Fukanzazengi*:

> First we learn to bring our bodies into harmony—we learn how to physically sit in the proper fashion. Then, sitting properly, our breathing settles into a harmonious cycle on its own—we stop panting and gasping and start to breathe easily, smoothly, and naturally. And as body and breath begin to settle down, and no longer create disturbances for us, we find that the mind too is given the opportunity to settle into its own smooth and natural functioning. The racket and babble of our noisy minds give way to the clarity and naturalness of our true selves.[161]

Central to his teaching was the need to appreciate one's life "just as it is"—rather than to seek it to be something different. This was, he said, the "essence of Zen practice."

> The point of our practice is not to become something other than what we already are, such as a buddha or enlightened person, but to realize or become aware of the fact that we are intrinsically,

originally, the Way itself, free and complete. If we practice to become something else, we simply put another head on top of our own.[162]

What hampers this realization is our

—limited, self-centered consciousness. With consciousness *per se*, there is nothing at all wrong. Consciousness is a plain, pure function of the body-mind, and not a matter of right or wrong, problematical or not problematical. But our trouble is that we give too much value, too much authority, to our conscious functioning. We think that we can figure out everything by our intelligence, by our thinking, by our ideas and thoughts and concepts. That's how we get into trouble.

So, in practicing zazen, set aside those ideas and preconceived notions. Just stop that entire process of analysis and idea formation.[163]

Koan study, for Maezumi, was an aid in overcoming this self-centered consciousness. Koan study in itself was not

—the main thing.
The main thing is always oneself.
And when oneself and the koan become identical
that's the moment of realization
of koan.[164]

Quoting Dogen, Maezumi reiterated that the proper way to study Self was to forget self. This was also the way to approach Mu.

Dogen Zenji says, "Forget the self."
Mu-ji,
the same, see?
Dissolve yourself into Mu-ji!
Don't hold on to yourself
when you are dealing with Mu.[165]

—when you work on koan,
the important thing is no I, my, me.

> How can you do that?
> Throw yourself into the koan.
> Be the koan yourself.
> So when we work on Mu-ji
> become Mu yourself.
> Either way it's okay—
> give yourself altogether away to Mu,
> or let Mu occupy yourself completely.
> Nothing but Mu!
> Give up yourself
> and let Mu-ji take care of it.[166]

When self-centered consciousness comes to an end, then "you recognize that you and the universe are one"[167]—which is enlightenment.

A student came to see Maezumi and asked, "What do you mean by 'Buddha-nature'?"
"Would you like some tea?" Maezumi asked.
The student nodded his head impatiently, then repeated his question.
"Do you use milk or lemon?" Maezumi inquired.

One evening, Maezumi was seated on the porch of the Zen Center with one of his students when a drunken and unhappy man walking along the street noticed them. He obviously recognized Maezumi and stumbled up to him. "What is it like?" he asked in a gloomy tone. "What's it like to be enlightened?"
"Very depressing," Maezumi told him gently.

Philomene Long, who had been a cloistered Roman Catholic nun before becoming a student of Maezumi, records this story:

> Anne Seisen Fletcher was reading about the times of Shakyamuni Buddha. According to legend, a group of women, led by Shakyamuni Buddha's stepmother, approached Buddha and begged him

to ordain them as nuns. The Buddha refused them again and again, but the women persisted with their request.

Finally, the Buddha said, "Yes, I will ordain women, but you should know that this action will set Buddhism back some five hundred years."

Seisen was appalled by the Buddha's apparent sexism and, being interested in Roshi's [Maezumi's] reaction, she relayed this story to him.

Roshi was silent for a moment, then said, "Well, it was worth it!"[168]

Sean Murphy, in *One Bird, One Stone*, includes this account of the first sesshin he participated in with Maezumi:

On the first day, distracted by thoughts and feelings for a woman I'd been dating, I went in for my private interview with the roshi despondent about my inability to keep my mind on my practice. I was expecting to be scolded for my poor efforts, but Maezumi responded: "You're in love! That's wonderful! Don't worry so much about your practice. Just relax and enjoy your sitting."

On the second day, troubled by serious pain in my back and knees, I was considering dropping out of the retreat entirely. I went to dokusan, expecting to be admonished to sit through the discomfort. Instead Maezumi said: "Don't try so hard! Practice is not asceticism. Take the next period off and rest yourself. Now, I'll give you a back massage." With that he directed me to turn around and proceeded to rub my back and shoulders.

By the third day I was struggling with constant sleepiness, since a painting crew had mixed up the screens on the building, and mosquitoes from the center's koi pond swarmed nightly into the dormitories, past the ill-fitting frames, keeping everyone awake. But when I tried to tell the roshi about these difficulties, he cut me off, saying: "Stop feeling sorry for yourself! Make some effort. You're not trying hard enough!"[169]

During the 80s, so many people came to Los Angles from Mexico City to attend sesshin that Maezumi decided to open a center there. Shishin Wick accompanied Maezumi to Mexico City three or four times a year, and they held sesshin in an empty house owned by a sangha member. During one of these, the neighbor's dog ran out into the street and was run over by a car. Maezumi told Wick

> —that we were responsible. I said, "Really? How are we responsible?" And he said, "Well, this was an empty house, then suddenly there were people here chanting and lighting incense, walking around. The dog's routine got distracted; it got frightened and went out in the street. So we need to give that dog a proper funeral." The main thing for me was not necessarily the funeral but that he said, "We're always responsible." That was a real teaching. "We're always responsible." So we talked to the owners of the dog, and they were willing. So we dug a grave, did a procession in robes with incense, bells, and chanting, and we buried the dog.

In 1995, Maezumi travelled to Japan to visit family members and Soto leaders. Although after 1983 he had stopped drinking in the United States, he allowed himself to relax and drink socially while in Japan where attitudes towards alcohol consumption were different. Alcoholism, for example, was not recognized as a disease, and drinking played a major role in social and family gatherings.

On May 14, Maezumi passed the evening with his brothers at the family temple in Otawara. He intended to spend the following day with another brother in Tokyo, and, although it was late and they had been drinking heavily, Maezumi took the train into the city. He fell asleep during the trip and missed his stop, so it was even later than he had planned when he finally arrived at his brother's house. He told the brother that he was going to take a bath in the large traditional Japanese tub and then retire; there was no need to wait up for him.

The next morning, when the brother got up, he discovered Maezumi had drowned in the tub. In order to protect Maezumi's reputation in America, the family told the students at ZCLA that their teacher had succumbed to a heart attack during his sleep. It was only two years later, when Maezumi's successor at ZCLA requested a copy of his death certificate for insurance purposes, that the actual details of his death were revealed.

Maezumi's sexual indiscretions, his drinking, and even the circumstances surrounding his death, raised questions and concerns among his students as well as in the wider community of both Buddhists and non-Buddhists in America. In some ways—as Robert Aitken had discovered when he met with Nakagawa and Yasutani in Japan to discuss Shimano's behavior—it was more an American than an Asian problem. However, unlike Shimano, Maezumi accepted responsibility for his failings and did not try to excuse his behavior. Still, the circumstances and the way in which students responded to them revealed a significant cultural chasm not only between Japanese and North American values but also between the fundamental metaphysical premises underlying the Judaeo-Christian worldview and that of Buddhism.

Japanese attitudes towards the use of alcohol and towards sexual behavior are very different from those in the US. As Aitken pointed out, there is no term as such for alcoholism in Japanese. Where North Americans might say that someone was an "alcoholic," the Japanese would say, "He likes Saki." More significant than the cultural differences is a differing understanding of the relationship between morality and spirituality as well as differing assumptions about what the term "enlightenment" refers to. It became apparent during the crisis at ZCLA that many Americans, whether Zen practitioners or not, had inflated expectations of how "enlightened" Zen masters should behave. Conversely, one of the most celebrated and respected Zen masters from Japan, Ikkyu Sojun,[170] brazenly frequented wine shops and brothels. In one of his poems he wrote that while his awakening experience had been profound, a night spent with a particularly talented prostitute provided an even deeper wisdom.

Arguably, the responsibility of Christians is to know and obey the will of a Divine Creator. Sins are not just human weaknesses; they are offences against God. In his essay "Beat Zen, Square Zen, and Zen," Alan Watts had suggested that one of the reasons young people were exploring Asian spiritual traditions was specifically to escape the onerous burden associated with the guilt of disobeying divinely decreed laws.

The Judaeo-Christian concept of sin is absent from Buddhism. Spirituality and morality are not equated in the same way as they are in the west. The purpose of spiritual activity in Zen is not to fall into step with a divinely revealed game plan but rather to overcome the reality of suffering (the first Noble Truth) by becoming aware of (enlightened about) one's Buddha-nature or True Self—one's inherent connection with all of Being. There are still appropriate and inappropriate, honorable and dishonorable behaviors, but these do not carry the weight of being directives from the Creator of the Universe. Adultery and the use of intoxicants are both prohibited in the precepts not because they transgress the directives of God but rather because they are recognized as impediments that perpetuate desire, which (according to the second Noble Truth) is the root cause of suffering—one's own and that of others.

The term "enlightenment" can also be misleading to Western students. In contemporary liberal parlance, "enlightened" essentially means "progressive" as when one is said to have an enlightened attitude about certain political or environmental concerns. In Buddhism, "enlightenment" has a much narrower meaning. To be "enlightened" is to be enlightened about one's True Self. One can realize one's Buddha-nature and remain "unenlightened" about a whole range of social and political issues. Many enlightened Zen masters in Japan, for example, had supported the country's imperialist ambitions which led to their engagement in the Second World War. Throughout the history of Buddhism, as far back as the Buddha himself, enlightened individuals were no more capable of overcoming contemporary social prejudices or traditional attitudes towards gender issues than anyone else.

The students who remained with Maezumi did so because they recognized that he was not only an awakened teacher but was also one genuinely concerned about their welfare. It helped that he lamented the damage his behavior had caused both to his family and to the spread of the Dharma and that he did not pretend that his enlightenment should in any way exonerate him from behaving in a responsible and decent manner. Consequently a reconciliation between Maezumi and some of his students had been possible.

In other communities and with other teachers this would not necessarily be the case.

Chapter Ten
Walter Nowick

THE ORIGINAL ZEN (CHAN) TEACHERS in China were difficult to access. Their temples were hidden away in the mountains, intentionally located far from larger population centers. Nor were they welcoming. Prospective students who made their way to the temple gates could be refused entry for days on end in order to test the sincerity of their aspiration. In the early 1970s, something similar was happening in a remote village in Maine.

Walter Nowick was a powerfully built man who could envelop people in his hugs. Balding and with pale blue eyes, he had a face which one of his students described as "vaguely resembling the round innocence of Charlie Brown."[171] He was the first American to receive authorization to teach in the Rinzai School. Before Robert Aitken finished his training under Yamada Roshi, Nowick had completed the koan curriculum under Zuigan Goto at Daitokuji.

Nowick lived in Japan for sixteen years and was wholly at home there. But his teacher believed it was his responsibility to return to the United States to promote the Dharma. So when Goto died in 1965, Nowick returned to America and to a farm his family had purchased for him on the Morgan Bay Road in Surry, Maine.

Goto had told Nowick to wait at least ten years before he began teaching in order to allow his Zen to deepen. Nowick was a professional musician and had no intention of teaching Zen at all. But well before the ten year period was up, people learned about him and started turning up at the Morgan Bay farm. Nowick did not make it easy for them.

When Hugh Curran arrived at the farm he had been Philip Kapleau's attendant at the Rochester Zen Center for several years. That made no difference to Nowick.

> The standard practice was to come to the tree in the front yard and stand there for a little while. I came here in 1975, and I asked what I should do and was told by a student, "You'll have to stand in front of the tree. And sometime Walter may come out and say, 'All right, come in.' Or he may keep you standing there." So, I did that for two or three days. He came out and said, "What do you want?" And I said, "Well, I'd like to be a student." And he said, "No. No, I've got too many."[172]

Curran came back twice more before being accepted. Another student, who had practiced at the San Francisco Zen Center for five years, had to wait two and a half months.

Gradually a small community of cabins—some better constructed than others—was built on the farm in which some of the students resided without electricity or running water and under living and training conditions unusually rigorous for

Americans, although not as harsh as those common in the Zen temples of Japan. Similar experiments were taking place elsewhere in the US, but Maui and Southern California were one thing; coastal Maine, with its frigid winters, was something else altogether.

Walter Nowick was the fourth of seven children born to Russian immigrants. Nowick's father had fled Russia at the age of 14 after getting into trouble with the local authorities for scrawling graffiti on the steps of the parish church. His parents sent him to relatives in New York, where he met a young girl who came from the same region of Russia as he had. They were married in 1912, when his was 19 and she 15. They became potato farmers on Long Island. Farming is labor intensive, and, as soon as the children were old enough, they were expected to help with the daily chores.

It was a cultured family. Walter's father played the piano by ear, and his mother insisted that her children take piano lessons. A local teacher came to the farm every Saturday from 9:00 in the morning until 6:00 in the evening to provide individual instruction to each of the children. Walter, who started his lessons at the age of four, showed the most talent, and the teacher encouraged him to apply to Juilliard while still in high school. He was accepted in 1940 at the age of fourteen.

Henriette Michelson, a woman he would revere throughout his life, was his piano coach at Julliard. Michelson spent her summers in Maine, where she taught at the Kneisel Hall Chamber Music Program. Each year, she brought some of her New York students with her, and Nowick was invited to be among them. While in Maine, he lodged at the farmhouse of Leverett and Addie Morgan in Surry.

On the afternoon of December 7, 1941, the day of the Japanese attack on Pearl Harbor, Nowick gave his first recital in Michaelson's apartment in New York. "I played Chopin," he recalled later. "It went well, and I had a wonderful time.... I was lucky that they didn't tell me about the attack until afterwards."[173]

He did not doubt where his duty lay when war broke out and enlisted as soon as he completed high school. He was sent to the Pacific Theater and was involved in the "mopping up" campaign on Okinawa, which followed one of the most prolonged battles of the war. The brutality Nowick witnessed there affected him profoundly.

> We walked south to north, shoulder to shoulder, the whole length of the island. We were supposed to shout "Come out!" in Japanese

and our orders were to only shoot soldiers. But our accents were horrible, there were no translators, and the locals didn't come out. So the Americans went into houses and caves where the people were hiding and dragged them out. Discipline was very poor and not only did a great many Japanese soldiers get killed but a great many civilians as well. A lot of them were old people who were just beaten to death.[174]

After the Japanese surrender, Nowick was among the troops stranded in the Philippines until transportation back to the United States could be arranged. During this time, he joined the American Male Chorus under the direction of Lieutenant Lewis Bullock. Nowick had wanted to audition for the chorus, but, when it was discovered he could play the piano, he was appointed the accompanist.

When the Chorus came to Tokyo to play for General MacArthur, Nowick had his first experience of Japan and the destruction wrought by the war. He saw the devastation left by the bombs dropped on Hiroshima and Nagasaki and found himself curious about and sympathetic towards the defeated people he met.

Henriette Michelson, who was a friend of Ruth Fuller Sasaki, was instrumental in introducing Nowick to Zen. After demobilization, he returned to Juilliard, and, one day in her waiting room, he found a copy of a booklet of translations Sokei-an Sasaki had made of the *Zenrin Kushu*. The sensibility expressed in one verse, in particular, struck Nowick:

> Bamboo shadows sweep the stairs, yet not a speck of dust is stirred;
> Moonlight penetrates the bottom of the lake, yet not a trace
>   remains.[175]

He began to accompany Michelson to zazen at the First Zen Institute which, following Sokei-an Sasaki's death during the war, was without a resident teacher. His commitment to practice caught Ruth Sasaki's attention, and, after he completed his music degree, she suggested that he consider traveling to Japan to study with the teacher with whom she had been working—Zuigan Goto at Daitokuji. Ruth provided the introduction and used her influence to help Nowick acquire the necessary documents to travel to Japan, then still occupied by US forces. He went to Kyoto in 1950. His stay there overlapped Gary Snyder's, who arrived later to study with Goto's successor, Oda Sesso.

Although he would eventually become proficient in the language, Nowick spoke no Japanese when he arrived. Goto, however, had been one of the monks who had accompanied Sokatsu Shaku and Sokei-an Sasaki to California in 1906, and he still retained a smattering of English. During his first sanzen meeting with Goto, Nowick—overwhelmed by the strangeness of everything around him and the formality of the occasion—stammered, "I may be a little slow."

"It doesn't matter," Goto told him. "Slow or fast. We will proceed."

Daitokuji was a training center for young men preparing to become temple priests. At 24, Nowick was older than most of his fellow students, but, because he was the most recent person to come to the temple, they were all considered his superiors. The training was rigorous. Depending on the time of year, the day began at either 3:00 or 4:00 a. m. with two hours of meditation and a chanting service; there was another four hours of meditation in the evening, which did not end until 10:00 p. m. During the day, the monks were engaged in various maintenance tasks. Once a day, each student met with Goto to report on his practice. As at other Zen Centers, all activities—whether meditation, chanting, preparing vegetables, or working on the grounds—were to be undertaken with full-attention. The monks slept in quarters which had paper walls and only small space heaters to ease the chill of winter. Toilet facilities were primitive by American standards. There was never enough to eat; monastic fare was modest to begin with, but there were still food shortages in Japan at the time and meals were sparse. During sesshin, the schedule and conditions were even more arduous.

When Sean Murphy asked Nowick if he had not found conditions at Daitokuji daunting, Nowick told him:

> If you want to play the piano in a certain style…you find the person who teaches that style best, and do what they say. If you want to do something else, you do something else. But if you want to learn what *they* have to teach, you follow their directions.[176]

After a period as a resident student at Daitokuji, he moved out of the temple and continued as a lay student. There was a strong interest in western classical music in Japan, and Nowick earned a living by providing music lessons to private students as well as teaching at the Kyoto Women's University and the Kyoto Music School. Over time he became a recognized and even a celebrated performer as a result of his public recitals and appearances on Japanese radio and television. The First Zen Institute, which followed his activities in Japan, reported in their newsletter for

April 1955 that he played before the Imperial Family as accompanist for the Ohtani Gakuen Chorus.

In all, Nowick spent sixteen years in Japan. He took the precepts from Goto and was given the Buddhist name Gessen, which translates as "Source of the Moon" or Moonspring. Nowick remained a lay person. It had never been his, or his teacher's, intention that he become a priest.

He made several visits back to the United States during his time in Japan, and, when the Morgans died, his family bought the farm on the Morgan Bay Road for him, possibly as an incentive for him to return home. He did not do so, however, until Goto died in 1965. When he returned to Maine, he brought one third of his teacher's ashes with him.

Nowick, then forty years old, moved into the Morgans' farm house and redesigned the second floor in Japanese style with tatami mats, shoji screens, and a Buddha altar. He maintained his personal practice but gave no thought to teaching Zen. Instead, he taught in the Music Department at the University of Maine at Orono and supported a number of music students from Japan who came to America in order to further their studies. These young people either lodged with Nowick or with one of the families in the area who were used to hosting students. The Morgans' barn proved to have unusually good acoustics and was converted into a concert hall where performances by the visiting students were given.

One of the Japanese youth who came to Surry was Masanobu Ikemiya, who had studied Zen with Soko Morinaga, Zuigan Goto's heir at Daitokuji. In 1967, Ikemiya was accepted at the Music Conservatory of Oberlin College in Ohio, and Morinaga arranged an introduction to Nowick. Nowick invited the young man to Morgan Bay for the Christmas break, and the two sat zazen together in the mornings.

Lenore Straus, a sculptor, had met Nowick while she had been supervising the installation of an exhibit in Japan. He gave her her first zazen instruction during that visit, and, when she returned to the US, she continued to attend sesshin with Haku'un Yasutani. She resolved the koan Mu during a retreat at Pendle Hill, Pennsylvania.[177] After achieving kensho, she wanted to maintain and deepen her practice. When she learned that Nowick was back in the United States, she made her way to Surry to ask him to be her teacher. The ten years Goto had told him to wait had not passed, but Nowick found it difficult to refuse her. Other students were referred to him by the First Zen Institute. Still others found their way to Maine on their own.

In 1968, with some reluctance, Nowick agreed to work with a small number of students he felt were sincere enough to commit themselves to practice. He established a board of directors, consisting of Lenore, himself, and a third member, and they incorporated "Moonspring Hermitage." Nowick still considered himself primarily a musician, and many of the students who came to Moonspring were musicians as well. The statement of purpose declared that Moonspring Hermitage had been established to "maintain, and support a religious, philosophical and cultural center or centers dedicated to teaching in regular meetings between students and teachers, the spirit, precepts, and practice of Zen Buddhism and to encourage and teach the practice of the arts." From the beginning "Moonspring Hermitage was to have a dual focus: Zen and the practice of the arts."[178]

Nowick tried to recreate something of the atmosphere of Daitokuji. There were two three-month training periods a year, run as formally as those in Japan had been. A woodshed was converted into a small zendo, and a sanzen room was improvised in Nowick's living quarters on the second floor of the farmhouse.

Ever since the eighth century Chinese Zen Master, Baizhang Huaihai,[179] had declared that "a day of no work is a day of no food," manual labor has been a traditional part of formal Zen training. So Nowick, guided by his experience working on his father's potato farm, revived the Morgan farm in order to provide work and income for the community gathered there. In addition to crops and extensive vegetable gardens, there were dairy cattle, hogs, and poultry. Nowick was not a vegetarian and took charge of slaughtering the poultry.

As more students arrived, Nowick routinely told them to go away. If they persisted and were finally accepted as students, he could be very generous. Some families were deeded an acre of land on which to build small houses. Single students usually lived in cabins they built near the zendo.

Nowick allowed students to call him by his first name, although those who preferred to be more formal addressed him as "Sensei." He did not insist upon rituals, seldom gave formal talks, and refused to discuss theory. For him, Zen consisted of zazen, sanzen, and mindful labor. He insisted that students give their full attention to whatever activity they were engaged in, whether in the zendo or the fields.

He also stressed that Zen training was not automatic and that following a certain discipline did not necessarily guarantee a particular result. "What you are doing here isn't easy," he is reported to have told students taking part in a sesshin:

> Your body hurts and your mind creaks with stress. The trouble you are going to, and which you think will release you in the end, is nearly maximal.

But…you must be aware that it is quite possible that this training may not give you any result whatever.[180]

In spite of the challenges, students continued to arrive, and by 1969 it was necessary to build a larger zendo to accommodate them. Nowick constructed a sawmill on the farm. The lumber was milled on site from trees harvested on the property. After allowing the boards to dry for a year, the community—under the supervision of a student who had worked on set-designs for motion pictures—completed the construction of the new zendo in 1971. Soko Morinaga came to Maine to take part in the official inauguration, bringing an image of Manjusri to adorn it.

Near the zendo, a short path—marked by a statue carved by Lenore Straus—led to a glacial rock known as the "Roshi Stone" where, three years prior, Nowick had interred the ashes of his teacher. A plaque, marking the spot, read:

> Here lie some of the ashes of the Japanese Zen Master Goto Zuigan, my teacher. They were placed here in October 1968, with hope that his teaching will continue.

With the completion of the new zendo, it appeared that that hope was being realized. The transition of an ancient spiritual tradition from Asia to America and from one generation to the next, however, was going to prove to be more challenging.

The surrounding Maine community was not entirely welcoming. They referred to the Zen center as the "command." "A guy who lived down the road was trying to say 'commune,' but he said 'command,'" one of Nowick's student explained.[181] Moonspring residents cheerfully adopted the term, which seemed to suggest something slightly sinister. The locals kept a wary eye on them.

There were a number of families with small children at Moonspring and eventually the matter of schooling became important. Nowick's first response was to establish the Nowick Corner School, based on Montessori guidelines, in 1970. When it was discontinued six years later, pupils were bused to public school in Surry. It was hard for the Command children to blend in with their fellows. Their families led a modest lifestyle. None of them had television sets, so their children were unfamiliar with the pop culture references which bind young people together.

Nowick did not tell students or their parents why he closed the school—whether he thought that families should take more responsibility for looking after their children or because he felt it was financial burden Moonspring could not afford. His abrupt decision and his refusal to explain himself were typical.

Nowick had a complex personality. He could be friendly, humorous, and enormously generous and caring. He enjoyed preparing meals for people, and he loved music. When he sang Schubert, it was with an exuberance which affected even people unfamiliar with classical music. But he was a demanding Zen teacher. While it was not a role he had sought, it was one he took seriously. Unfamiliar with what was happening elsewhere in the United States in the still fledgling Zen movement, he developed his own style of teaching and working with students, bringing to it the single-minded, autocratic perspective of an orchestra conductor—or of the Japanese teachers with whom he was familiar.

Those who came to Moonspring did so because they were in search of something. The Vietnam War had polarized the generations, and there was still anxiety about a possible nuclear conflict. Young people throughout the western world, but particularly in the United States, were questioning the values and standards of their elders. They recognized the underlying racism and sexism that existed in contemporary society and sought to address them. Many abandoned the religious traditions of their parents.

Driven by what Buddhists term "suffering," they sought teachers who—they hoped—could show them a better way. They made sacrifices to come to Maine and put up with hardships their peers would have scorned. It was not so much the actual living conditions as the master-student relationship which was the challenge. As with the piano student in Nowick's analogy, Zen students across American sought teachers they believed could help them attain their goals. They would accept the idiosyncrasies of the teachers because they believed them to be enlightened beings who saw things from a different, higher, perspective. If the student hoped to achieve enlightenment, they submitted to the training.

Japanese Zen is hierarchal and, in that sense, ran counter to the prevailing egalitarian attitudes of the youth movement of the 1970s. The situation was the same in San Francisco and Los Angeles, but, with Japanese teachers, students could rationalize the imported structures. It would prove to be different when the teacher, himself, was also American.

Nowick was both the spiritual leader and the administrative leader at Moonspring. Some students came to feel that he micro-managed all aspects of the community, even when it was evident that some of his decisions about issues beyond his expertise—farm management or construction, for example—showed poor judgment. The students ceded him control over areas of their lives in which he had no training. They came to him for advice about personal relationships or how to raise their children even though he was unmarried and childless.

There was enough information about Zen available that students understood that the training was intended to guide them to discover their "True Nature"—that innate wisdom which is separate from, or underlies, the individual's personal history. The personal history—the ego, the "I"—is an impediment to that realization. The sense of "I" is what creates the feeling of being separate from everything else, and the sense of being separate, of dualism, is the root of the suffering identified in the Buddha's First Noble Truth. So an integral part of Zen training is to overcome or see through the impediment of the ego and the dualistic way of seeing the world associated with it. One way the Zen teacher accomplishes this is by leading the student to recognize that what he thinks of as a permanent self is actually empty—merely a role being played, conditioned by external factors.

In *A Brief History of Moonspring Hermitage*, there is an example from a student who was a social worker in Ellsworth, Maine, where he wore a suit and tie and was frequently on the phone. The student described an occasion when he and Nowick were walking to the barn. Nowick began to tease him:

> "Out in the world he dresses up and has so much responsibility, making calls, doing so many important things. And then he comes home and just shovels shit."
>
> I responded somewhat flippantly, "Yeah, this here is much better." And he turned to me strongly and said, "Not better, not worse. It's that a man can switch from one mode to another!"[182]

Janwillem van de Wetering, who first met Nowick at Daitokuji, recorded a similar conversation. When van de Wetering was a new student at the monastery in Japan, Nowick explained to him that each person plays multiple roles in the course of his life—child, parent, employee, employer, spiritual seeker, seducer—none of which are real, each of which is a part played according to the circumstances in which one finds oneself. Each role is like a layer of an onion.

> When he goes into himself, by meditation and other exercises, by discipline, by fighting his "self," the layers of the onion drop away, one by one, till the last layer disappears and nothing remains.[183]

One of the goals of Zen practice is to be fully present to what is occurring, so that one responds to things as they are rather than as one thinks about them or imagines them. That includes awareness of one's own prevarications and rationalizations. The majority of the students who came to Moonspring were young, and while they came seeking wisdom or enlightenment, they often lacked basic self-awareness. Nowick was ruthless in pointing out pretensions. Van de Wetering—who called Nowick "Peter" in his book—provided this example:

> I remembered one of Peter's lessons in the Kyoto temple. I had only just moved in with him and had some difficulty in adjusting to his rhythm and way of doing things. He had been washing the dishes one afternoon and I had intended to go out somewhere. I was looking for the key to my scooter and rummaging about for it in the kitchen.
>
> "Can I be of any help?" I asked.
>
> Peter mumbled a word which resembled "idiot" but I thought I had misheard and asked him again, in the same cheerful manner, if I could be of any help.
>
> "Idiot!" Peter said, very clearly this time.
>
> The insult angered me and I pointed out that his behavior was ridiculous. I had politely offered to help him and he called me names.
>
> "Of course I am calling you names," Peter said. "The mere fact that you are asking me if you can be of help proves that you have learned nothing at all during the long year you have been with us."
>
> "Yes?" I asked, really angry now.
>
> Peter had put the dish towel down and looked at me.
>
> "Yes," he said, "you learned nothing. You know damn well you can be of help because I am doing the washing-up and you know I have a lot to do. But you don't want to help at all because you are going out somewhere. You are only asking because you want to make a good impression, to show your so-called helpfulness. If you want to be of help, you would *be* of help and pick up a dish towel,

which is right here on the table, we do have two dish towels, and you would start drying up."[184]

Persistent assaults on the ego are an essential part of Zen training, but they are difficult for the student. Their effectiveness is dependent upon the student's faith in the teacher. Nowick followed the Japanese form, refusing to explain why he behaved a certain way or made certain demands of his students, leaving it to the student to come to his own understanding.

By the late '70s—whether it was because of Nowick's teaching style, the difficulty of raising families, or the harsh Maine winters—a number of long time Command members became disaffected and left. A few years later, some of the remaining students began to wonder if Nowick's heart was in the teaching any longer.

In 1984, while the Cold War between the US and the Soviet Union was still simmering, Nowick saw a television program about the probable after-effects of a nuclear war. The program stunned him. A student, who was with him at the time, reports: "He said, 'I actually realized everything could come to an end: Mozart, Beethoven, Zen, Buddhism, everybody could stop.'" He felt it particularly strongly because of his Russian heritage, and he looked for some way he could help ease the tensions between the nations and promote greater understanding.

He told Sean Murphy:

> I just couldn't feel comfortable any longer…with sitting here pursuing our own practice while out there tensions were building that could destroy the planet. In former times Zen could afford to be apolitical, even during times of conflict, because whatever the damage, it was going to be limited. But when you have war machines out there that can destroy everything—well, at a certain point I just had to do something. What I knew how to do was music.[185]

Nowick performed all thirty-two Beethoven piano sonatas as well as others by Haydn in Ellsworth, Maine, to raise funds for Ground Zero, an organization that sought to reduce the threat of nuclear war. That same year, he formed the Surry Opera Company which performed Verdi's *Aida* and Mozart's *The Magic Flute* in the barn. Launching the Opera Company with non-professional singers was just as improbable an endeavor as establishing a zendo in rural Maine, but within a year of its inception, the Company was invited to perform at Wolf Trap near Washington DC. The following year the Opera Company performed Mussorgsky's *Boris Godunov* in Russian and, in 1986, made the first of several trips to the Soviet Union, inaugurating more than two decades of musical collaboration between Nowick's Company and musicians from Russia, Japan, France, and elsewhere.

Several Moonspring students were members of the chorus, but others felt that Nowick was spending too much time with music and not enough time teaching. They wrote him a letter in which they expressed their concerns. He responded with a brief hand-written reply:

> It has become distinctly clear to me that I have fully involved myself in music and that it has taken me from my work with you as a teacher. Because of this situation, I wish to inform you without further delay of my decision to resign from Moonspring as teacher. I will help in any way I can to support its growth. I hope you will accept this decision along with me as the wisest one for all of us concerned.

A handful of former students formed a board in order to maintain the zendo, and Nowick formally turned Moonspring Hermitage over to them in 1993 with the request that the name—which had been derived from his Dharma name—be changed. They reincorporated as the Morgan Bay Zendo and evolved into a center for meditation practice unaffiliated with any particular school of Buddhism.

Nowick continued to live in Surry. As Cold War tensions eased after the collapse of the Soviet Union, the Surry Opera Company gradually faded. For the remainder of his life, Nowick's energy was focused on music. He still gave piano recitals in the barn as well as in Russia and Japan. Russian musicians continued to come to the farm in Maine each summer.

Nowick maintained his personal Zen practice, but, although he visited occasionally, he remained separate from the operations of the zendo and did not resume formal teaching.

Walter Nowick died in February 2013 at the age of 87. That April, a memorial service was held at the zendo where friends and former students—many of whom had taken turns at his beside during the last weeks of his life—shared stories. The following November, a portion his ashes were buried at the Roshi Stone alongside those of his teacher, Zuigan Goto Roshi. Another portion were flown to Japan and scattered near the plot where the remainder of Goto's ashes had been interred.

Chapter Eleven
Philip Kapleau

The Three Pillars of Zen, compiled and edited—with assistance—by Philip Kapleau, was first published in Japan in 1965. One of the most influential books ever written on Zen, it has remained in print ever since and has been translated into Dutch, French, German, Italian, Polish, Portuguese, Spanish, Swedish, Vietnamese, and even Chinese. It was unique, when it first came out, in presenting Zen not as a theory or a philosophy but as a practice with a clearly defined goal.

The book consists of translations of a series of introductory lectures given by Haku'un Yasutani to beginning Zen students, a teisho by Yasutani on the koan Mu, transcriptions of private interviews with students in dokusan—something which had never previously been available in any language—and the personal accounts of eight lay practitioners, Japanese and American, who had achieved kensho. The focus of the book was specifically on zazen.

No other book on Zen then available in English had dealt with zazen in a significant way. The works which were popularly read and discussed at cocktail parties portrayed what Kapleau called "a pseudo-Zen which is little more than a mind-tickling diversion of highbrows and a plaything of beatniks."[186] These books, he stated, clogged the mind "with splinters of koan and irrelevant fragments of philosophy, psychology, theology, and poetry which churn about"[187] in the brain ultimately creating an impediment to genuine Zen practice. *The Three Pillars of Zen*, on the other hand, provided step by step instructions on how to begin the practice of zazen and was "nothing less than a manual of self-instruction."[188]

In San Francisco, Shunryu Suzuki seldom talked about enlightenment and taught his students to sit without expectations. In contrast, kensho was all important to Kapleau's understanding of Zen, as it had been to his primary teachers Haku'un Yasutani and Daiun Sogaku Harada. Without enlightenment, Kapleau declared in his outspoken manner, Zen practice was meaningless.

Kapleau's descriptions of the sesshins in which he took part in Japan were intimidating—shouting monitors, kyosakus flailing down on the shoulders of participants, and students bellowing *Mu!* with all their might. But the process was effective. The enlightenment narratives in *The Three Pillars* demonstrate that not only is kensho achievable, it is within the reach of Western lay practitioners as well as Japanese monks.

Each of the six sections of *The Three Pillars of Zen* is prefaced by an introduction by Kapleau. While he writes with the authority of someone who had attained enlightenment himself, his tone, at times, is grating. He had a strong personality. He has been described as aggressive and uncompromising as well as kind and generous. He was noted for being down to earth and yet could also be naïve, as in his belief that psychic powers were a natural by-product of zazen.

In a memorial tribute written in 2004, Rafe Martin noted that while Kapleau could

> —be tough as nails…and sprout horns and fangs to reveal, in Zen parlance, the "black piercing eyes of a devil," he could also be as sweet and gentle and subtle and sensitive and wonderfully able to bless with his presence as a spring breeze after harshest winter. He had his particular failures and shortcomings. Sometimes his maverick strength (that firm, unyielding jaw and solid chin were perfectly made for stubbornly sticking out into the wind) was, at the same time, his greatest weakness…. He had a knack for making waves. His style was to call a spade "a damn shovel!"[189]

He insisted on strict ethical standards, had strong opinions, and could be impatient and blunt with people who he thought were wasting their time (for example, by working with Soto teachers – none of whom, he held, were enlightened). He also enjoyed playing the harmonica and leading members of the Rochester Zen Center in sing-a-longs.

He was born in 1912, the fifth of six children of a working-class family in Connecticut. Neither of his parents was particularly religious. His mother attempted to enroll him in a Sunday School program, but he resisted it. By the time he had entered high school, he had progressed through agnosticism to atheism. He read Voltaire and Robert Ingersoll and tried to form an "Atheists' Club," desisting only when the school threatened to expel him.

After graduating high schoool, he took courses in shorthand and found work as a court reporter. A medical deferment kept him from being drafted during the Second World War, but, when the fighting ended, he became the Chief Allied Court Reporter at the Nuremburg Trials. Kapleau wrote that:

> The testimony at the trials was a litany of Nazi betrayal and aggression, a chronicle of unbelievable cruelty and human degradation. Listening day after day to victims of the Nazis describe the atrocities they themselves had been subjected to or had witnessed, one

was shocked into numbness, the mind unable to comprehend the enormity of the crimes.

> The grim evidence of man's inhumanity to man, plus the apparent absence of contrition on the part of the mass of Germans, plunged me into the deepest gloom.[190]

When the trials were drawing to a close, Kapleau applied to go to Tokyo to cover the war crimes trials there. The situation there, he thought, could not be worse than it had been in Germany. In fact, he found the atmosphere of the Japanese trials very different. The Japanese, unlike the unrepentant Nazis, seemed to have accepted responsibility for their actions. Kapleau wondered what caused this difference in attitude and was told by acquaintances that it was the result of the Buddhist understanding of karma—which held that the current sufferings of the people of Japan were the direct consequence of their behavior during the war.

This was Kapleau's introduction to Buddhist thought, and it intrigued him enough that he accepted the invitation of a friend, Dick DeMartino, to visit D. T. Suzuki at his cottage at Engakuji. Kapleau was impressed both by the Japanese scholar and by the serenity of the temple grounds. The discussion, however, did not go beyond theoretical. The Americans were less interested in Zen practice than they were in Buddhist philosophy and its influence on Japanese culture.

Before returning to the United States, Kapleau visited China where his interest in Buddhism was deepened after visiting the temples of Beijing. By this time he had acquired a rudimentary understanding of basic Buddhist teachings, and the conditions he had encountered in Germany, Japan, and now China resonated with the Buddha's first noble truth—that all life is characterized by suffering.

Back in Connecticut, Kapleau established a successful firm of court reporters but remained distressed by what he had seen and heard in Europe and Asia. He described his life as vacuous. In his diary entry for April 1953—included in *The Three Pillars of Zen*—he complained about stomach ulcers, allergies, and the inability to sleep at night without the aid of drugs.

He searched out books on Buddhism and Zen, attended meetings of the Vedanta Society, and investigated the Bahá'í faith. When he learned that Suzuki was giving a series of lectures at Columbia University, Kapleau drove into the city to attend them. But his study did nothing to alleviate his personal suffering.

Then a Japanese friend pointed out that Zen was not something which could be learned through books. If Kapleau were serious, the friend said, he should go back to Japan and find a transmitted teacher. "It won't be easy," the friend told him, "but you can rely on this: once you enter upon the Buddha's Way with sincerity and zeal, Bodhisattvas will spring up everywhere to help you."[191]

So in August of 1953, at the age of 41, he quit his business, gave up his apartment, sold his furniture, and returned to Japan.

It took a while for the promised Bodhisattvas to appear. Kapleau arrived in Japan with letters of introduction to two Zen masters, neither of whom was willing to accept him as a student because he did not speak the language. After a month of frustration, he ran into an American university professor, then teaching in Japan, whom he had met at Suzuki's Columbia lectures. The two of them finally received an invitation to spend two days with Soen Nakagawa at Ryutakuji.[192]

The professor and Kapleau spent the train ride from Kyoto to Ryutakuji drawing up a list of questions they proposed to ask Nakagawa in order to determine if he were a genuine Zen master. It was evening when they arrived, and Nakagawa suggested that they must be tired after their journey. They explained that there were some questions they would like to ask him, and he nodded politely, saying, "By all means. But first you must collect yourselves. I have some other matters to which I must attend, so please spend a little time in zazen, and afterwards we will talk."

He brought them to the meditation hall and indicated the cushions they were to use.

"But we don't know how to meditate," the visitors complained. "No one has ever shown us how."

"It doesn't matter," Nakagawa assured them. "Just sit still and don't speak until I return."

For two hours, Kapleau and his friend struggled unsuccessfully to find a tolerable sitting posture. They were thoroughly exhausted and dispirited by the time Nakagawa returned and did not have the energy to put their questions. "One look at me," Kapleau later told Sean Murphy, "and he had me pegged. *That* was my first lesson in Zen."[193]

The professor returned to Kyoto, but Kapleau accepted an invitation to remain at Ryutakuji, where he began his formal practice of Zen. Nakagawa made allowances for Kapleau's lack of physical flexibility. He could use a chair if necessary, or sit on his heels in the traditional Japanese seiza style, but he was kept separate from the monks in the zendo. The only meditation instruction Nakagawa gave him was, "Put your mind in the bottom of your belly, there's a blind Buddha there, make him see!"[194]

Three weeks after arriving at Ryutakuji, Kapleau was introduced to Yasutani, who was paying a visit to Nakagawa accompanied by Nakagawa's friend—and the man who would later become Yasutani's chief disciple and heir—Koun Yamada. They talked about the upcoming Rohatsu Sesshin which was to take place at Hossinji, in the city of Obama, under the direction of Yasutani's teacher, Daiun Harada. Kapleau asked Yasutani if he believed it were possible for an American to achieve satori in a seven day retreat. Yasutani replied, "You can get it in *one day* of sesshin if you're genuinely determined to and you surrender all your conceptual thinking."[195]

Nakagawa was uncertain whether Kapleau could withstand the rigors of Harada's methods, especially since the Rohatsu sesshin was the most demanding retreat of the year. He was finally convinced to take Kapleau to Hossinji after receiving a letter from Yasutani which included a report of the enlightenment experience Yamada had after their visit to Ryutakuji. Nakagawa believed the coincidence was evidence of a karmic link between Kapleau and Yamada.

Harada was a more severe and demanding teacher than Nakagawa, and the rules governing the sesshin were strict. For seven days, the participants would not speak, bathe, or shave. Kapleau was assigned the koan Mu and was told to forget all the theories he had about Buddhism and focus solely on *Mu!* "Put your mind in the *hara*, the pit of your stomach," Harada instructed, "and breathe only *Mu!* in and out."

The physical pain of sitting on cushions, even with frequent changes of posture, was agonizing. The blows of the kyosaku were more distracting than encouraging. And Harada's manner during dokusan was intimidating. But Kapleau persisted.

On the fourth day, he was given a chair and, grateful for this concession, threw himself with renewed vigor into the practice, focusing with such energy that he passed out. When he came to, he was in bed, Nakagawa seated beside him. Nakagawa congratulated him, and Kapleau asked if that meant he had achieved satori. "No, but I congratulate you just the same," Nakagawa said.[196]

After Rohatsu, Kapleau returned to Ryutakuji. The following April, he took part in a second sesshin at Hossinji following which, with Nakagawa's encouragement, he was accepted as a student by Harada and spent three years with him as a lay monk. During this time, his allergies vanished, but the severe conditions and the diet, which was inadequate for one used to Western food, left him physically exhausted. In November of 1956, health problems forced him to leave, and he came back to Ryutakuji.

That Rohatsu, Nakagawa arranged for Kapleau to participate in a sesshin presided over by Yasutani. Because Yasutani's students were all lay persons, Nakagawa believed it would be a more suitable environment for Kapleau. Although the atmosphere of the sesshin was taut, it was not as severe as that at Hossinji, and Kapleau felt he had finally found his teacher.

Between December 1956 and July 1958, Kapleau took part in nineteen sesshins under Yasutani's direction. The week long sesshin of the following August would be his twentieth, and he entered it with the conviction that he was close to a breakthrough. By the third day, he had attained such a degree of concentration that his responses to the Roshi's questions during dokusan came quickly and spontaneously.

The crisis came on day four. The previous evening he had continued his practice late into the night, completely focused on Mu. At one point he stood up to go to bed and "staggered into a nearby fence. Suddenly I realized: the fence and I are one formless wood-and-flesh Mu."[197] Energized, he continued sitting until the morning gong rang. When Kapleau next went into dokusan, Yasutani could see that he was on the verge of a deep realization. He asked a number of testing questions, many of which Kapleau responded to immediately. Yasutani smiled and pointed out that some roshis would accept Kapleau's replies as evidence of awakening. Before Yasutani finished speaking, however, Kapleau interrupted him and said:

> I wouldn't accept sanction of such a picayune experience even if you wanted to grant it. Have I labored like a mountain these five years only to bring forth this mouse?[198]

Kapleau threw himself "into Mu for another nine hours with such utter absorption that *I* completely vanished."[199] Kapleau did not eat breakfast, Mu did; Kapleau did not sweep the floor during the work period, Mu did. Then in the afternoon dokusan, Yasutani told him:

> "The universe is One.... The moon of Truth—" All at once the roshi, the room, every single thing disappeared in a dazzling stream of illumination and I felt myself bathed in a delicious, unspeakable delight.... For a fleeting eternity I was alone—I was alone.... Then the roshi swam into view. Our eyes met and flowed into each other, and we burst out laughing....
>
> "I have it! I know! There is nothing, absolutely nothing. I am everything and everything is nothing!"[200]

Years later, a student would ask Kapleau whether, relatively speaking, the koan Mu was easy or hard to solve. "Both," Kapleau answered. "Easy in this sense: When you resolve it you realize that the 'answer' was there all the time. And hard because it takes longest to see what is closest to you.""[201]

Kapleau remained with Yasutani for another six years, doing further koan work. Over time, his command of Japanese became proficient enough that he was able to act as translator for western students who came to study with Yasutani. He married one of these students, and they had a daughter.

While at Hossinji, Kapleau had had the idea of writing a book about actual Zen practice to balance the idealized portraits of Zen more commonly available. As he continued his training, he began work on it with the assistance two of Yasutani's students, including Koun Yamada, with whom, according to Soen Nakagawa, he was karmically linked."[202]

In addition to Yasutani's talks and dokusan, the book included a sampling of the letters of the 14th century master, Bassui[203] and a chapter from Dogen's *Shobogenzo*. But the most compelling part of the book was the section which presented eight personal enlightenment accounts.

Yasutani began his introductory talks by explaining that there were several types of Zen practice ranging from *bompu* Zen—in which the goal is simply to improve one's ability to concentrate—through practice undertaken solely for one's own benefit and onto the higher forms by which the practitioner seeks enlightenment not only for himself but for the benefit of others as well. The fundamental instrument for all forms of Zen is zazen.

Zazen has three aims: first, the development of the powers of concentration, which leads—second—to kensho or awakening, and, finally, the integration of the enlightenment experience into all aspects of one's life. *The Three Pillars of Zen* provided enough detailed information about zazen—posture, regulating the breath, focusing attention—that readers without access to a qualified Zen teacher were able to begin practice on their own.

Zazen, they were told, differed from other spiritual practices in

> —that the mind is freed from bondage to *all* thought-forms, visions, objects, and imaginings, however sacred or elevating, and brought to a state of absolute emptiness, from which alone it may one day perceive its own true nature or the nature of the universe.[204]

It was also pointed out that Zen practice was not limited to the time spent in seated meditation. "Being attentive in the details of your daily life," Yasutani insisted, "is also training in Zen."[205]

The goal of practice was enlightenment, the first experience of which was *kensho*:

> —the direct awareness that you are more than this puny body or limited mind. Stated negatively, it is the realization that the universe is not external to you. Positively, it is experiencing the universe as yourself. So long as you consciously or unconsciously think in terms of a distinction between yourself and others, you are caught in the dualism of I and not-I. This I is not indigenous to our True-nature, being merely an illusion produced by the six senses.[206]

Kapleau and Yasutani are careful, however, to stress that kensho in itself is not the culmination of Zen practice. "Enlightenment," as Kapleau would explain in another book, "is not a static condition; it is capable of endless enlargement."[207] This was something he recognized within his own life. As one of his heirs, Mitra Bishop, later remarked:

> He never quit practicing, never quit working on himself. He sat zazen daily without fail, and as soon as he could see where he was caught in some negative habit pattern, that was simply the end of it; I never saw it again in him. It was remarkable. There he was, growing older and older—a time in life when so many people get frozen in their negative habit patterns—and he continued to practice zazen and he continued to practice The Long Maturation; he continued to grow.[208]

In 1965, Kapleau—who by then had completed about half of the 800 koans used in the Harada-Yasutani school—was ordained a Zen priest by Yasutani and was given permission to teach. He was not, however, given *inka*, or transmission, the "formal acknowledgement on the part of the master that his disciple has fully completed his training...."[209] Given the increasing numbers of westerners coming to Japan to study Zen, both Yasutani and Kapleau felt it appropriate that the latter should return to the United States and introduce authentic Zen practice there.

Before he left Japan, Kapleau received a visit from Ralph Chapin, an American who had heard that one of his countrymen was studying Zen and was curious meet him. When Chapin came to Kapleau's apartment, the galley proofs for *The Three Pillars of Zen* were spread out on the floor. He read a few paragraphs and asked Kapleau to send him twenty copies once it was in print. When Chapin received them, he passed them out to members of a Vedanta group to which he belonged in Rochester. Chester and Dorris Carlson were also members of the group, and they were so impressed with *The Three Pillars* that they distributed another 5000 copies to libraries throughout the country.[210]

Kapleau accepted an invitation from the Carlsons to come to Rochester, which then became his home base in the United States. His first students were members of the Vedanta group organized by Dorris consisting largely of women in their forties who were exploring various religious traditions. Kapleau taught them how to sit zazen and set up a regular schedule of sittings. The group, however, did not show up on Sunday mornings because most of them were also regular church attendees.

Then younger people, who had read *The Three Pillars,* began to make their way to Rochester. Some had begun to follow the instructions provided in it. When the numbers were sufficient, in 1966, Kapleau rented a larger house and converted one of the rooms into a zendo. Most of the members of the Vedanta studies group fell away, but the young people stayed and formed the nucleus of the Zen Meditation Center of Rochester. Yasutani Roshi came to the city to lead sesshin. Soon a residential program was initiated. Kapleau attempted to establish a monastic community as well but was unsuccessful. Like Yasutani, his work would be with lay people.

And there were more than enough of these making their way to Rochester: both single individuals and couples, sometimes with young children, from across the United States, Canada, Mexico, and even Europe. They came expecting the training to be rigorous, and it was. In the early years of the Rochester Center, people talked of "boot-camp Zen." The kyosaku was used robustly. When the dokusan bell rang, meditators exploded off their cushions in order to get into line because there was never time for all of them to meet with the teacher. Sunyana Graef described the atmosphere:

> In the moments before dokusan began, the inspiring words of the monitors, followed by the vigorous whacking of the stick, created an intensity bordering on hysteria. The zendo filled with crackling energy, adrenaline surging, hearts pounding, as everyone waited for Roshi's handbell to signal the start of dokusan. The instant the bell rang, students flew off their mats to be first in the waiting line. Races to dokusan resulted in more than a few injuries over the years. Once Bodhin Kjolhede and I, responding to the bell, jumped off our mats at precisely the same instant. As we hurtled though the zendo doors, we collided, falling to the ground in a heap. The people coming from behind did not even slow down; they just

ran around us like a stream flowing past a rock. As for us, we helped each other up, dusted ourselves off, and resumed the race.

The highly charged atmosphere of sesshin was often compared to a pressure cooker, an apt analogy. The pressure was so great that people occasionally broke under the strain. The sound of the kyosaku alone, even without feeling its stinging bite, was enough to dissuade some sitters from attending a second sesshin. All this was done for the purpose of helping students come to awakening. And it worked. It was a rare sesshin conducted by Roshi Kapleau when no one "broke through."[211]

Kapleau experimented with the ritual forms of Zen, seeking adaptations which seemed appropriate for Americans. Instead of the traditional Japanese takahatsu begging rounds undertaken to foster humility, Zen Center students cleaned up sidewalks and street gutters in the blocks around the center. In addition to maintaining the area, the clean-up won the respect of the center's neighbors.

Not all of his adaptations, however, were successful. Rafe Martin recounts the following story:

> Once he had a turkey brought into the Buddha Hall at Thanksgiving. It had been purchased by the Zen Center to be released, but now the bewildered bird flapped about anxiously. Roshi got us all chanting and, sure enough, the frightened bird grew calm. Then Roshi put his hands together and bowed deeply to the turkey in gassho style saying, "Turkey bows to turkey."[212]

At an introductory workshop in Rochester, one of the attendees asserted with confidence, "All religions are one."

"One what?" Kapleau inquired.

At another workshop, a young man told Kapleau, "I'm Jewish, and I'm proud of my Jewish heritage. Can one practice Zen and remain a Jew?"

"What were you before you were a Jew?" Kapleau asked.

Mitra Bishop was older than many of the other members of the Zen Center and, during one retreat, had difficulty making her way through the rush to the dokusan line, besides which she did not feel she had anything to report. So when the bell rang, she remained on her cushion. After couple of days of that, a monitor pulled her out of the kinhin line[213] and ordered her to dokusan.

> I went in, several feet off the floor, assuming I'd had kensho. Kapleau Roshi said, "Why haven't you been to dokusan?" And I said, "I didn't have anything to say." He pulled himself up and roared at me, *"Don't you think I might have had something to say to you!"*

When Kapleau and his eventual successor—Bodhin Kjolhede—were in Mexico, Bodhin found a scorpion in their quarters and asked, "Should I kill it?"

"If you can do so completely without malice," Kapleau said, "go ahead. Otherwise you should find some other way of getting rid of it."

Kapleau developed Parkinson's Disease in his 80s. He turned his teaching responsibilities over to senior students and retired to two rooms at the Center. One day he fell in his bedroom and struck his head against the wall. A student, Victoria Kieburtz, visited him not long after and noticed the indentation in the wall where Kapleau had hit it.

> "I heard you took a fall," I said, continuing lightly, "Well, it's a good thing you have a hard head."
>
> Roshi's smile widened, "Oh," he replied, as if relishing the opportunity, "I had another breakthrough."[214]

Dosho Port, who became a student and heir of Dainin Katagiri, tried to visit the Rochester Zen Center when he was young but was unable to find it. Many years later, while attending a meeting of the American Zen Teachers' Association hosted by the Rochester Center, he at last had an opportunity to meet Kapleau.

> He was very old and sick by then, and they wheeled him out into the courtyard, with blankets wrapped around him. We all lined up and came to greet him. When I met him, I smiled and told him I'd read his book and how important it was and how it changed my life. He looked up, sized me up a little bit, and then said, "For the better, I hope."[215]

In his efforts to adapt Zen practice to North America, Kapleau minimized traditional Japanese ritualism and arranged for English translations of the chants, in particular the *Heart Sutra*.[216] Yasutani was not happy with the changes his student was making, and Kapleau, on his part, stubbornly refused to make concessions. Yasutani further took offence when Kapleau suggested he should not make use of Eido Shimano—about whom he had reservations—as a translator during a scheduled tour of the United States. The two became estranged, and Yasutani died not long after, precluding a chance for a reconciliation.

Later Kapleau would express regret over his intransigence, but the immediate question was his status within the traditional Zen establishment. Because he had not completed koan training or received transmission (inka), he was not formally recognized by either the Soto or Sanbo Kyodan hierarchies. On the other hand before Kapleau had returned to the United States, Yasutani had given him permission to teach and had presented him with a robe and bowl symbolic of that authorization. Kapleau decided that this was adequate endorsement to continue teaching. He was careful not to claim to be a transmitted Zen master although—after he learned that Richard Baker was using the term—he, too, adopted the title "roshi." He pointed out, however, that the word only meant "venerable teacher":

> —that is, one who commands respect and reverence by reason of age or great dignity. The abbot of a monastery, the chief priest of a temple, or a lay teacher beyond the age of, say, fifty could be addressed as roshi and the title would simply imply deep respect....
> —it is not a title signifying completion of a prescribed course of study or in recognition of high spiritual accomplishments.[217]

There were people in the emerging American Buddhist community for whom the formalities of transmission were of primary importance. They would question Kapleau's legitimacy, but most of his students remained loyal to him. A bigger challenge, however, came from within the Rochester sangha itself.

Although the boot-camp Zen practiced at the Rochester Center in the early years was effective with some people, it was not for everyone. Many of the sitters in the late 1960s and into the 70s were in their twenties, a time of life when it is perhaps easier to undertake that type of physical and psychological challenge. But by the start of the 1980s, some members were raising questions.

In 1981, Kapleau took a group of students to Santa Fe in order to establish a new center there. He was tired of the winters in Rochester and was considering retiring to the Southwest. In his absence, he left his senior disciple, Toni Packer, in charge of the Zen Center. Once she was on her own, Packer found herself increasingly uncomfortable with some of the forms used at the center, in particular the practice of having students prostrate themselves before her. She instituted a number of changes which some other senior members believed subverted the taut atmosphere necessary for Zen practice. Then, shortly before Kapleau was scheduled to return to Rochester, Packer flew down to Mexico City—where he was working on a new book—and informed him that she could no longer continue to work within the Buddhist tradition. She left the Zen Center and established her own group, which would eventually settle at Springwater, about an hour south of Rochester. Nearly half of the Center's members went with her. Others, discouraged by the divisions in the community, fell away from practice altogether.

When he returned, Kapleau supported some of the changes that Packer had implemented, and the samurai atmosphere of the 1960's and 70's began to mellow. He

> —eliminated the shoving, pushing, and shouting, reduced the severity and frequency of the encouragement stick, and at the same time pruned the encouragement talks of their blood-and-guts quality. More Americans, we found, responded well to this training atmosphere than to the strictly Japanese version that preceded it.[218]

Kapleau acknowledged several heirs who—regardless of the question of his transmission—have been recognized as significant and effective teachers in their own right.

He died in May 2004 in the garden at the Rochester Zen Center, surrounded by grateful students and disciples. When his body, dressed in Zen robes and rakusu, was laid out, students placed a few parting gifts in the coffin. Included among them were some of his favorite chocolate bars and a harmonica. He was buried at the country retreat of the Zen Center at Chapin Mill. The grave is marked by the former mill's large grind stone.

Chapter Twelve
Dainin Katagiri

Dainin ("Great Patience") Katagiri established his Zen Center neither on the west coast nor in New York state, where virtually all other centers at that time were located, but in Minneapolis. It was at least as unexpected a location as Surry, Maine. Unlike Nowick, however, Katagiri was not returning home; he chose the mid-west city because he hoped that there he would be able to bring Zen to ordinary American students, instead of to the counter-culture youth—hippies and flower children—who were tenanting other centers.

Katagiri could be a stern, at times intimidating, teacher. His Dharma heir, Dosho Mike Port, credited him with having a "world-class frown," emphasized by heavy black eyebrows, when formally seated in dokusan or giving a lecture. He could also be exuberant, frequently exclaiming, "How sublime life is!" He enjoyed television, drank cheap red wine—indifferent to whether it came from a bottle or a box—and did not adhere to a strict vegetarian diet. He taught a more formal style of Soto Zen than did Shunryu Suzuki, in spite of which, he elicited great affection and loyalty from his students.

He was born in Osaka in 1928. His birth name—Yoshiyuki—means "Good Luck." He was the last of ten children, and his family believed him to be the reincarnation of an elder sister who had drowned. He apparently shared this belief. Years later, when a student in Minneapolis confessed that he could not accept the idea of reincarnation, Katagiri replied, "Perhaps you will in your next life." He was surprised when the students thought he was making a joke.

The family were devout Pure Land (Shin) Buddhists, who gathered every morning to chant in front of the family shrine before beginning their daily chores. When Yoshiyuki was five, his father—Kashichi—opened a restaurant in Tsuruga on the coast. The business kept both parents occupied. Yoshiyuki grew up with a youngest child's fervent love for a mother who was so overwhelmed with family and business responsibilities that she had little time to give her son any individual attention. He would later treasure those few moments they had alone together, and he was deeply affected by her death when he was fourteen years old.

The War in the Pacific was raging by then. Soon the young Yoshiyuki's name belied him, and, a year after his mother's death, he was drafted into the armed forces. The Japanese government had called up all males over the age of twelve. He went into the air force and, for a time, hoped to become a pilot but was unable to qualify. He became, instead, a battlefield mechanic. He was conflicted about his military service and later said that there were times in battle when he could not bring himself to aim his weapon at the enemy but, rather, fired over their heads.

In spite of his reservations about the war, Katagiri was as devastated by the Japanese surrender as were the rest of his countrymen, especially the young. Many felt betrayed by those leaders who had demanded enormous sacrifices but whose policies had culminated in defeat and occupation. His family's restaurant had been destroyed by Allied bombing runs, and they were destitute. Katagiri found work, drawing on his experience as an air force mechanic, but he was depressed and unsure what value or significance his life held.

Everything in Japan changed after the surrender. Some 500 Japanese officers immediately committed ritual suicide following the Emperor's radio broadcast announcing the end of the war. Hundreds more would be executed as war criminals. American soldiers patrolled the streets and were in control of all national activities. Every major city in the country—except Kyoto which Allied forces had spared because of its religious importance—had been devastated by bombing; the manufacturing industry was in shambles. Poverty was the norm even for families which had been well-off; food shortages would continue for years.

The only place where things seemed to continue as they had before the war were the Buddhist temples such as Eiheiji. Here monks spent their days, as they always had, in meditation and labor, in chanting and performing rituals for the benefit of others. Here there was the illusion of something permanent and stable in a world which—as Buddhism teaches—is characterized by impermanence. Katagiri was drawn to Zen as much out of a nostalgia for a lost way of life as from a hope that it would help him find peace and a sense of meaning.

At the age of 18, Katagiri sought out his first teacher, Daicho Hayashi. Hayashi was a temple priest in the small fishing village of Taizoin in Fukai Prefecture. Later Katagiri would explain that Hayashi did not so much teach Zen as exemplify it in the way he served the needs of his community not only as a Buddhist priest but as the local soothsayer. Katagiri was trained to perform memorial rituals and to chant sutras; he also spent time grooming the grounds and the small cemetery attached to the temple.

In 1946, Katagiri received the precepts from Hayashi and was given the Buddhist name Jikai Dainin, Ocean of Compassion, Great Patience. Katagiri did not feel very patient and for a long while avoided using the name Dainin.

After a short time, Hayashi determined that Katagiri should undergo formal training. It had been his intention to send his student to Hossinji, which was then under the direction of Sogaku Harada. Katagiri, however, felt drawn to the more formal training temple, Eiheiji, and Hayashi ultimately granted him permission to go there. "Remember, however," he instructed the young man, "no one else can change you. You alone can change yourself."

Eko Hashimoto was the novice master at Eiheiji. At their first formal meeting, Hashimoto gave his new charges this simple instruction, "Sit. Become Buddha." Katagiri was not entirely certain what was being asked of him, but he threw himself into the practice of shikan taza with all his will.

The first retreat he participated in happened to be the strenuous Rohatsu Sesshin. Monks rose at 2:00 in the morning and did not go to bed until 10:00; the more earnest students even sacrificed those few hours for further zazen practice. Katagiri was unused to such uninterrupted sitting and, at one point, passed out from the pain in his legs. The other monks carried him out of the zendo and threw him into the snow. When he revived, he returned to his cushion and continued meditating.

His commitment to practice was noticed, and he was appointed Hashimoto's attendant, a post usually reserved for more experienced students. It was a demanding position. Without being told what to do, the attendant was required to anticipate each of his master's needs—when to bring out his slippers, when to take them away, when to provide tea, when to clean up. The attendant was reprimanded whenever he failed to act promptly; there was no praise for carrying out the duties as expected. Successful attendants needed to be alert.

Direct instruction was seldom provided at the temple. Younger monks simply emulated older monks. There were appropriate ways to carry out every activity—even walking. One senior monk scolded the students for their undue haste when moving about. When the monastery was shaken by an earthquake, Katagiri observed this monk maintain his usual attentive pace while others rushed from the area, even taking time to blow out a burning candle by an altar before leaving the temple.

Katagiri studied Dogen's writings and sought to follow the instructions he found there—even Dogen's arcane directives on how to properly use the privy. First one snapped one's fingers

> —three times (to alert any god-realm beings in the vicinity to move out of harm's way) and then afterward wiping your butt using small, damp clay balls about one inch in diameter—though this latter practice had not been maintained for a really long time. [Katagiri], however, did his best to follow the instructions to the letter. The other monks thought this was going too far.[219]

After three years at Eiheiji, Katagiri received transmission from Hayashi, then went to Tokyo where he earned a Master's Degree in Buddhist studies at Komazawa University. While studying there, he lived with Kakudo Yokoi under whom he continued his training. It was also in Tokyo that he met Tomoe, the woman who would become his wife. They both studied English with the same teacher.

Training under Yokoi was much as it had been with Hashimoto; the student's personal identity was to be dissolved in service to his master. Nor was the rigorous shikan taza practiced by the Soto school undertaken to attain anything. It was done, as Dogen had specified, for its own sake. Katagiri was fond of telling the story of a time when he was studying the *Lotus Sutra* and came upon a passage that struck him so with such impact he was certain he had attained awakening. Exhilarated, he rushed to Yokoi and announced, "I have attained enlightenment!"

Yokoi looked up from the work he was doing and replied, pithily, "Don't be stupid."

After graduation from university, Katagiri worked in the International Division of the Soto headquarters, Sotoshu Shumucho. He had responsibility for the temples that had been established in the United States, and one of his early duties was to see Shunryu Suzuki off at the airport when he left to go to San Francisco. Brief as it was, it was their first meeting.

In 1963, Bishop Reirin Yamada of Zenshuji in Los Angeles requested that Sotoshu Shumucho send a priest to assist him. Katagiri applied for the position and was accepted. He did not have adequate funds to bring Tomoe and their infant son with him, so they remained behind when he went to the United States.

He was 35 and pictured himself as a missionary to the Americans. There was a large Japanese congregation at Zenshuji and several priests, including Taizan Maezumi. The bishop wanted Katagiri to work with the English-speaking second and third generation members. So Katagiri had no contact with Western students and found his time at Zenshuji tedious.

During a visit to San Francisco, he was re-introduced to Shunryu Suzuki. Although Sokoji was not as large as Zenshuji there seemed a lot more going on, and, when Suzuki invited Katagiri to be his assistant there, the younger man accepted with alacrity. His first duties were to the Japanese congregation at Sokoji which was pleased to have him, but he saw that Suzuki's interest was in the young Western students who showed up at the door seeking instruction in meditation. These students were unlike anything with which Katagiri was familiar. They were largely undisciplined, morally lax, used drugs, and often lacked even basic hygiene. He did not believe they could be serious students of Buddhism.

Katagiri proved to be more formal than Suzuki in many ways and might have sought to establish stricter guidelines for the American students. For example, when

Tassajara was opened, Katagiri opposed having both men and women train there. He was overruled but accepted without question that each temple had only one abbot or teacher. Sokoji was under Suzuki's direction, and Katagiri set aside his own inclinations in order to follow the lead of the abbot.

Although many things in America remained strange to him, Katagiri was happy to be there and within a year arranged for his wife and son to join him. The Japanese community welcomed them as well, and the Katagiris received frequent invitations to dine, which were accepted with gratitude because his income was wholly inadequate to meet the family's needs.

In Japan, Zen was increasingly seen as one of the archaic institutions young people sought to shed in their quest to reestablish their nation as a modern industrial and intellectual power. In the United States, on the contrary, youth were turning to Zen as a way of seeking release from what they perceived as stifling social conditions. Katagiri struggled to overcome his distaste for the counter-culture members and committed himself to work with them. When Katagiri arrived in San Francisco, Suzuki had about fifteen American students. That number increased steadily, and soon the zendo needed to be expanded. Katagiri was given responsibility for overseeing the renovations.

Katagiri worked with Shunryu Suzuki from 1963 until 1971. In 1969, when Suzuki left Sokoji to focus on his American students at their new facilities on Page Street, Katagiri went with him. Suzuki appointed him Master of Training, and told the students that Katagiri was now to be formally addressed as Roshi. Suzuki depended on Katagiri and trusted him but also took him for granted. When it became clear that Richard Baker was Suzuki's intended heir, Katagiri wondered what future he had at Zen Center.

Then a guest teacher, Sotan Tatsugami, was brought from Japan in 1970 at Baker's invitation in order to lead some practice periods at Tassajara, and Katagiri was asked to serve as his translator. He resented it. He began to think about starting his own zendo. He had the idea of operating one where what he considered ordinary Americans could learn the Dharma. As much as he had come to respect the commitment of the hippies at SFZC, he recognized that they did not represent mainstream America.

In 1971, while Suzuki was recovering from an operation to remove his gall bladder, Katagiri sent him a get-well card in which he enclosed a letter announcing that he was leaving Zen Center. It caught Suzuki off guard, and he implored Katagiri to stay a while longer, pleading ill health and even arranging for Tatsugami to be sent back to Japan. Katagiri remained reluctant, and it was not until various students told him that they considered him as much their teacher as Suzuki that he agreed to stay a while longer.

Suzuki's plan was for Baker to become abbot and for Katagiri to function as senior teacher, but that was not enough for Katagiri. He took part in Baker's Mountain Seat Ceremony, even acted as Suzuki's proxy during portions when the older teacher—debilitated by cancer—was too weak to continue. But with Baker's installation as abbot, Katagiri knew it was time to leave SFZC.

Katagiri's first attempt to establish his own zendo was at his own home in Monterey. Then, in 1972, he received an invitation from a small group in Minneapolis which included Robert Pirsig, author of the bestselling *Zen and the Art of Motorcycle Maintenance*.

The Katagiris packed their few possessions into a U-Haul trailer and, with the help of some Zen Center students, made the move to Minnesota. There Katagiri would have an opportunity to be a trailblazer. He pictured a Sangha of working people coming to the center before or after they went to their jobs.

He specifically asked his former students in California not to follow him; a few ignored that request and came anyway. Then, ironically, other young people from throughout the Midwest heard that a Zen master had moved to Minnesota and sought him out. The numbers were never large—at the time Katagiri left San Francisco, SFZC was already huge; Minneapolis would remain small—nor were they kind of students Katagiri had imagined, but they were committed. The first major influx was made up of members from Stephen Gaskin's commune in Tennessee. Gaskin, an activist and counter-culture leader, was one of the inspirations behind a number of communal efforts, including Robert Aitken's early community on Maui.

Pirsig donated $20,000 for the purchase of a building to house the center and provide accommodations for the teacher and his family. A former half-way house for drug addicts was found on Lake Calhoun. It was in poor repair, but the Tennessee commune members had sufficient carpentry skills to put things in order. The zendo, located in what had been the living room, became redolent with the incense Katagiri had sent from Eiheiji in Japan. Rows of zabutons and zafus were arranged before a small altar adorned with a figure of the Buddha. The Center was officially inaugurated on February 1, 1976.

Two years later, Katagiri also opened a training center on 280 acres of former grazing land in the hills two miles from the Mississippi. He called the center Hokyoji—Catching the Moon.

The form of Zen Katagiri taught was demanding. For him, Buddhist practice was the practice of clear seeing, of perceiving things as they are rather than as one wishes or imagines them to be. One of the most basic characteristics of being, Buddhism teaches, is impermanence. Nothing remains static. Nor does anything have a permanent identity. Katagiri, who had a facility with analogies, used the example of water:

> —all phenomena in the world are constantly appearing, disappearing, and changing based on the conditions functioning in the moment. If you study water according to Buddhism, you may say, "Well, as a human being I think it is water for me to drink, but if I were a fish I would think that it is my house, my world. To me it is water, but to a fish it is not water." There are a hundred different ways to understand water, because a moment of existence is really complicated.
>
> The understanding that water has no permanent identity is the difference between Buddhism and our usual sense of things.[220]

Suffering (the Buddha's First Noble Truth) is essentially the result of the human desire (Second Noble Truth) that things be other than they are, the desire for permanence and stability in a world where they do not exist. People generally respond to that suffering in one of two ways. The more common is to seek relief through the pursuit of pleasure and a futile quest for physical security. The other is to develop what Katagiri calls "a way-seeking mind" and the quest for spiritual security (Third and Fourth Noble Truths).

> Spiritual security means you are fully alive and comfortable in your life as it is, without expecting anything. With a calm, way-seeking mind, you can face the naked nature of time, whatever happens, without escaping into your own ideas of progress or meaning, relief or satisfaction. This is the way to find real relief and satisfaction, but it's not so easy to do.[221]

This spiritual security is acquired through zazen.

> As a human being, you inherently have a great capability that enables you to realize…truth and to experience your life with deep joy.
>
> To know this joy we practice looking at ourselves with a calm mind. That is Zen meditation, called *zazen*.[222]

But this "deep joy" can only come about if one undertakes zazen without expecting anything from it. If one takes up the practice with expectations, those expectations cloud the ability to see clearly. Like Shunryu Suzuki—and in stark contrast to Philip Kapleau—the student is told not to strive for anything in particular. "When you do zazen, don't have any expectations. You don't know what will happen. Zen Masters always tell you, 'Don't expect enlightenment—just sit!'"[223]

> Buddhism is really hard, particularly Dogen's teaching. He gives you a very hard practice: Keep your mouth shut and look directly at impermanence! This living practice is called zazen. Zazen is not a way to escape from life by being mindful of something that is apart from the human world; it is the practice of being present in the real stream of time and looking directly at life itself. Zazen enables you to plunge below the surface and leads you to touch the core of your life. It's not so easy. But even so, you have to do it, because spiritual life originates from the direct observation of impermanence.[224]

In 1983, the San Francisco Zen Center was in crisis. In a situation unprecedented in Zen anywhere in the world, the students had dismissed their teacher.[225]

Richard Baker had built SFZC into a multi-million dollar empire. In addition to owning their practice center at Tassajara and several buildings in the area around their City Center zendo, they owned and operated the premier vegetarian restaurant in San Francisco (Greens), a bakery, a stitchery (zafus and zabutons), and an organic farm (Green Gulch). SFZC also had the largest membership of any Zen center in the country and numerous wealthy donors.

Baker was a huge personality. In addition to being an often inspiring teacher, he was an astute businessman. But as SFZC grew and administrative issues preoccupied him, he had less time for direct contact with his students. He also had a number of sexual relationships—often with vulnerable women—which were known about but overlooked until it was discovered that he was having an affair with the wife of a major donor to SFZC. The donor threatened a law suit, and the board was finally compelled to act. Although the sexual affair precipitated the rupture between Baker and SFZC, other factors contributed as well. Whereas Shunryu Suzuki had washed Elsie Mitchell's windows, Baker held elaborate dinner parties for entertainment celebrities and political figures during which Zen Center students were expected to serve as silent wait-staff. His management style was one which left senior members of SFZC feeling their contributions to the center were undervalued.

Baker still had loyal students; but, in the end, his critics outweighed his supporters, and he was forced to resign. In 1984, finding themselves without a teacher and still unclear about the direction they wanted to go, the board contacted Katagiri and asked him to return to the city in the capacity of "Interim Abbot" for one year.

Katagiri was proud of what he had accomplished in Minnesota, but there was no doubt that being abbot of the San Francisco Zen Center was the most prestigious position in North American Zen. He came fully expecting to be appointed permanent abbot after the year was up. Katagiri told the board he was willing to work with Tenshin Reb Anderson, Baker's only transmitted Dharma heir, and help him develop his capacity to take over the duties of abbot. Anderson was still relatively young, and Katagiri assumed it would be some time yet before Anderson would be considered qualified. Some board members, however, were eager to have Anderson assume the position of abbot immediately. He was in Shunryu Suzuki's direct lineage; Katagiri was not. When the year was up, Katagiri was not asked to remain. People close to him believed that it broke his heart.

In *Shoes Outside the Door*, Michael Downing reports that one of the reasons some SFZC board members decided not to invite Katagiri to remain was the anger of Minnesota students that their teacher had been poached. By 1985, Katagiri was back in Minneapolis, and, if he was disappointed, he never let it show.

As word of Katagiri's prowess as a teacher spread, high caliber students made their way to Minnesota. He was committed to their training and wanted to ensure that the center remained in the official Soto tradition. He even arranged for appropriate students to pursue additional training in Japan.

For Katagiri, zazen was shikan taza. "In Rinzai Zen," he asserted, "they sit with many questions, many koans. In Soto Zen, we have just one big koan, so called *shikantaza*."[226] Students sat shikan taza and adhered to the four vows. By doing so, they were to overcome their own desires and learned to live in service to others. Katagiri called this "Selfishnessless." It was a practice which required perseverance and promised, as Katagiri put it, "no sweet candy." He kept admonishing his students to "continue under all circumstances!"

James Ishmael Ford's first experience of Zen practice took place at the San Francisco Zen Center when Katagiri was assisting Shunryu Suzuki. On his first visit, he was directed to the dokusan room where Katagiri was seated. "How long have you been practicing Zen?" Katagiri asked.

"About half an hour," Ford admitted truthfully.

"Good! Keep that mind!"

Arnold Kotler also described a dokusan experience with Katagiri at SFZC. He was attending sesshin and on the fifth day:

> —I felt myself having a breakthrough that seemed to be similar to the *satori* experiences described in *The Three Pillars of Zen*. I sat on my cushion, clenched my teeth, tightened all the muscles on my face, and felt waves of nausea traversing through me. I was sure this was "It." So I asked to see one of the teachers, Dainin Katagiri Roshi, to tell him of my extraordinary accomplishment.
>
> Waiting outside the *dokusan* (interview) room, I thought about the laudatory response the teacher would give me when I told him what had happened. The bell from the teacher's room rang. I stood up, bowed from the waist at the door, bowed again inside the door, did three full prostrations, sat down, and told Katagiri about my experience. He looked at me deeply and finally said, "Not so good. Please go take a warm bath and rest for a while."[227]

Katagiri's bluntness and precise use of English frequently caused problems. An often repeated story tells of a fund-raiser members of the Minneapolis Zen Center put together. In Yvonne Rand's version, quoted by Sean Murphy, she explains that the center members decided to host an old-fashioned tea party.

So they got all their grandmothers' linen tablecloths, and silver and tea cups, and made sandwiches with the crusts cut off. They invited what were described as the "Minneapolis/St. Paul Swells"—all the people of wealth and prestige, none of whom had ever gone to the Zen Center, or were ever likely to.

At a certain point, after the guests had arrived, Katagiri Roshi came down the stairs, looking radiant, as he could in his robes. He looked at everyone, welcomed them, and began, "You know, of course, we all will die."[228]

The guests left early, and the hoped for donations did not materialize.

Katagiri was asked to give a seminar at a conference in Chicago on yoga and related matters. Katagiri entitled his presentation: "Zazen Is Useless." No one attended the talk.

During a discussion period for new students at the Minneapolis Zen Center, a number of beginners talked about the physical pain they suffered during zazen, complaining about aching legs and backs. Katagiri listened with his eyes lowered, seated formally in full lotus posture and dressed in his ceremonial robes. After a while he cleared his throat, and the discussion stopped. Without raising his eyes, he said, "You will not know how much pain you're in until you are awakened."

According to Dosho Port, none of the students returned.

Dosho also describes a trip he took with Dainin Katagiri during which they a nine-hour delay at the San Francisco airport. Katagiri found one of

> —those awful blue-colored plastic airport chairs, and he just sat down and waited, and every few hours he would get up and go to the bathroom. There were other people with us, but I saw myself as his attendant, so I was trying to do what he did. But after two or three hours, I told him, "I'm going to take a walk." So I walked

around a bit and came back, and he was still sitting there, so I sat down next to him. A moment or two later, he leaned over and said, "You're not a very patient person."[229]

Natalie Goldberg was one of the students who, in spite of the challenges of practice, kept coming back. She recorded her experiences with Katagiri in *Long Quiet Highway: Waking Up in America.* As a new student at the Center, she did not have much personal contact with the teacher. Her first extended conversation came when she was asked to interview him for the Center's newsletter. The editor of the newsletter thought the interview would also provide an opportunity for Goldberg to get to know Katagiri better.

> I agreed to do it, but I wasn't very interested. Roshi had yet to captivate me. The morning of the interview, I woke up obsessed with what color material to get for curtains. After all, I had just gotten married and we were making a home for ourselves.
>
> I drove to Zen Center to interview Roshi with that curtain obsession blazing in my mind. I planned to get the interview over with and then rush to the fabric store.
>
> I parked in front of Zen Center and dashed out of the car. I was a few minutes late. I was halfway up the walk when I realized I'd left my notebook on the front seat. I dashed back to the car, grabbed the notebook, and ran to the back entrance of Zen Center. I flung open the door, spun around the corner, and came to a dead stop: Roshi was standing in the kitchen by the sink in his black robes, watering a pink orchid. That orchid had been given to him three weeks before. Someone had brought it from Hawaii for a Buddhist wedding I had attended. It was still fully alive.
>
> "Roshi," I said in astonishment and pointed at the orchid.
>
> "Yes." He turned and smiled. I felt the presence of every cell in his body. "When you take care of something, it lives a long time."

My mouth fell open. Suddenly, I didn't know anything, but for a moment I knew I didn't know anything, and that was a great opening. This human being before me was present. We could say, "Be here now," my generation, but I'd never encountered anyone before who was present.[230]

In January of 1989, Katagiri was diagnosed with terminal cancer. He determined that he needed to ensure his work continued after his death, so in the autumn of that year, even though he was severely ill, he began formal ceremonies to give transmission to twelve of his students. He chose not to identify any of them as his principal heir; it was his intention that they remain peers, equally responsible for continuing the spread of the Dharma. The ceremonial process lasted from October 5th until December 8th.

By the end of the year, he was spending longer periods in the hospital. He received chemotherapy and radiation as well as traditional Asian medicines, but the disease continued to spread. Students who no longer lived in Minnesota returned to see their teacher one last time. He remained inspirational; even in his hospital bed, he continued zazen. One day when he was no longer able to come downstairs to the zendo, he asked his students to come to his bedside. "You are all observing me," he noted, "waiting to see how a Zen master dies. I will show you." Then he began kicking his legs and throwing his arms about, screaming, "I don't want to die! I don't want to die!"

The students stared, speechless.

Katagiri settled down and looked at each one of them. "I don't know how I will die. Maybe I will die in fear or in pain. Remember, there is no right way."[231]

Dainin Katagiri died on March 1, 1990, at the age of sixty. For three days before its cremation, the body lay in a plain wood coffin in the Zendo. The crematorium allowed his students to place the coffin in the oven and turn on the gas which fed the flames that burned the body.

A portion of his ashes was buried near those of Shunryu Suzuki at Tassajara; another was buried on a hilltop overlooking Hokyoji.

When Katagiri first went to Minnesota, other than Walter Nowick's community in Maine, all the other Zen Centers in the continental United States were in New York state or on the West Coast. By the time of his death, active communities had been established in Nebraska, Iowa, Wisconsin, North Carolina, and even Alaska. It appeared that the work of the early pioneers—both Japanese and American—who worked to establish Zen in North America had borne fruit. It did not take long, however, to discover how fragile their success was.

In *Long Quiet Highway,* Natalie Goldberg described some of the things that she had valued in Katagiri as a teacher.

> I could go into dokusan, speak to him straight, and be answered straight. And never for a moment did I have to be concerned about him crossing a sexual boundary. I did not have to close down or protect myself. This is no small feat given the sexual transgressions of many spiritual teachers today.[232]

In addition to the sexual indiscretions of Eido Shimano in New York, Maezumi in Los Angeles, and Baker in San Francisco, it turned out that one of the factors behind the departure of students from Moonspring Hermitage in Maine had been unwanted sexual advances Walter Nowick made to certain of his male students. By 1990, Zen centers across the country were engaged in controversy. Rochester still had not wholly healed after Toni Packer left, taking a large number of students with her. An eminent Japanese teacher in California was infamous for touching female students inappropriately during sanzen. A second generation teacher suffered an apparent descent into mental illness. And the problems in San Francisco continued: The teacher who had been chosen abbot instead of Katagiri made national headlines after brandishing a gun in a low-income housing project.

Then, after his death, it was revealed that Katagiri had also had affairs with female students. Natalie Goldberg remembered, after her book had been published, an awkward pass he had made at her. She felt betrayed. Many other people in many other centers throughout the United States did as well.

Zen had made the difficult journey across the Pacific to North America; it had spread from one coast to the other. The early teachers—whatever their faults—had been strong and charismatic, effective and compassionate. But they left unanswered questions that their successors would need to deal with: questions about ethical issues, about financial matters, about management styles, about transmission and succession, about who was authorized to teach and who had the sanction to authorize, about the degree to which Zen needed to retain Japanese cultural characteristics, about the differences between lay and ordained practice, about what training Zen teachers should have.

Zen was established in North America, but it still remained to be seen if it would survive.

Epilogue in Clatskanie

In 2002, the people of the small, self-professed Christian community of Clatskanie, Oregon, were dismayed to learn that the former elementary school just outside of town had been purchased by a group of Zen Buddhists from Portland. Residents of Oregon still remembered the Rajneesh Movement in Wasco County which, twenty years earlier, had been found guilty of using salmonella against their perceived enemies in the largest bio-terror act ever perpetrated within the United States. More than 700 people had been poisoned. Now another cult was trying to establish itself in their state and in their town.

The Buddhists invited the people of the community to a gathering so they could introduce themselves. "We expected about fifty people to come," Jan Chozen Bays, the principal teacher of the center, remembers, "because this is a community of about 1700 people. And we had tea and we had cookies and we had name tags; we had little tables to sit and chat. But when I came in, everybody was lined up. Nobody would wear name tags, and they were afraid to drink the tea, afraid that it was poisoned Kool-Aid. They wouldn't eat the cookies. All lined up in chairs. 200 people."

Chozen is a pediatrician, a deeply compassionate woman, and a Dharma heir of Taizan Maezumi. She was also one of the students with whom Maezumi had been sexually involved. After the crisis at the Los Angeles Zen Center in the '80s, Chozen left California and spent a great deal of time trying to understand the dynamics of appropriate and inappropriate behavior within religious communities. Reflecting on her own situation and on some of the things that had taken place in Los Angeles, she questioned what "enlightened behavior" was and whether she wanted anything to do with it.

In 1984, she moved to Oregon because her sister lived there and she felt a need for family support. It was not her intention to establish a Zen Community.

"I wanted to get the kids out of LA and into a more healthy environment. LA was not a healthy environment for them. There was a lot of bullying in school, and they went backwards academically. So that was a motive. I felt like the family had, to a certain extent, been neglected while we were at the Zen Center because we were so focused on getting enlightened. And I had divorced, too, so there was that trauma to the kids. And so I felt I needed to gather the family together and be closer to other family members.

"And then this thing of, 'Wow! If that's enlightened behavior, I don't want anything of it.' So I reacted against practice for several years. I didn't sit at all. Got a job. 'Cause I had to support the kids now that I was divorced and left the Zen Center. Worked back in medicine again, including academic medicine. Just hunkered down and took care of family and lived an ordinary life."

She and her second husband explored other religious traditions. She had only done Zen for such a long time that she no longer felt she had any perspective. But nothing they attended satisfied them, and slowly they began to sit again, at first by themselves and then with an existing sitting group in Portland. When the leader of that group moved to Mexico, other members approached her.

"The group was without a leader, and they asked would I be willing to lead the group. So the way I would say it is, I built up the practice again step by step. I sat and sat, and 'Oh, yeah, I can see how sitting is helpful.' I had to learn everything afresh. 'Yeah. Sitting is helpful and I can understand now.' Then they wanted services, would we lead the services? So, I did some services. Then they wanted to know would I do a talk once a month? I did a talk once a month. It was only by request. I didn't move forward at all myself. Then would I do interviews? I started doing interviews. And each time, I was saying, 'Is this valuable? And on what basis does it need to be founded on?'"

She was supported in her return to practice by Maezumi, who had reconciled with enough members of the Los Angles community to keep that center operating. He even came to Oregon to assist her when the community asked her to perform a jukai ceremony for those who wanted to formally profess Buddhism.

The Portland Community grew and eventually opened a small training center on Larch Mountain in the Colombia Gorge. When that property was declared part of a federal protective area, they searched for another location. They learned that the school district in Clatskanie had been reconfigured and that the Quincy-Mayger Elementary School with its surrounding grounds was for sale.

Chozen was working at the hospital the night of the meet-and-greet, so she arrived late. "And when I walked in, this woman was saying, 'I would not speak unless my husband had given me permission to speak. And he has given me permission to speak. And I just want to say: What's wrong with all you Christians out there? Can't you feel the hand of darkness? Can't you feel the aura of Satan? These people are here to steal the souls of our children!' I thought, 'Wow! Have we made a mistake!' But then I could see some people rolling their eyes as if, 'There she goes again.' And I thought, 'Okay, they don't all believe this.'"

The Buddhists stayed and slowly won the trust of the community. Chozen's husband and fellow teacher, Hogen, joined the local Kiwanis Club. Chozen taught marimba to local school children.

"And we send our young men down when the old guys can't set up the tent for their 4th of July barbecue, or on Clatskanie Clean Up Days, when people bring in their old appliances, our young guys go down and throw appliances in dumpsters. But they have revealed over the years—we've been here I think twelve years—they have revealed what they thought about us at the beginning. So one year, when we'd been here about three years, at the Clatskanie Clean Up Day they were having coffee and donuts with some of our young men, and they said, 'Oh, when you first came here they said you'd steal all the cars and eat babies. Ha! Ha!'"

I stayed at the Clatskanie River Inn during my visit to Great Vow Monastery. In the morning as I set out to interview Chozen, I asked the desk clerk what the people of the town thought about the monastery. "Very good neighbors," she told me. "They bring a lot of business to the community. We're glad to have them."

During our interview, Chozen told me that what she calls the prime directive of Zen is to ensure that the Dharma—the teaching—continues. Zen has established a foothold in North America, but it remains to be seen how firm that foothold is. The fact that Chozen and Hogen were able to overcome local anxieties and establish a practice in rural Oregon is a good first indicator. But Zen practice is challenging and difficult, and the numbers of people drawn to it remain still small. And there is the issue of succession. If Great Vow is able to survive Chozen and Hogen, when they eventually have to cease teaching, that will be an even stronger indicator.

Within fifty years of Shunryu Suzuki's arrival in San Francisco, the American Zen Teachers Association listed 224 members leading centers, temples, and monasteries throughout the US, Canada, and Mexico. They represent a range of teaching, practice, and social engagement well beyond what the pioneers who brought Zen across the Pacific could have imagined, and they continue to find new and unique ways of adapting Zen to contemporary situations. In addition to regular zazen schedules, sesshin, and other traditional practices, they have found applications which go well beyond the zendo.

Sunyana Graef, one of Philip Kapleau's Dharma heirs, dedicated her Vermont Zen Center to Kannon, the Bodhisattva of Compassion. The kyosaku is not used at the Center, and one of Sunyana's senior students—Dharman Rice—regularly offers workshops on "Loving-Kindness Meditation" which draw people who frequently have no other interest in Zen.

Bernie Tetsugen Glassman has led street retreats in New York City in which participants experience the conditions of homelessness. He has held "Witnessing

Retreats" at Auschwitz and in Rwanda. A Witnessing Retreat is being considered for Wounded Knee. Many of the participants are not Zen students at all.

John Tarrant, of the Pacific Zen Institute, views koans as a "designed learning system" which transcends the culture in which they were developed, and he uses them in psychological counseling as well as in retreats where participants may have no meditation practice whatsoever.

Chozen Bays has become recognized in Europe as well as in America for her success in using Zen mindful eating practice as a way to help people with eating disorders.

Zen Mountain Monastery in the Catskills offers Wilderness Training programs with a zazen component. Zen centers operate hospices and offer prison outreach programs.

The questions left by the pioneers who brought Zen to America continue to be considered and addressed. The way these teachers and others are seeking to resolve them is a fascinating story, but it is a story to be told elsewhere.

COMING SOON FROM SUMERU BOOKS

Cypress Trees in the Garden

The Second Generation of Zen Teaching in America

Cypress Trees in the Garden continues the story of the establishment of Zen in North America, with profiles on many of the leading 21st Century teachers, including:

Jan Chozen Bays	Genjo Marinello
Mitra Bishop	Eshu Martin
Melissa Blacker	Toni Packer
Josh Bartok	Bobby Rhodes
Shinge Sherry Chayat	David Rynick
James Ford	Joshu Sasaki
Bernard Tetsugen Glassman	Richard Shrobe
Sunyana Graef	Henry Shukman
Shodo Harada	Steve Stucky
Blanche Hartman	Joan Sutherland
Taigen Henderson	John Tarrant
Robert Kennedy	Mel Weitsman
Bodhin Kjolhede	Gerry Shisshin Wick
John Daido Loori	. . . and others
Elaine MacInnes	

Acknowledgements

Charles E. Tuttle Publishing for permission to quote material from Taizan Maezumi, *Teaching of the Great Mountain*.

Shinge Roko Sherry Chayat Roshi, Abbot of the Zen Studies Society for permission to quote material from Louis Nordstrom (ed.), *Namu Dai Bosa*. New York: Theatre Arts Books, 1976.

Nyogen Senzaki, excerpts from *Like a Dream, Like a Fantasy: The Zen Teachings and Translations of Nyogen Senzaki* copyright © 2005 by the Zen Studies Society. Excerpts from *Eloquent Silence: Nyogen Senzaki's Gateless Gate and Other Previously Unpublished Teachings and Letters* copyright © 2008 by the Zen Studies Society. Both reprinted with the permission of The Permissions Company, Inc., on behalf of Wisdom Publications, www.wisdompubs.org.

The Rochester Zen Center for their rendition of the Four Vows.

Endnotes

1. Alan W. Watts, *The Way of Zen* (New York: Vintage Books, 1957), p. 3.
2. Richard Bryan McDaniel, *Zen Masters of Japan: The Second Step East* (Rutland, VT: Charles E. Tuttle Co., Inc., 2013), Chapter Three.
3. *Gongan* in Chinese.
4. Richard Bryan McDaniel, *Zen Masters of China: The First Step East* (Rutland, VT: Charles E. Tuttle Co., Inc., 2012), Chapter Twelve.
5. Cf. *Zen Masters of China,* Chapter Nineteen.
6. Sticks, rather than paper, were used for personal hygiene.
7. The suffix "ji" means "temple"
8. D. T. Suzuki, *The Field of Zen* (New York: Perennial Library, 1970), pp. 1-2.
9. Cf. *Zen Masters of Japan,* Chapters Sixteen and Seventeen.
10. The term *roshi* in Japanese means "venerable old one;" it is essentially a title of respect. In North American Zen, *roshi* has come to mean someone authorized to teach Zen.
11. Quoted in Rick Fields, *How the Swans Came to the Lake* (Boulder: Shambala, 1981), p. 138.
12. Suzuki, op. cit., p. 10.
13. D. T. Suzuki, *Essays in Zen Buddhism: First Series* (London: Rider and Company, 1973), p. 261.
14. Cf. *Zen Masters of China*, Chapter Six.
15. Pinyin: *Daodejing.*
16. Quoted in Peter Matthiessen, *Nine-Headed Dragon River* (Boston: Shambala, 1998), p. 14.
17. Cf. *Zen Masters of China,* Prologue.
18. "Buddha and Zen" in Suzuki, *The Field of Zen*, pp. 13-20.
19. Bodhi roughly means wisdom—to see things are they actually are rather than as one thinks of them.
20. Suzuki's first book, *A New Theory of Religion,* had been published in Japan in 1896. He was 26 years old and had not yet come to awakening. The book has

been cited as evidence that Suzuki supported Japanese militarization during the Meiji Era and the Sino-Japanese War. It is unfair, however, to maintain that the essays in this volume reflected the point of view of the more mature Suzuki during the Second World War and afterwards.

21. D. T. Suzuki, "An Autobiographical Account" in Masao Abe (ed.), *A Zen Life: D. T. Suzuki* (New York: Weatherhill, 1986), p. 24.
22. Robert Aitken, "Openness and Engagement: Memories of Dr. D. T. Suzuki" in Masao Abe (ed.), *A Zen Life: D. T. Suzuki*, pp. 211-12.
23. Alan Watts, "The 'Mind-less' Scholar" in in Masao Abe (ed.), *A Zen Life: D. T. Suzuki* (New York: Weatherhill, 1986), p. 190.
24. D. T. Suzuki, *Essays in Zen Buddhism: First Series* (London: Rider and Company, 1973), p. 268.
25. Nyogen Senzaki, *Eloquent Silence* (Boston: Wisdom Publications, 2008) p. 367.
26. Sutras (the teachings of the Buddha), the Abhidharma (commentaries on the Sutras), and Vinaya (rules regulating Buddhist, in particular monastic, life).
27. Cf. *Zen Masters of Japan,* Chapter Fourteen.
28. Deshan Xuanjian; cf. *Zen Masters of China*, Chapter Sixteen.
29. Pinyin: Lungtan.
30. Senzaki, op. cit., pp. 170-171.
31. Ibid., p. 370.
32. Ibid., p. 238.
33. Guishan Lingyou and Deshan Xuanjian in Pinyin. Cf. *Zen Masters of China*, Chapter Fourteen.
34. Senzaki, op. cit., p. 41.
35. Ibid.
36. Ibid., p. 102.
37. *Chants and Recitations* (Rochester: Rochester Zen Center, 2005), p. 36.
38. Quoted in Louis Nordstrom, *Namu Dai Bosa* (New York: Theatre Arts Books, 1976), p. 24.
39. Cf. illustrations of Chapters Eleven through Twenty of *Zen Masters of China*.
40. Senzaki, op. cit, p. 329.
41. Ibid., p. 332.
42. Ibid., p, 335.
43. The Bodhisattva of Compassion.
44. Senzaki, p. 338.
45. Quoted in Fields, op. cit, p. 194.
46. Quoted in Nordstrom, op. cit., p. 90.
47. Ibid., p. 107.

48. Ibid., p. 89.
49. Ibid., p. 59.
50. Quoted in Fields, op. cit., pp. 218-19.
51. Michael Hotz (ed.), *Holding the Lotus to the Rock*. (New York: Four Walls Eight Windows, 2003) e-edition, location 452.
52. Ibid., location 462.
53. Ibid., location 469.
54. Cf. *Zen Masters of China*, Chapter Three.
55. Sokei-an Sasaki, "The Transcendental World" in *Zen Notes,* I:5, First Zen Institute of America, New York, 1954 [http://www.firstzen.org/1954.php], p. 1.
56. Hotz, op. cit., location 1216.
57. Mary Farkas, "Zen Talks, II" in *Zen Notes,* XIII:6, First Zen Institute of America, New York, 1966, [http://www.firstzen.org/ZenNotes/1966/196606_Vol_13_No_06_June_1966.pdf]p. 4.
58. Ibid., p. 6.
59. Hotz, op. cit. location 1230.
60. Ibid., locations 2010-2016.
61. Ibid., location 240.
62. Ibid., location 250.
63. Ibid., location 562.
64. Ibid., location 1556.
65. Ibid., location 1850.
66. Alan Watts, *In My Own Way* (New York: Vintage Books, 1973), p. 166.
67. The Four Noble Truths are: 1) All of existence is characterized by suffering (dukkha); 2) Suffering is caused by craving; 3) Suffering can be ameliorated by overcoming craving; 4) Craving can be overcome by following the Noble Eightfold path, which consists of right view, right intention, right speech, right action, right livelihood, right effort, right mindfulness, and right meditation.
68. Cf. *Zen Masters of China*, Chapter Ten.
69. Jack Kerouac, *The Dharma Bums*. (New York: Signet Books, 1959). p. 6.
70. Ibid., p. 52.
71. Cf. *Zen Masters of China*, Chapter Ten for samples of Snyder's renderings.
72. Quoted in John Suiter, *Poets on the Peaks* (Washington D C: Counterpoint, 2002), p. 245.
73. I take refuge in the Buddha; I take refuge in the Dharma; I take refuge in the Sangha (community).

74. Gary Snyder, "Spring Sesshin at Shokoku-ji" in *The Gary Snyder Reader* (Washington D C: Counterpoint, 2012), electronic version, location 513.
75. Van de Wetering's impressions of Snyder and Walter Nowick, as well as the training they underwent, is recorded in his book, *The Empty Mirror*.
76. Gary Snyder, Jim Harrison, Paul Ebenkamp (ed.), *The Etiquette of Freedom* (Berkeley: Counterpoint, 2010), p. 32.
77. Rick Fields, *How the Swans Came to the Lake* (Boulder: Shambhala, 1981), p. 361.
78. "The East West Interview" in *The Gary Snyder Reader* (Washington D C: Counterpoint, 2012), electronic version, location 1400.
79. Jim Dodge, "Ten Snyder Stories" in Jon Halper (ed.), *Gary Snyder: Dimensions of a Life.* (San Francisco: Sierra Club Books, 1991), p. 156.
80. Jack Kerouac, op. cit., p.11.
81. Quoted in John Suiter, *Poets on the Peaks* (Washington D C: Counterpoint, 2002, p. 109.
82. Ibid., p. 111.
83. Cf. *Zen Masters of China*, Chapter Five.
84. Hisao Kanaseki, "An Easy Rider at Yase" in Jon Halper (ed.), *Gary Snyder: Dimensions of a Life.* (San Francisco: Sierra Club Books, 1991), p. 73.
85. Suiter, op. cit., p. 245.
86. Helen Tworkov, *Zen in America* (San Francisco: North Point Press, 1989), p. 224.
87. Sean Murphy, *One Bird, One Stone* (New York: Renaissance Books, 2002), p. 63.
88. Isshu Miura and Ruth Fuller Sasaki, *Zen Dust* (New York: Harcourt, Brace & World), p. 4.
89. Alan Watts, "Beat Zen, Square Zen, and Zen" in *This Is It* (New York: Collier Books, 1967), p. 91.
90. "Great Buddha."
91. Alan Watts, *In My Own Way*, pp. 96-97.
92. Ibid., pp. 152-53.
93. Ibid.
94. Kerouac, op. cit., pp.153-54.
95. Alan W. Watts, *The Way of Zen*, pp ix-x.
96. Ibid.
97. Ibid.
98. Ibid., p. 111.
99. Pinyin: Mazu.
100. Pinyin: Nanyue.

101. See *Zen Masters of China*, Chapter Five, for the complete story.
102. Philip Kapleau, *The Three Pillars of Zen* (Boston: Beacon Press, 1969), p. 22.
103. James Ishmael For, *Zen Master Who?* (Boston: Wisdom Publications, 2006), pp. 64-65.
104. Monica Furlong, *Zen Effects* (Woodstock, VT: Skylight Paths, 2010), p.188.
105. Interview with author, June 24, 2013.
106. Alan Watts, *In My Own Way*, p. 426.
107. R. H. Blyth, *Zen in English Literature and Oriental Classics* (Mineola, NY: Dover Publications, 2003), p. vii.
108. Ibid.
109. Cf. *Zen Masters of Japan*, Chapter Fourteen.
110. Robert Aitken, *Taking the Path of Zen* (New York: North Point Press, 1982), p. 118.
111. John Tarrant quotations from an interview with the author, March 24, 2013.
112. "The Fellowship of the Three Treasures" which are the Buddha, the Dharma, and the Sangha. In 2014, the school was renamed Sanbo Zen.
113. A traditional but meaningless shout.
114. Robert Aitken, op. cit. 123.
115. There are two ranks of "Zen Master" in the Sanbo Zen school. The first is *junshike*, roughly equivalent to "associate Zen Master." The second, *shoshike*—which Aitken received in 1985—conveys full transmission. Aitken was the only American to receive full transmission from Yamada, and that was later questioned by Yamada's heirs. The issue eventually resulted in the Diamond Sangha separating from the Sanbo Kyodan School, in what Aitken described as an "amicable divorce," in 1995.
116. Robert Aitken, op. cit., p. 14.
117. Ibid., p. 10.
118. Ibid., p. 11.
119. Ibid., p. 24.
120. Robert Aitken, *Encouraging Words*. (New York: Pantheon, 1993). p. 22.
121. Helen Tworkov, op. cit., p. 47.
122. Dale Pendell, "A Raven in the Dojo: Gary Snyder and the Dharma" in Jon Halper (ed.), *Gary Snyder: Dimensions of a Life*. San Francisco: (Sierra Club Books, 1991). pp. 315-16.
123. Cf. *Zen Masters of Japan*, Chapter Two.
124. Shunryu Suzuki, *Zen Mind, Beginner's Mind* (New York: Weatherhill, 1994), p. 21.
125. Cf. *Zen Masters of Japan*, Chapter Fifteen.
126. Cf. *Zen Masters of China*, Chapter Eight.

127. Shunryu Suzuki, op. cit., pp. 26-27.
128. Ibid., p. 28.
129. Ibid., p. 49.
130. Ibid., p. 29.
131. Ibid., p. 53.
132. Elsie P. Mitchell, *Sun Buddhas, Moon Buddhas* (New York: Weatherhill, 1973), pp. 189-90.
133. David Schneider, *Street Zen* (Boston: Shambhala, 1993), pp. 99-100.
134. Kazuaki Tanahashi and Roko Sherry Chayat (eds.), *Endless Vow* (Boston: Shambhala, 1996), p. 8.
135. As quoted by Soen Nakagawa, in Tanahashi and Chayat, Op. Cit., pp. 10-11.
136. Cf. *Zen Masters of Japan*, Chapter Fourteen.
137. Cf. *Zen Masters of Japan*, Chapter Seven.
138. Trans. by Nyogen Senzaki, Op. cit., p. 55.
139. See page 24 above.
140. Quoted in Nordstrom, Op. cit., p. 129.
141. Peter Matthiessen, Op. cit., p. 3.
142. Ibid., pp. 32-33.
143. Cf. *Zen Masters of Japan*, Chapters One and Two.
144. *San* is an honorific roughly equivalent to Mr.
145. Nordstrom, Op. cit., p. 189.
146. Kapleau, Op. cit., p. 242.
147. Referring, at least in part, to the koan of the *Mumonkan* in which Nanquan Puyuan [J:Nansen], the teacher of Zhaozhou [J:Joshu], cuts a cat in two. Cf. *Zen Masters of China,*, Chapter Eleven.
148. Nordstrom, Op. Cit., p. 213.
149. A detailed description of the inauguration is provided in Nordstrom, pp. 215-16.
150. From an interview with the author, Februay 19, 2014.
151. Matthiessen, Op. cit., p. 275.
152. Helen Baroni, *Love, Roshi* (Albany: State University of New York Press, 2012), e-edition, location 678.
153. From an interview with the author, July 15, 2013.
154. Jan Chozen Bays quotations from an interview with the author, March 28, 2013.
155. Matthiessen, Op. cit, p. 240.
156. Joan Yushin Derrick quotations from an interview with the author, June 8, 2013.

157. Gerry Shishin quotations from an interview with the author, October 12, 2013.
158. Taizan Maezumi, *Teaching of the Great Mountain* (Rutland, VT: Tuttle Publishing, 2001). p. 14.
159. Taizan Maezumi and Bernie Glassman, *On Zen Practice*. (Boston: Wisdom Publications, 2000), p. 3.
160. Ibid., p. 20.
161. Ibid., p. 4.
162. Ibid., p. 22.
163. Ibid.
164. Maezumi, *Teaching of the Great Mountain*, p. 4.
165. Ibid., p. 61.
166. Ibid., p. 81.
167. Maezumi and Glassman, Op. Cit, p. 25.
168. Philomene Long, *American Zen Bones* (Los Angeles: Beyond Baroque Books, 1999), p. 11.
169. Sean Murphy, Op. cit., p. 77-78.
170. Cf., *Zen Masters of Japan,* Chapter Eight.
171. Janwillen van de Wetering, *A Glimpse of Nothingness* (New York: St. Martin's Griffin, 1975), p. 10. Van de Wetering wrote three semi-fictional books on Nowick; in the first two (*The Empty Mirror* and *A Glimpse of Nothingness*), Nowick is called "Peter." In the third (*Afterzen*), he is called "Sensei."
172. Hugh Curran quotations from an interview with the author, June 5, 2013.
173. Sarah LeVine, *A Brief History of Moonspring Hermitage* (Surry, ME: Morgan Bay Zendo, 2008), p. 6.
174. Ibid., p. 6.
175. Nordstrom, Op. cit., p. xii.
176. Murphy, Op. cit., p. 150.
177. Lenore Straus's description of her kensho is included in Kapleau, Op. cit., pp. 250-54.
178. LeVine, Op. cit., p. 17.
179. Cf. *Zen Masters of China,* Chapter Eleven.
180. Van de Wetering, *A Glimpse of Nothingness*, p. 132.
181. From an interview with the author, June 5, 2013.
182. LeVine, Op. cit, 35-36
183. Janwillem van de Wetering, *The Empty Mirror* (Boston: Houghton Mifflin Company, 1974), p. 36.
184. Van de Wetering, *A Glimpse of Nothingness,* pp. 37-38.
185. Murphy, op. cit., pp. 150-51.

186. Kapleau, *The Three Pillars of Zen*, p. xv.
187. Ibid., p. 84.
188. Ibid., p. xvi.
189. http://www.rafemartin.com/articles7.html.
190. Philip Kapleau, *Zen: Merging of East and West* (New York: Anchor Books, 1989), p. 261.
191. Kapleau, *The Three Pillars of Zen*, p. 209.
192. See Chapter Eight, pages 171-72, for two stories from this visit.
193. Sean Murphy, Op. cit., p. 22.
194. Kapleau, *The Three Pillars of Zen*, p. 213.
195. Ibid.
196. Ibid., p. 219.
197. Ibid., p. 227.
198. Ibid.
199. Ibid.
200. Ibid., p. 228.
201. Kapleau, *Zen: Merging of East and West*, p. 84.
202. Philip Kapleau is given title page credit for editing and "writing" *The Three Pillars of Zen*, but the issue remains a touchy one within the Sanbo Zen school, where it is widely believed that both Yamada and Akira Kubota should have received equal credit.
203. Cf. *Zen Masters of Japan*, Chapter Seven.
204. Kapleau, *Zen: Merging of East and West*, p. 13.
205. Kapleau, *The Three Pillars of Zen*, p. 77.
206. Ibid., p. 137.
207. Kapleau, *Zen: Merging of East and West*, p. 69.
208. Mitra Bishop quotations from an interview with the author, October 8, 2013.
209. Kapleau, *The Three Pillars of Zen*, p.333.
210. Bodhin Kjolhede recounted this story during an interview with the author, June 20, 2013. Ralph Chapin became a sometime member of the Rochester Zen Center and, at the end of his life, donated to it a country property now known as Chapin Mill.
211. Sunyana Graef, "Seeing the Ox: A Second Look" in Kenneth Kraft (ed.), *Zen Teaching, Zen Practice* (New York: Weatherhill, 2000), p. 110.
212. http://www.rafemartin.com/articles7.html.
213. *Kinhin* is the period of walking meditation which take place between rounds of sitting.

214. Victoria Kieburtz, "The Authoritative Gaze," in Kenneth Kraft (ed.), *Zen Teaching, Zen Practice* (New York: Weatherhill, 2000), p. 84.
215. From an interview with the author, July 14, 2013.
216. Cf. *Zen Masters of China*, pp. 126-27, for the Rochester translation.
217. Kapleau, *Zen Merging of East and West*, p. 30.
218. Ibid., pp. xxvi-xxvii.
219. Dosho Mike Port, *Keep Me in Your Heart a While* (Boston: Wisdom Publications, 2009), p. 43.
220. Dainin Katagiri, *Each Moment Is the Universe* (Boston: Shambhala, 2011), p. 27.
221. Ibid., p. 13.
222. Ibid., p. 4.
223. Ibid., p. 14.
224. Ibid., p. 10.
225. The story of Richard Baker and Zen Center is recorded, in what James Ishmael Ford called "excruciating" detail, in Michael Downing's *Shoes Outside the Door*.
226. Dosho Port, *Keep Me in Your Heart a While*, p. 21.
227. Arnold Kotler, "Philip Kapleau, Shunryu Suzuki, and Thich Nhat Hanh" in Kenneth Kraft, *Zen Teaching, Zen Practice* (New York: Weatherhill, 2000), p. 86.
228. Sean Murphy, *One Bird, One Stone* (New York: Renaissance Books, 2002), pp. 103.
229. From an interview with the author, July 14, 2013.
230. Natalie Goldberg, *Long Quiet Highway*. (New York: Bantam, 1994). pp. 110-12.
231. Jack Kornfield, *After the Ecstasy, the Laundry* (New York: Bantam, 2001), p. 150.
232. Goldberg, Op. cit., 197.
233. Jan Chozen Bays quotations from an interview with the author, March 28, 2013.

Bibliography

Abe, Masao (ed.), *A Zen Life: D. T. Suzuki Remembered.* New York: Weatherhill, 1986.

Addiss, Stephen and Stanley Lombardo and Judith Roitman (eds.). *Zen Sourcebook.* Indianapolis: Hackett Publishing Company, 2008.

Aitken, Robert. *Encouraging Words.* New York: Pantheon, 1993.

Aitken, Robert. *Taking the Path of Zen.* New York: North Point Press, 1982.

Baroni, Helen J. *Love, Roshi.* Albany: State University of New York Press, 2012.

Blyth, R. H. *Zen in English Literature and Oriental Classics.* Mineola, NY: Dover Publications, 2003.

Chadwick, David. *Crooked Cucumber.* New York: Broadway Books, 1999.

Coleman, James William. *The New Buddhism.* New York: Oxford University Press, 2002.

Cook, Francis Dojun. *How to Raise an Ox.* Boston: Wisdom Publications, 2002.

Downing, Michael. *Shoes Outside the Door.* Washington D. C.: Counterpoint, 2002.

Fields, Rick. *How the Swans Came to the Lake.* Boston: Shambhala, 1992.

Ford, James Ishmael. *Zen Master Who?* Boston: Wisdom Publications, 2006.

Furlong, Monica. *Zen Effects.* Woodstock, VT: Skylight Paths Publishing, 2001.

Goldberg, Natalie. *Long Quiet Highway.* New York: Bantam, 1994.

Goldbert, Natalie. *The Great Failure.* New York: HarperOne, 2005.

Halper, Jon (ed.). *Gary Snyder; Dimensions of a Life.* San Francisco: Sierra Club Books, 1991.

Heine, Steven and Dale S. Wright (eds). *Zen Masters.* New York: Oxford University Press, 2010.

Hotz, Michael (ed.). *Holding the Lotus to the Rock.* New York: Four Walls Eight Windows, 2003.

Kapleau, Philip. *Straight to the Heart of Zen.* Boston: Shambhala, 2001.

Kapleau, Philip. *The Three Pillars of Zen.* New York: Anchor, 1989.

Kapleau, Philip. *Zen: Merging of East and West.* New York: Anchor, 1989.

Katagiri, Dainin. *Each Moment Is the Universe.* Boston: Shambhala, 2011.

Katagiri, Dainin. *Returning to Silence.* Boston: Shambhala, 1988.
Kerouac, Jack. *The Dharma Bums.* New York: Viking Adult, 2008.
Kornfield, Jack. *After the Ecstasy, the Laundry.* New York: Bantam, 2001.
Kraft, Kenneth (ed), *Zen Teaching, Zen Practice.* Boston: Weatherhill, 2000.
Kraft, Kenneth (ed.). *Zen: Tradition and Transition.* New York: Grove/Atlantic, 1988.
LeVine, Sarah. *A Brief History of Moonspring Hermitage.* Surry, ME: Morgan Bay Zendo, 2008.
Long, Philomene. *American Zen Bones.* Los Angeles: Beyond Baroque Books, 1999.
Low, Albert, *Hakuin on Kensho.* Boston: Shambala, 2006.
Low, Albert, *What More Do You Want.* Rutland, VT: Tuttle Publishing, 2013.
Low, Albert. *Zen Meditation Plain and Simple.* Rutland, VT: Tuttle Publishing, 2000.
Maezumi, Taizan. *Teaching of the Great Mountain.* Rutland, VT: Tuttle Publishing, 2001.
Martin, Andrea. *Ceaseless Effort: The Life of Dainin Katagiri.* Published by the Minnesota Zen Meditation Center: http://mnzencenter.org/katagiri/bio_pdf/katagiri_biography.pdf.
Matthiessen, Peter. *Nine-Headed Dragon River.* Boston: Shambala, 1998.
McDaniel, Richard Bryan. *Zen Masters of China: The First Step East.* Rutland, VT: Tuttle Publishing, 2012.
McDaniel, Richard Bryan. *Zen Masters of Japan: The Second Step East.* Rutland, VT: Tuttle Publishing, 2013.
Mitchell, Elsie P. *Sun Buddhas Moon Buddhas.* New York: Weatherhill, 1973.
Miura, Isshu and Ruth Sasaki. *Zen Dust.* New York: Harcourt, Brace and World, 1966.
Morgan, Bill. *The Typewriter Is Holy.* Berkeley: Counterpoint, 2010.
Murphy, Sean. *One Bird, One Stone.* New York: Renaissance Books, 2002.
Nordstrom, Louis (ed.). *Namu Dai Bosa.* New York: Theatre Arts Books, 1976.
Oppenheimer, Mark. *The Zen Predator of the Upper East Side.* The Atlantic Books, 2013.
Port, Dosho Mike. *Keep Me in Your Heart a While.* Boston: Wisdom Publications, 2009.
Reps, Paul and Nyogen Senzaki. *Zen Flesh, Zen Bones.* Rutland, VT: Tuttle Publishing, 1998.
Schneider, David. *Street Zen.* Boston: Shambhala, 1993.
Senzaki, Nyogen. *Eloquent Silence.* Boston: Wisdom Publications, 2008.
Senzaki, Nyogen. *Like a Dream, Like a Fantasy.* Boston: Wisdom Publications, 2005.

Shodo Harada. *The Path to Bodhidharma.* Rutland, Vermont: Tuttle Publishing, 2000.
Snyder, Gary and Jim Harrison and Paul Ebenkamp (ed.). *The Etiquette of Freedom.* Berkeley: Counterpoint, 2010.
Snyder, Gary. *The Gary Snyder Reader.* Washington D C: Counterpoint, 2012.
Snyder, Gary. *Riprap and Cold Mountain Poems.* Berkeley: Counterpoint, 2010.
Suiter, John. *Poets on the Peaks.* Washington D C: Counterpoint, 2002.
Suzuki, D. T. *Essays in Zen Buddhism, First Series.* New York: Grove Press, 1994.
Suzuki, D. T. *The Field of Zen.* New York: Harper & Row, Perennial Library, 1970.
Suzuki, D. T. *Zen and Japanese Culture.* Princeton: Princeton University Press, 2010.
Suzuki, D. T. *The Zen Doctrine of No-Mind.* Newburyport, MA: Samuel Weiser, 1991.
Suzuki, Shunryu. *Zen Mind, Beginner's Mind.* Boston: Shambhala, 2011.
Tanahashi, Kasuaki (ed. and trans). *Endless Vow: The Zen Path of Soen Nakagawa.* Boston: Shambala, 1996.
Tworkov, Helen. *Zen in America.* New York: Kodansha USA, 1994.
Van de Wetering, Janwillem. *Afterzen.* New York: St. Martin's, 2001.
Van de Wetering, Janwillem. *The Empty Mirror.* New York: St. Martin's, 1999.
Van de Wetering, Janwillem. *A Glimpse of Nothingness.* New York: St. Martin's, 1999.
Victoria, Brian Daizen. *Zen at War.* Oxford: Rowman and Littlefield, 2006.
Watts, Alan. *In My Own Way.* Novato, CA: New World Library, 2007.
Watts, Alan. *This Is It.* New York: Vintage, 1973.
Watts, Alan. *The Way of Zen.* New York: Vintage, 1999.
Zen Notes published by the First Zen Institute of America, http://www.firstzen.org/ZenNotesOnLine.php

Index of Names

Aitken, Anne Hopkins – 38, 115-17, 118, 119, 124, 151, 154
Aitken, Mary – 112-13
Aitken, Robert – **109-12**; 38, 47, 127, 135, 138, 147, 151, 152, 154, 156, 157, 158,161, 163, 169, 181, 185, 222, 241
Aitken, Thomas – 113
Akiba, Gengo – 175
Alpert, Richard – see Ram Dass, Baba
Anderson, Reb Tenshin – 225
Amida Buddha – 25
Ashvaghosha – 29
Avalokitesvara – 53
Bach, J. S. – 112
Baháʼuʼlláh – 31
Baizhang, Huaihai – 190
Baker, Richard – 9, 86, 90, 107, 136, 137, 139, 144, 161, 171, 174, 212, 221, 222, 224-25, 230, 245
Baker, Virginia – 136
Baroni, Helen – 163
Barrows, John Henry – 21
Basho, Matsuo – 44, 112, 113, 148
Baso – 103-04
Bassui – 148, 207
Bays, Hogen – 233
Bays, Jan Chozen – 170, 171, 172, 173-74, 175, 231-33, 234
Beck, Charlotte Joko – 170, 171, 174
Beethoven, Ludwig van – 154, 195
Bernard, Pierre – 66
Bishop, Mitra – 208, 211
Blake, William – 78

Blavatsky, Helena – 98
Blyth, Reginald Horace – 111-12, 113, 122
Bodhidharma – 18-19, 45, 79, 114, 116
Boyington, William – 29
Buddha – 17, 18, 19, 21, 25, 31, 32-34, 45, 48, 56, 69, 78, 112, 113, 130, 131, 150, 159, 176, 178-79, 182, 203, 204, 222
Bullock, Lewis (Lieutenant) – 187
Burroughs, William – 77
Carlson, Chester – 159, 209
Carlson, Dorris – 159, 160, 209
Carus, Paul – 21-22, 27, 28, 29, 30
Cassady, Neil – 85
Chapin, Ralph – 208-09, 244
Coppens, Anton Tenkel – 175
Corso, Gregory – 77
Crowley, Aleister – 62
Curran, Hugh – 185
DeMartino, Richard – 36, 203
Derby, Marian – 137, 140
Derrick, Joan Yushin – 170, 172-73
DeWitt, Dorothy – see Watts, Dorothy DeWitt
Dharmapala, Anagarika – 21, 29
Dodge, Jim – 87
Dogen Kigen – 18, 19, 127, 129, 140, 141, 155, 168, 176, 177, 207, 219, 220, 224
Dorsey, Issan – 90-91, 143-44
Downing, Michael – 225, 245
Eckhart, Meister – 39, 48, 49, 112, 113, 114
Eisai, Myoan – 18, 155
Erskine, Beatrice – see Suzuki, Beatrice (Erskine)
Everett, Eleanor – see Watts, Eleanor Everett
Everett, E. Warren – 66-67
Everett, Ruth – see Sasaki, Ruth Fuller
Farkas, Mary – 65
Ferlinghetti, Lawrence – 83
Fletcher, Anne Seysen – 178-79
Ford, James Ishmael – 7, 104-05, 226, 245
Franklin, Benjamin – 43
Freeman, Annis – 38
Fromm, Erich – 38

Fudo-myoo – 25
Furlong, Monica – 100, 105
Ganesh – 89
Gaskin, Stephen – 222
Gautama, Siddhartha – see Buddha
Ginsberg, Allen – 10, 37, 77, 78, 79, 81, 83, 86, 87, 88, 92, 105, 137
Glassman, Bernie Tetsugen – 169-70, 171, 172, 175, 234
Goddard, Dwight – 78
Goldberg, Natalie – 228-29, 230
Goto, Kengan – 155
Goto, Zuigan -71, 72-73, 185, 187-88, 191, 197
Graef, Sunyana – 209-10, 233
Hakuin Ekako – 26, 27, 63, 135
Hamerstrom, Davis – 160
Hanshan – 78, 84
Harada, Daiun Sogaku – 116, 127, 151, 168, 201, 205, 220
Hashimoto, Eko – 219, 220
Hawk, Patrick – 124
Hayashi, Ekyo – 160
Hayashi, Daicho – 218-19
Haydn, Joseph – 195
Hearn, Lafcadio – 97
Hegeler, Edward – 29
Hojo, Jikei – 26
Hopkins, Anne – see Aitken, Anne Hopkins
Huineng – 63, 64, 114
Humphreys, Christmas – 34, 36, 97, 98, 107, 153
Ikemiya, Masanobu – 189
Ikkyu Sojun – 181
Ingersoll, Robert – 202
Isan Reiyu – 48
Jesus Christ – 17, 33, 112, 154
Joshu Jushin – 19, 114
Joyce, James – 62
Jung, Carl – 36
Kangetsu – see McCandless, Ruth Strout
Kannon – 233
Kant, Immanuel – 47

Kapleau, Philip – **199-214**; 9, 36, 39, 103, 117, 154-55, 158, 159, 161, 185, 224, 244
Katagiri, Dainin – **215-30**; 136, 212
Katagiri, Kashichi – 217
Katagiri, Tomie – 220
Katsube, Keigaku -148-49
Kennedy, Robert – 106
Kennett, Jiyu – 105
Kerouac, Jack – **77-80**; 10, 37, 81, 83, 85, 87, 88, 92, 101, 106, 144
Khan, Hazrat Inayat – 49-50
Kieburtz, Victoria – 211
Kishizawa, Ian – 133
Kjolhede, Bodhin – 209-10, 211, 244
Kosen, Imakita – 20, 26, 27, 60
Kotler, Arnold – 226
Krishna – 31
Krishnamurti, Jiddu – 102, 112, 115
Kriyananda, Swami – 86
Kubota, Akira – 244
Kubota, Kitako – 59
Kurodo, Hakujun – 167, 169
Kurodo, Kojun – 167
Kwong, Bill – 137
Kyger, Joanne – 85, 87
Kyogen – 48
Lamantia, Philip – 83
Leary, Timothy – 105
Long, Philomene – 178
Loori, John Daido – 170, 171, 175
Loori, Joan – see Derrick, Joan Yushin
MacArthur, Douglas (General) – 187
Maezumi, Taizan – **165-82**; 9, 119, 161, 220, 231, 232
Mahakasyapa – 32
Manjusri – 113, 191
Marinello, Genjo – 162
Marks, Annette – 158
Martin, Rafe – 202, 210
Matsuno, Mitsu – see Suzuki, Mitsu Matsuno
Matthiessen, Peter – 152, 161, 172

Mazo Daoyi – 89
McCandless, Ruth Strout – 53, 55
McClure, Michael – 83
Merzel, Dennis Genpo – 170, 175
Muhammad - 31
Michelson, Henriette – 186, 187
Michizu, Setsumon – 26, 148
Mitchell, Elsie – 142-43, 225
Mitrinovic, Dmitrije – 98
Miura, Isshu – 72, 73, 84, 85, 86
Morgan, Addie – 186, 189
Morgan, Leverett – 186, 189
Morinaga, Soko – 189, 191
Mozart, Wolfgang Amadeus – 195
Mumon – 149
Muramatsu, Chie – see Suzuki, Chie Muramatsu
Murphy, Sean – 91, 179-80, 188, 195, 204, 226
Mussorgsky, Modest – 196
Nakagawa, Kazuko – 147, 152
Nakagawa, Soen – **145-163**; 51, 55, 56, 114, 115-16, 117, 118, 119, 181, 204-05, 207
Nakagawa, Suketaro – 147
Nakamura, Taiyo – 72
Nangaku – 102-04
Nanshinken – 66-67, 72
Nowick, Walter – **183-97**; 9, 73, 84, 217, 229, 230
Okamura, Mihoko – 10, 37-38, 39, 79
Oom the Magnificent – see Bernard, Pierre
Orlovsky, Peter – 79
Osaka, Koryu – 167-68, 169
Otsubo, Monk – 133
Packer, Toni – 213, 230
Pangyun – 29
Parker, Charlie – 78
Patanjali – 88
Pendell, Dale – 123
Petchey, Grahme – 136, 137
Pirsig, Chris – 138
Pirsig, Robert – 222

Port, Dosho Mike – 212, 217, 227-28
Prabhavananda, Swami – 102
Ram Dass, Baba – 105
Rand, Yvonne – 226-27
Ransom, Nona – 130-31, 135
Reps, Paul – 47, 51, 53
Rexroth, Kenneth – 77, 83, 90
Rhys-David, Thomas William – 21
Rice, Dharman – 233
Rinzai – 56
Rohmer, Sax – 96
Roosevelt, Theodore – 30
Russell, Ida – 30, 46
Ryutan – 44
Saiko-an
Sakyamuni – see Buddha
Sasaki, Joshu – 10
Sasaki, Ruth Fuller – **66-68, 71-73**; 83, 84, 95, 98-99, 100, 106, 116, 187
Sasaki, Sokei-an – **57-71**; 9, 10-11, 73, 89, 100, 111, 127, 187, 188
Sasaki, Tomeko – 9, 61-62, 63
Sasaki, Tsunamichi – 59
Schopenhauer, Arthur – 147
Shubert, Franz – 192
Sekida, Katsuki – 119
Senzaki, Nyogen – **41-56**; 9, 59, 61, 67, 69, 102, 111, 113, 114, 115, 116, 122, 127, 138, 148, 149, 150-52, 156, 161, 163, 168, 172
Sesso, Oda – 85, 187
Seung Sahn – 161
Shaku, Sokatsu – 10, 60-62, 63-64, 70, 71, 188
Shaku, Soyen – 9, 10, 20-22, 27-29, 30-31, 43, 44, 45, 46-47, 53-54, 55, 60, 127
Shakespeare, William – 112
Shakyamuni – see Buddha
Shide – 78
Shimano, Eido Tai – **155-61**; 55, 56, 115, 117, 118, 119, 147, 152, 153, 181, 212, 230
Shoju Rojin -135
Snyder, Gary – **81-88**; 9, 73, 77, 78-79, 80, 90, 92, 95, 105, 106, 123, 127, 137, 187
Snyder, Lois – 81

Sogen, Asahina – 113-14
Sokatsu – see Shaku, Sokatsu
Sokei-an – see Sasaki, Sokei-an
So-on, Gyokujun – 128-29, 130, 131, 132
Soulé, Jan – see Bays, Jan Chozen
Spiegelberg, Frederic – 101
Stowe, Harriet Beecher – 160
Straus, Lenore – 189, 190, 191, 243
Suzuki, Beatrice (Erskine) – 31-32, 35
Suzuki, Chie Muramatsu – 132, 133
Suzuki, D. T. – **23-39**; 9, 10, 21-22, 43, 56, 59, 66, 68, 78, 79-80, 82, 88, 95, 97, 98, 101, 102, 103, 112, 113, 121, 127, 135, 147, 148, 158, 168, 172, 203, 204, 237-38
Suzuki, Hoitsu – 132, 133, 140
Suzuki, Kantaro (Admiral) – 150
Suzuki, Mitsu Matsuno – 133-34, 135, 136
Suzuki, Omi – 133
Suzuki, Otohiro – 133, 135
Suzuki, Paul – 31
Suzuki, Shunryu – **125-44**; 9, 20, 86, 90, 102, 105, 107, 152, 167, 168, 169, 201, 217, 220-22, 224, 225, 226, 229, 233
Suzuki, Sogaku – 128, 130, 131
Suzuki, Gyokujun So-on – see So-on, Gyokujun
Suzuki, Yasuko – 132, 133, 140
Tanahashi, Jimmy – 50-51
Tanahashi, Shubin – 50-51
Tanahashi, Shuji – 50
Tarrant, John – 115, 120, 234
Tatsugami, Sotan – 139, 221
Thoreau, Henry David – 78
Tojo, Hideki – 36
Tokusan – 44
Tozan – 156
Trungpa, Chogyam – 161
Tworkov, Helen – 91, 122
Ummon Bun'en – 19
Unmon – 156
van de Wetering, Janwillem – 85, 193-94, 243
Verdi, Giuseppe – 195

Vishnu – 89
Vivekananda, Swami – 21
Voltaire – 202
Watson, Burton – 73
Watts, Alan – **93-107**; 17, 34, 38, 39, 66, 67, 70, 82-83, 85, 121, 127, 134, 135, 137, 144, 168, 181
Watts, Dorothy DeWitt – 101, 102, 104
Watts, Eleanor Everett – 66, 98-101, 104
Watts, Emily – 95-96, 97
Watts, Joan – 100
Watts, Lawrence – 95, 97, 98
Watts, Mary Jane (Jano) – 104, 106
Welch, Lew – 81, 86
Whalen, Philip – **88-91**; 81, 82, 83, 85, 92
Weitsman, Mel – 137
Wick, Gerry Shishin – 170, 174, 175, 180
Wordsworth, William – 112
Yamada, Koun – 119, 120, 121, 147, 148, 149, 151, 185, 205, 207, 241, 244
Yamada, Reirin (Bishop) – 168, 220
Yamamoto, Gempo – 114, 148-49, 150, 151, 152
Yamaoka, George – 158
Yampolsky, Philip – 73
Yasutani, Haku'un – 116, 117, 118, 119, 127, 151, 152, 156-57, 158, 159, 168, 169, 181, 189, 201, 204-208, 209, 212
Yates, Mary Jane – see Watts, Mary Jane (Jano)
Yogananda, Paramahansa – 86
Yokoi, Kakudo – 219-20

About the Author

Richard Bryan McDaniel taught at the University of New Brunswick and Saint Thomas University before starting a 27 year career in International Development and Fair Trade. He is the creator of the YMCA Peace Medallion.

A long time Zen practitioner, he is the author of *Zen Masters of China: The First Step East* and *Zen Masters of Japan: The Second Step East*.

The sequel to this volume, *Cypress Trees in the Garden: The Second Generation of Zen Teaching in America*, will be released by The Sumeru Press in the autumn of 2015.

Rick McDaniel can be reached at rickmcdaniel@bellaliant.net.

About Sumeru

For more information about The Sumeru Press, visit us at www.sumeru-books.com, or use this QR code:

www.ingramcontent.com/pod-product-compliance
Lightning Source LLC
Chambersburg PA
CBHW030137170426
43199CB00008B/99